# WEALTH IN AMERICA

Wealth ownership in the United States has long been concentrated in the hands of a small minority of the population. Because data on wealth ownership have been scarce, the nature of the wealth distribution has received relatively little attention from social scientists, and knowledge about the processes that lead to wealth inequality has been even more elusive. In this book, Lisa A. Keister synthesizes theory and data from various sources to present a detailed picture of household wealth distribution from the early 1960s through the 1990s. The author utilizes existing survey data and a unique simulation model to isolate and examine some of the processes that create this distribution, paying particular attention to the wealth ownership and accumulation of top wealth holders, those who control the bulk of household wealth. She also identifies trends in wealth mobility that are not possible to estimate with traditional research methods. The results underscore the importance of wealth as an indicator of well-being, identify important causes of wealth inequality, and propose some methods of lessening the recent increase in the concentration of wealth.

Lisa A. Keister is Assistant Professor of Sociology at The Ohio State University. She is the recipient of the National Science Foundation Faculty Early Career Development Award and author of *Chinese Business Groups: The Structure and Impact of Interfirm Relations During Economic Development* (forthcoming).

# WEALTH IN AMERICA
## Trends in Wealth Inequality

LISA A. KEISTER
The Ohio State University

CAMBRIDGE
UNIVERSITY PRESS

PUBLISHED BY THE PRESS SYNDICATE OF THE UNIVERSITY OF CAMBRIDGE
The Pitt Building, Trumpington Street, Cambridge, United Kingdom

CAMBRIDGE UNIVERSITY PRESS
The Edinburgh Building, Cambridge CB2 2RU, UK   http://www.cup.cam.ac.uk
40 West 20th Street, New York, NY 10011-4211, USA   http://www.cup.org
10 Stamford Road, Oakleigh, Melbourne 3166, Australia
Ruiz de Alarcón 13, 28014 Madrid, Spain

First published 2000

Printed in the United States of America

*Typeface* Garamond 3 11/13 pt.      *System* QuarkXPress [BTS]

*A catalog record for this book is available from the British Library.*

*Library of Congress Cataloging in Publication Data*
Keister, Lisa, 1968–
Wealth in America : trends in wealth inequality /
Lisa A. Keister.
p.   cm.
Includes bibliographical references and index.
ISBN 0-521-62168-2 (hbk.). – ISBN 0-521-62751-6 (pbk.)
1. Income distribution – United States.   2. Equality – United States.
3. Wealth – United States.   4. Income – United States.   I. Title.
HC110.I5K38   2000
339.2′ 0973 – dc21                                    99-40250
                                                              CIP

ISBN   0 521 62168 2   hardback
ISBN   0 521 62751 6   paperback

*To JWM*

# CONTENTS

# PREFACE

This is a project that I started several years ago when I became curious about the uses of simulation modeling and their application to the study of wealth inequality. It seemed at the time that wealth ownership was an important, albeit little-studied part of well-being. When I began to explore the reasons that more people did not study wealth ownership, I quickly realized that the lack of data made it nearly impossible to ask many of the questions about wealth for which we would like answers. In this book, I use survey data to estimate patterns in wealth ownership and inequality given the data that are available, presented in what I hope is a single, consistent story. I also use simulation modeling to extrapolate in various ways from what the survey data tell us. Simulation modeling of the sort I do here makes it possible to use available data to explore some of the questions about wealth ownership and inequality that we otherwise might not be able to explore. Using this type of modeling, I am able to ask questions about how changes in historical patterns would have affected more recent distributional outcomes, to explore patterns in wealth ownership for times for which survey data do not exist, to extrapolate to future periods, and to estimate life-course patterns of ownership and mobility despite large gaps in data.

The methods I use are more widely used in policy circles than by those doing basic social science research, so they may at first seem unusual to some of the readers of this book. I hope, however, that the benefits of these methods become obvious. I have enjoyed posing new questions throughout the book and pondering the answers that the model has produced. At the same time, an important caveat is necessary. While I discuss the simulation estimates as if they are fact, they are, of course, only simulated estimates. They are my best guess about what the world would look like if we did, indeed, have comprehensive, longitudinal survey data on wealth.

I do not intend for these estimates to replace survey estimates. In fact, I hope this book raises more questions than it answers. If it does, the questions it raises will most likely require high-quality longitudinal survey data to answer. Perhaps these questions will be a catalyst for the collection of such data.

As with all books, I created a large number of debts in writing this. I am grateful to Rob Bentley, Naomi Calvo, Michael Chermside, Joshua Cope, Tom Johnson, Yooki Park, Aaron Peromsik, and Mark Wright for research and programming assistance at various stages of this project. I am also grateful to the Department of Sociology at Cornell University, where I began work on the project, particularly to Steve Caldwell for his assistance with the simulation modeling. My colleagues at the University of North Carolina, especially Glen Elder, Howard Aldrich, and Rachel Rosenfeld, provided priceless support and advice as I wrote the bulk of the book. Stephanie Moller and Natalia Deeb-Sossa provided excellent research assistance and critical comments during the analysis and writing stages. Grants from the University Research Council and the Institute for Research in the Social Sciences at the University of North Carolina provided financial assistance.

# *Part I*
## INTRODUCTION

# I

# WEALTH AND INEQUALITY

The love of wealth is therefore to be traced, as either a principal or accessory motive, at the bottom of all that the Americans do.

(de Tocqueville 1841)

One of the most astute observers of American life, Alexis de Tocqueville noted that wealth accumulation is perhaps the fundamental motivator of American behavior. At the same time, wealth ownership is thought to be concentrated in the hands of a small minority of the population. It is no secret that wealth ownership has advantages and that these extend beyond the obvious economic benefits to such areas as general social standing and political power. Political influence, for example, is typically exercised indirectly, through lobbying, private funding of research and policy institutes, and campaign financing (Domhoff 1990; Dye 1995; Useem 1984). To the extent to which economic power can be converted into political power, those who own wealth also influence the making of important decisions. As Spencer pointed out more than a century ago, "Even before private land-owning begins, quantity of possessions aids in distinguishing the governing from the governed" (Spencer 1882:401). While the nature of the economic and political systems in which wealth is accumulated has changed dramatically since Spencer's time, there is still a strong association between control of material possessions and political influence. Thus those who have wealth have every incentive to maintain that wealth, while those who own little are motivated to acquire wealth. Moreover, the notion of the American dream suggests that such upward mobility is, indeed, possible. Researchers have long suspected, however, that in addition to motivating much of what Americans do wealth ownership is the single dimension on which American families are most persistently unequally distributed. While disparities in income and educational attainment are

3

extreme, disparities in the ownership of wealth are likely worse and apparently more enduring across generations.

Yet information on the distribution of family wealth in the United States has been relatively scarce, and understanding of the processes that lead to wealth inequality has been even more elusive. As a result, knowledge of the role that wealth ownership plays in motivating and constraining behavior has remained relatively limited. Over the last decade, data improvements have allowed researchers to begin outlining a few of the more salient descriptive features of the distribution of wealth, and while the evidence is still preliminary, the picture that has emerged is disquieting. Wealth inequality, already highly concentrated in the early 1960s, became even more so during the 1980s and 1990s. Estimates indicate that the top 1 percent of wealth owners enjoyed two-thirds of all increases in household financial wealth during the 1980s, while the bottom 80 percent actually owned less real financial wealth in 1989 than in 1983 (Wolff 1995b). In the past, Americans smugly assumed that European societies were more stratified than their own, but it now appears that the United States has surpassed all industrial societies in the extent of its family wealth inequality (Wolff 1995b). Interpreting these reports, the press has realized that wealth inequality may be as harmful as income and educational inequality, which have attracted so much more attention. Pondering new wealth distribution estimates in its lead editorial, the *New York Times* worried that "Some inequality is necessary if society wants to reward investors for taking risks and individuals for working hard and well. But excessive inequality can break the spirit of those trapped in society's cellar – and exacerbate social tensions" (4/18/95).

While improvements in wealth data began to cast new light on this fundamental social problem in the 1980s, understanding of both wealth inequality and its causes remains far from complete. Researchers have begun to create a picture of household wealth distribution, particularly for the years in which surveys were conducted (Wolff 1987b, 1995a, 1995b, 1998; Wolff and Marley 1989). Demographic, social, and financial characteristics of families in various portions of the distribution have also become increasingly clear, again particularly in the years for which survey data are available (Avery, Elliehausen, Canner, and Gustafson 1984b; Avery, Elliehausen, Canner, Gustafson, and Springert 1986; Avery, Elliehausen, and Kennickell 1987; Avery and Kennickell 1990; Kennickell and Shack-Marquez 1992; Kennickell and Starr-McCluer 1994). Yet this research appears in disparate places and has seldom been accumulated into a single story of wealth inequality in America. At the same time, and perhaps more importantly, our understanding of the processes that create these distributional outcomes is limited. Family-level demographics and processes, such as racial differences, aging, and inheritance, are likely to affect wealth accumulation and thus inequality (Ando and Modigliani 1963; Blau and Graham 1990; Danziger, VanDerGaag, Smolensky, and Taussig 1982; Oliver and Shapiro 1995). Likewise, social and economic trends, such as baby booms and stock market fluctuations, are likely to influence distributional outcomes (David and Menchik 1988; Goldsmith 1962; Wolff 1979). While researchers have certainly addressed these subjects, empirical support for arguments has been somewhat limited by the availability of longitudinal data with adequate coverage.

My aim in this book is to begin to fill some of these gaps. I synthesize theory and data from various sources to present a detailed picture of household wealth distribution from 1962 to 1995. Furthermore, I isolate and examine some of the aggregate and family-level processes that create this distribution. I examine trends in the overall distribution of wealth among families, the movement of families among segments of the wealth distribution over time, and the distribution of the components of wealth (i.e., specific financial assets and real assets versus debts). To identify trends in wealth distribution even more clearly, I isolate and examine specific segments of the wealth distribution. I pay particular attention to top wealth holders, those who control the bulk of household wealth. I also identify trends in wealth ownership among both the middle class and the poor. Finally, in an effort to create a more unified picture of the processes that underlie trends in wealth ownership than has been available in the past, I explore the factors that have contributed to changes in wealth distribution, including both macroeconomic influences and microlevel influences.

To accomplish this, I synthesize data from various sources. I use basic data sources, including survey data (the 1962 Survey of the Financial Characteristics of Consumers, and the Surveys of Consumer Finances for more recent years), estate tax data on top wealth holders, and aggregate flow of funds data on household wealth holdings (e.g., the total amount of stocks, bonds, and housing assets owned by households in a given year). I also use a simulation model to literally synthesize these data sources into a single model of household wealth ownership. I draw on existing theory and research to identify potential sources of wealth inequality, and I use the simulation model to examine the feasibility of these ideas. The simulation model allows me, for example, to ask questions about the distributional outcomes of stock market booms and busts. It also allows me to ask family-level questions such as whether the distribution of wealth would be different today if middle-class families had begun investing in the stock market decades ago. In addition to investigating the basic processes that lead to inequality, the simulation model allows me to address the implications of policies designed to lessen inequality. We know historically that the distribution of wealth has fluctuated dramatically with economic trends and changes in demographics. This might suggest that, in time, current levels of wealth inequality are likely to be lessened without intervention. Previous research cannot address this question, but it is one for which a simulation model is a highly useful tool.

## *What Is Wealth and Why Should We Study It?*

When social scientists discuss financial well-being, they usually refer to income. However, I want to make a clear distinction between income and wealth. Wealth is property; it is the value of the things people own. Wealth is measured as net worth, defined as total assets (such as stocks, bonds, checking and savings accounts, the value of the family home, vacation homes, and other real estate) minus total liabilities (such as mortgage debt, the balance on credit cards, student loans, and car loans). Income is a *flow* of financial resources, such as wages or a salary received for work, interest and dividends from investments such as pensions, or transfer payments from the government. In contrast, wealth refers to the *stock* of resources owned at a particular point in time.

Income can, of course, be saved to produce wealth, but the two are not equivalent. Unlike income, wealth is not used directly to buy necessities such as food and clothing, but it can be used to generate income for these purposes. Assets such as stocks and bonds and, to a lesser degree, checking and savings accounts can produce interest and dividend income that can be used to satisfy either short- or long-term consumption needs. In the short term, wealth can be converted wholly or in part to produce income to meet consumption needs or to reduce liabilities. Similarly, wealth can satisfy long-term consumption desires through investment for long-term income streams, as in the accumulation of pension wealth to meet consumption needs after retirement. While there is a clear relationship between wealth and income, having one does not necessarily imply having the other.

In addition to producing income, wealth generates more wealth, allowing the rich to get richer. Because wealth appreciates, saving and reinvesting interest and dividends allows wealth to grow. Wealth can also be used as collateral to secure loans for further investment; many of the wealthiest people leverage their assets this way to produce even greater wealth. Wealth also allows its owner to combine consumption with investment, as in the purchase of houses and other real estate, land, vehicles, paintings, thoroughbred horses, or jewels. Frank (1999) used the term "luxury fever" to highlight the extravagant consumption that is possible, and that was increasingly obvious in the 1980s and 1990s, with great wealth. One of the most famous rich people of the 1990s, Bill Gates, Chairman of the Microsoft Corporation, built a 45,000-square-foot house on the shores of Lake Washington that cost more than $100 million and included a $6.5-million swimming pool. When new construction is considered "luxury" at $200 per square foot in many regions, the Gates mansion seems even more extravagant given that it cost more than $2,000 per square foot to build. Equally extravagant were the homes of Microsoft cofounder Paul Allen and Oracle CEO Laurence Ellison. Allen's 74,000-square-foot house and Ellison's $40-million, 23-acre complex have drawn nearly as much attention as Gates's new home (Frank 1999:21–22).

In addition to the material luxuries it can buy, there are other more basic advantages of wealth ownership. Wealth not only allows the direct purchase of a home, but it also allows its owner to purchase advantages such as physical protection and a safe and pleasant living environment. Wealth can buy leisure, that is, it can allow its owner to decide whether to work or not. While there may be pressures associated with wealth ownership, it certainly removes the stresses associated with meeting very basic needs. In the words of Rebecca Jacobs, a woman who became rich as an entrepreneur, "Money can't give you health, friends, love. But it can give you peace of mind" (Schervish, Coutsoukis, and Lewis 1994:47). Because assets can be used to lessen the impact of a financial emergency, wealth also provides economic security to its owners. Wealth can be used to indirectly gain advantages such as political influence, social prestige, flexibility, leisure, and improved educational and occupational advantages for oneself and one's children.

Naturally there are also potential disadvantages associated with the ownership of wealth. Excess wealth can attract unwanted media attention and solicitations of various kinds. In some cases, wealth can invite security threats and may produce social isolation. Moreover, wealth ownership may dampen achievement motivation and performance in both those who have created wealth and those who stand to inherit it. A recent investigation provides detailed qualitative accounts of the privileged lives of the American super-rich as well as insights into how the wealthy portray themselves (Schervish, Coutsoukis, and Lewis 1994). The authors attempt to depict both the advantages and disadvantages of wealth ownership. The people they interview do seem to encounter various inconveniences associated with owning great amounts of wealth. However, the authors only succeed in demonstrating that, on balance, the advantages of having wealth far outweigh the potential disadvantages. In the words of Sophie Tucker, a famous entertainer who lived from 1884 to 1996, "I've been rich and I've been poor. Believe me, rich is better."

In the context of these advantages, it seems even more remarkable that the majority of wealth is owned by less than 10 percent of the population. In recent decades, most people have not owned stocks, mutual funds, bonds, or even less-risky assets such as certificates of deposit. Most American families own checking and savings accounts, a vehicle or two, and tend to keep most of their assets in owner-occupied housing. In a common scenario, many middle-class Americans first use their income to make payments on a house to take advantage of tax breaks and the combination of consuming and investing that is available in homeownership. After a mortgage payment, however, there is often little left over to save in other forms. Americans do tend to buy their homes and vehicles with credit, and they finance other expenditures with debt as well. In recent years, in fact, Americans have been willing to accumulate tremendous amounts of such debt, including large amounts of mortgage debt, car loans, loans for vacations, and home improvement loans. While such liabilities may ease short-term financial woes, their long-term effect is to diminish overall wealth along with the advantages associated with wealth.

In many cases, debt accumulation is unavoidable. Many middle-class and poor families are forced to take loans for daily survival and thus erode the small amount of wealth they may have accumulated. In their study of racial inequality in wealth ownership, Oliver and Shapiro interviewed a rather typical American couple. Albert and Robyn are both college graduates and Albert also has a master's degree. They have been married five and a half years, have a two-year-old daughter, and both are currently employed. They bought a house when their daughter was born to make sure they had a suitable place to raise their child and also to take advantage of tax credits for homeowners. Since the birth of their daughter and the purchase of their home, however, they have been unable to save money. They regularly borrow money at very high interest rates to pay short-term bills. As a result, they have diminished their small savings and have accumulated more debt than they feel comfortable with owning (Oliver and Shapiro 1995:71–72). Like many Americans, Albert and Robyn are at high risk of financial disaster as U.S. society virtually requires two incomes to meet even modest financial obligations. Unlike the wealthy, most Americans could not rely on their assets to replace lost earnings if they were suddenly unemployed. Likewise, most Americans, like Albert and Robyn, are not accumulating assets to pay for potential future expenses such as college educations for their children and a comfortable retirement for themselves.

## Wealth, Income, and Inequality

In this book, I treat wealth as an intrinsically important indicator of family well-being and one quite different from income. When wealth (rather than income) is used as an indicator of family economic well-being, a different picture of advantage and disadvantage emerges; this suggests that our understanding of social inequality and social mobility has been limited by our nearly total focus on income. Moreover, because of the financial security and other advantages associated with wealth ownership, the control of wealth has been an important determinant of well-being throughout history, and the truly advantaged are still signaled by high net worth. Despite the important role wealth plays in stratifying society, however, existing studies of financial well-being generally use income to indicate the relative status of families. Advantage and disadvantage are usually measured in terms of current earned or total income or, less commonly, the present value of potential future income. The recent emphasis on income as an indicator of financial well-being has been the result of empirical convenience because, in the words of one economist, "with the advent of the income tax and the ever widening scope of census questioning, the government began to accumulate vast stores of data concerning the incomes of individuals and families in America" (Winnick 1989:160). Information regarding wealth holdings, in contrast, has not been investigated as successfully by the government, in part because the wealthy have strong incentives to conceal the details of their holdings from such agencies as the Internal Revenue Service.

9

Using income alone as an indicator of the financial well-being of families would be adequate if income and wealth were highly correlated. In reality, however, the correlation between the two indicators is relatively low. One study found that the correlation coefficient between income and wealth was 0.49 in 1983; while this correlation is already low, much of it is attributable to the inclusion of asset income (income generated by wealth) in the definition of total income. When asset income is removed from total income, the correlation between income and net worth dropped to 0.26 (Lerman and Mikesell 1988:779)! This suggests that the wealthy have rather low earnings, probably because they are able to support current consumption with income derived from assets. It also suggests that studies that focus solely on income miss a large part of the story of advantage and disadvantage in America.

Not only is the correlation between wealth and income low, but there is also substantial dispersion of wealth within income categories (Radner 1989). At all income levels, some families have acquired substantial wealth and own asset and debt portfolios that will maximize future wealth accumulation. Likewise at all income levels, there are those whose wealth is meager and whose portfolios indicate minimal potential for future wealth accumulation. In fact, many families, particularly nonwhite families, with both relatively low and relatively high incomes, have zero or negative net worth (Radner 1989; Winnick 1989). In contrast, many elderly households have low incomes but substantial net worth because they have had years to accumulate assets but no longer have earned income. For these reasons, many families found to be below the poverty line based solely on current income may be living quite comfortably on assets acquired during more prosperous years (Wolff 1990).

Moreover, wealth is even more unequally distributed than income. In 1989, the share of wealth of the top 1 percent of wealth owners was estimated to be 38.9 percent, while the share of the top 1 percent of income recipients was estimated to be 16.4 percent. The top quintile of wealth holders owned almost 85 percent of total household wealth, and the top quintile of income recipients received just over 50 percent of total family income. Another report (based on the Survey of Consumer Finances) found that wealth is more highly concentrated than income (Avery, Elliehausen, Canner, and Gustafson 1984b). This report demonstrated that the top 2 percent of wealth owners owned 28 percent of total wealth in 1983, and the top 10 percent owned 57 percent of wealth. In contrast, in the same year, families with the highest incomes earned 14 percent of total income, and those in the top 10 percent earned 33 percent. Moreover, the Gini coefficient for wealth increased from 0.80 in 1983 to 0.84 in 1989 (Wolff 1994). In contrast, the Gini coefficient for income in 1989 was 0.52. This evidence clearly illustrates that income tells only part of the financial story.[1]

When wealth is used as an indicator of family well-being, a new picture of advantage and disadvantage emerges. For example, studies of income inequality suggest that a black middle class is emerging, and that the gap between the races is closing. Others, however, have argued that when family wealth is included, the existence of a black middle class is highly questionable (Oliver and Shapiro 1995). Oliver and Shapiro's studies of racial differences in wealth ownership, in particular, provided strong evidence that black families have considerably less net worth than white families even when income is controlled. Similar differences are evident when wealth is included in other studies of wealth inequality, including those that focus on such indicators as age and cohort differences in well-being.

In addition to telling a different story about advantage and disadvantage, wealth comes closer both theoretically and empirically to our general understanding of well-being. When we talk about economic well-being, we are referring to how prosperous people are, to how financially secure they are. Income is an indicator of short-term security, a type of security that may be lost if markets change abruptly, if the income earner becomes ill or dies, or if one relocates with a spouse. Wealth implies a more permanent notion of security and an ability to secure advantages in both the short and long terms. It is this latter concept that likely fits our shared conception of well-being. This is also perhaps why most people, including social scientists, use the terms *income* and *wealth* interchangeably. It is the latter concept, however, that we should probably understand if we are to understand how well people are doing and what it really means to be disadvantaged.

How much wealth are we talking about when we refer to family wealth? Table 1–1 provides some indication of the total amount of family wealth outstanding in the United States. The first column in this table indicates

---

[1] The Gini coefficient is an indicator of inequality that is commonly used to indicate levels of income inequality. The Gini coefficient ranges from 0 to 1, with 0 indicating perfect equality and 1 indicating perfect inequality. Conceptually, if a single household were to own all wealth, the Gini coefficient would equal unity. Avery, Elliehausen, Canner, and Gustafson (1984a) compare the Gini coefficient for income to the Gini for wealth ownership. I discuss the Gini coefficient more in Chapter 3.

Table 1–1. *Total Household Wealth in the United States (trillions of 1990 dollars)*

|  | Total Assets | Total Housing Assets | Home (% of total assets) | Total Stock Assets | Stocks (% of total assets) |
|---|---|---|---|---|---|
| 1960 | $6.6 | $1.3 | 19 | $1.6 | 24 |
| 1970 | 9.3 | 1.8 | 20 | 2.2 | 24 |
| 1980 | 12.3 | 3.2 | 26 | 1.8 | 14 |
| 1990 | 13.8 | 3.6 | 26 | 2.5 | 18 |
| 1992 | 16.6 | 3.8 | 23 | 3.7 | 22 |
| 1995 | 17.2 | 3.7 | 22 | 5.8 | 34 |
| 1997 | 17.5 | 3.8 | 21 | 6.2 | 35 |

*Note*: Estimates from the Federal Reserve Board's *Balance Sheets for the U.S. Economy* (Federal Reserve System 1995).

the total assets (the sum of all assets such as houses, cars, stocks, bonds, and savings accounts) that families owned between 1960 and 1997. As this table indicates, families owned only $6.6 trillion in 1960 (in 1990 dollars), however, by 1990 this number had risen to nearly $14 trillion dollars. By 1997, total assets had grown to more than $17 trillion, and estimates indicate that continued stock market booms in the late 1990s will push this number even higher by the end of the decade. Just how much money is this? For comparison, in 1990, the Gross Domestic Product (GDP) of the People's Republic of China was only $364 billion, and the GDP of the United States was $5.4 trillion (World Bank 1992). A number that has attracted considerable attention in the United States, the national debt, was $3.2 trillion in 1990. A particularly interesting story told by this table is the change American families have made in this decade in asset ownership. As the table indicates, in 1990, 26 percent of assets owned by households was in the family home, and only 18 percent was in stocks. By 1997, only 21 percent of assets was in the home and a full 35 percent was in the stock market. Some think that this increase in the relative importance of stocks may be accounted for by the tremendous growth of the stock market that has characterized the 1990s, but it is also true that American families are making fundamental changes in their asset ownership patterns that are reflected in these figures (Norris 1996).

## A Model of Wealth Inequality

It is nearly impossible to discuss the wealth accumulation of individuals and families without speculating about the implications this behavior has on inequalities in the macrolevel distribution of wealth. Common phrases such as "the rich get richer" imply not only that wealth creates wealth but also that as the wealthy increase their wealth, the poor become worse off. Similarly, research that explores relationships between demographic characteristics of microactors and wealth accumulation, without explicitly making such claims, often implies that certain behaviors of actors result in the concentration of wealth within particular demographic groups. It is likewise difficult to discuss the aggregate-level distribution of wealth among families without speculating about how the behavior of members of the society affects this distribution. Researchers discover these same difficulties in their efforts to identify, whether theoretically or empirically, the processes that create wealth accumulation at the microlevel (i.e., individual or household level) or wealth distribution at the macrolevel.

Yet most research on wealth accumulation and distribution focuses either on the microlevel or the macrolevel. Specifically, existing research on wealth accumulation processes and wealth inequality has been concerned either with describing the distribution of wealth among families or with explaining how families acquire their wealth, usually with little regard for how processes at one level of aggregation affect outcomes or processes at other levels. While research focused on aggregate processes has made considerable strides in describing wealth inequality and trends in the distribution of wealth among families, relatively little research has explored the factors that account for changes in wealth distribution (Kennickell and Shack-Marquez 1992; Smith 1987; Wolff 1987a, 1993, 1994, 1995b). Some have implied that market trends (such as fluctuations in the stock market), legal changes (such as the introduction of new financial instruments), and other macrophenomena coincide temporally with changes in the distribution of wealth.

Moreover, existing research has not addressed the role that behaviors at the level of individuals and families play in determining the distribution of wealth among families. For example, we suspect that the increased propensity for middle-class families to invest in the stock market in recent years has tilted the wealth distribution away from the super-wealthy. Existing approaches to understanding wealth inequality, however, have been unable to isolate the causes of distributional changes because such research is generally based on data from a single level of aggregation, usually the family level. Because this research does not, for example, integrate knowledge about the processes by which families accumulate wealth in discussions of distributional outcomes, it tells only part of the story.

Similarly, research that explores the accumulation of wealth by families does not account for the impact of structural constraints and incentives on this behavior, nor does this literature examine the distributional outcomes of the processes explored. Research on family-level processes has examined the effects of age and life-course patterns on the accumulation and depletion of wealth stocks (Mirer 1979; Modigliani 1986; Osberg 1984); it has investigated the impact of family background and parents' social status on wealth accumulation (Campbell and Henretta 1980; Henretta 1984; Henretta and Campbell 1978); and it has investigated the role race plays in determining wealth accumulation processes and its components (Brimmer 1988; Henretta 1979; Horton 1992). However, this literature has not addressed the impact of macrolevel processes (such as market fluctuations) on family wealth accumulation or the impact of accumulation patterns on subsequent aggregate outcomes (such as the distribution of wealth among families).

One empirical approach at integrating macroprocesses and microprocesses is that used by Steckel and Krishman (1992) to estimate changes in individuals' percentile positions in the wealth distribution based on demographic characteristics. Steckel and Krishman used the National Longitudinal Survey to regress changes in individuals' positions in the wealth distribution (a macromeasure) on characteristics of the individuals such as age and gender (micromeasures). While commendable in its focus, this method of linking micro and macro is not grounded theoretically, nor is it able to incorporate existing knowledge about the way families accumulate wealth because it is based on survey data. Moreover, it does not account for the effect of the accumulation of wealth by actors on the distribution of wealth among actors. Essentially, such an approach overlooks the role of the accumulation of wealth by individuals and families in an effort to make a simple micro–macro connection.

Angle (1986, 1993) suggested an alternative micro–macro link in his work that argued that the surplus theory of social stratification, that is, the tendency for wealth to flow into the hands of those who already have wealth, could be used to explain wealth inequality. The surplus theory of social stratification posits that where "people are able to produce a surplus, some of the surplus will be fugitive and leave the possession of the people who produce it" and that wealth "confers on those who possess it the ability to extract wealth from others. So netting out each person's ability to do this in a general competition for surplus wealth, the rich tend to take surplus away from the poor" (Angle 1986:298). Again, however, this approach does not take into account existing knowledge about the effect of demographic characteristics such as age and race or the effect of family background on wealth ownership and accumulation. Like other existing approaches to understanding wealth ownership, the surplus theory of stratification approach does not integrate all components of the socioeconomic system that combine to produce wealth accumulation and distribution.

The failure to adequately link microlevel and macrolevel processes in building an explanation of wealth accumulation and distribution is problematic because there is evidence that influences on both levels of aggregation are important. Market fluctuations, population trends, and other aggregate influences are clearly related to trends in wealth distribution. Likewise, it is no surprise that demographic characteristics of wealth owners (such as age, race, marital status, number of children, and educational attainment) influence savings and investment behavior, both of which either directly or indirectly (e.g., through earnings and occupation) affect wealth ownership and trends in wealth ownership over the life course. In addition to demographics, attitudes toward saving and investing, including such factors as willingness to postpone consumption and tolerate risk, directly influence wealth accumulation. Perhaps more important, however, macrolevel and microlevel forces are likely to interact with each other to produce many of the trends in wealth accumulation and distribution that have been evident in recent history. For example, regular rises in stock values (an aggregate force) are likely to encourage investment in stocks, perhaps at the expense of other savings or investments (a microlevel decision) in ways that are not evident if either level of aggregation is studied in isolation.

Because of its concern with both individual action and structural constraints, a sociological approach to human behavior can contribute to answering questions about wealth accumulation and the distribution of wealth. Coleman (1990) posited a two-level model of a social system that includes both microlevel actors and structural constraints and attempts to identify the links between the levels.[2] Coleman's model is useful in

---

[2] Coleman's conception of the micro–macro link is, not surprisingly, quite similar to Merton's conception (Stinchcombe 1975).

understanding wealth accumulation and distribution because it clearly identifies both the relevant behaviors and influences at both levels of aggregation and the mechanisms that account for the relations between levels.

In Coleman's model, social structure, including networks of actors and institutional constraints, such as laws, and informal institutions affect microlevel behavior such as whether to have children, how many children to have, decisions about education, decisions about divorce and separation, and decisions specifically related to the family's wealth portfolio. Portfolio behavior includes decisions about whether or not to own particular assets and debts, how much to invest in assets, how much debt to assume, and how to divide investments and liabilities across particular assets and debts. Within families, some decisions are made collectively and some are made by the individuals who comprise the family. For example, individuals make independent decisions about careers, employment, and sometimes about divorce and separation. Similarly, individuals become ill, disrupting family income, and individuals also die. All of these behaviors are influenced by the behavior of the family (e.g., family enforcement of norms) and all of these behaviors affect both individual and family outcomes. These behaviors, in turn, affect the microlevel outcomes such as the amount of wealth owned.

Coleman (1990:20–21) discussed several ways in which microlevel behaviors and outcomes combine to produce macrolevel outcomes, including the production of externalities by microbehavior, bilateral exchange, market outcomes, social choice, and the development of formal organizations. Market mechanisms, of course, do determine many of the social outcomes, such as interest rates, that feed back into this system to produce wealth behavior. Researchers use standard rules to construct other society-level outcomes by aggregating individual and family outcomes and discussing the particular ways these outcomes (such as net worth) are distributed across all actors. Modeling a multilevel system of this sort is an added challenge. I take up that challenge in the next chapter.

## Overview

The purpose of this book is to improve our understanding of how wealth is distributed among families, how families accumulate wealth, and the processes that account for wealth accumulation and distribution. In the second chapter, I introduce the methods that I use to study wealth, including both the data sources I use and the techniques I use to analyze the data. In that chapter, I also discuss the simulation model I use to synthesize and manipulate traditional data sets as I investigate the processes that create wealth inequality. I use a combination of survey data, aggregate household wealth data, data from estate tax records, and simulated data that synthesizes information from each of these traditional data sources. Traditional empirical methods of studying complex social and economic systems have generally sought to isolate portions of the system and make inferences about the larger system based on findings in the subsection. As Chapter 2 details, I take a different approach. Rather than focusing on a small portion of the complex system, I use a large-scale model to represent the whole system, including interactions among the subsections. My general modeling strategy is to incorporate into an existing model a module that re-creates the accumulation and distribution of 14 components of wealth by American families beginning in 1962 and extending through the year 1992 (and into the later 1990s and future as part of experiments).

The full simulation model begins in 1960 and includes a variety of modules (each similar to the wealth module) that separately represent individual demographic processes such as birth, death, and immigration, as well as family demographic processes such as family formation, assortative mating, and family dissolution. The model also includes income generation, taxation, savings, consumption, family-based transfers, and a variety of other individual and family-level processes. Each of these processes interacts with the wealth module directly or indirectly affecting the ownership and accumulation of each wealth component. In reality, multiple, complex processes interact to create the distribution of wealth among families. The model that I use achieves a high degree of realism because many (if not most) of the processes that actually affect wealth accumulation and distribution are modeled together.

I use the traditional data in conjunction with the simulation model to provide a detailed social history of wealth accumulation and distribution trends and to investigate the processes that account for these trends. The empirical results fill three broad gaps in our understanding of wealth and wealth inequality. First, these results fill temporal gaps in our understanding of wealth accumulation and distribution patterns. Data availability has forced existing research to concentrate on select historical years. In contrast, I am able to provide estimates of wealth indicators for every year between 1962 and 1995 (with some projections past that point).

Second, existing research generally focuses on static aspects of wealth ownership, neglecting dynamic accumulation processes, again because even the best data on wealth is often cross-sectional. When data is available for more than a single year, the range of years is usually quite limited. My estimates are fully dynamic. For example, I follow the same families until factors such as death, divorce, or children leaving home separate them. When the family separates, I continue to track the individual members as separate families. For these reasons, I am able to address very specific questions about changes in wealth ownership and distribution over time.

Finally, as I mentioned above, existing research tends to focus either on aggregate-level wealth patterns or patterns at the level of individuals and families. This tendency is at least partially a result of inadequacies in the data on wealth that have been available to study these patterns. In contrast, I link aggregate-level wealth outcomes (such as the total amount of stock owned by families) to the behaviors and processes at the level of individuals and families (such as changes in marriage behaviors) that account for these outcomes. As a result, I am able to answer a wide variety of questions about wealth ownership and accumulation patterns that until now have been unanswerable.

In Part II, I explore the social history of wealth ownership in America between 1962 and 1995. Chapter 3 provides an overview of changes in the distribution of household wealth over that period. That chapter asks what proportion of total wealth has been owned by top wealth holders (the top 1 percent, top 5 percent, top 10 percent, and top 20 percent of net worth holders), what has been left for the remaining families, and how families have moved among segments of the wealth distribution. Chapter 4 provides a profile of the wealth ownership patterns of the wealthiest American families. This chapter examines trends in the ownership patterns of these families over the entire 1962–1992 historical period, by looking at their demographic characteristics (such as income level, marital status, educational level, and race) and portfolio behavior. Chapter 4 also provides a detailed account of the accumulation patterns of these families. The following chapter provides a similar account of the wealth ownership and accumulation patterns of middle-class and poor families.[3]

---

[3] In these chapters, I profile families that are rich, middle class, and poor by *wealth* ownership. In the chapter on wealthy families, I profile those in the top 20 percent of wealth holders, with a special emphasis on those in the top 1 percent. In the chapter on middle-class and poor families, I profile those in the rest of the wealth distribution.

In Chapter 6, I ask whether Americans have been getting richer over time. That is, I ask whether the distribution of wealth in each new generation of Americans (starting with those who were adults in the 1960s) has been more or less equal to the distribution of wealth in previous generations. Recent literature has begun asking how baby boomers are doing financially, relative to their parents. The majority of this research is forced by data availability to make broad statements about the well-being of whole generations of individuals, often from different data sources that may not be comparable. I extend this literature by comparing the well-being of adult children with their *actual*, same-sex parent at a comparable age. For example, I isolate members of the baby boom generation at age 50 and compare their wealth (total wealth as well as individual asset and debt holdings) with that of their actual parents at age 50.

In Part III, I explore the processes that lead families to be among the wealthy or the not-so-wealthy. Chapter 7 addresses the role of the stock market, real estate market, and other macroeconomic trends in producing patterns of wealth distribution. This chapter reveals that the wealthiest Americans tend to hold more of their wealth in stocks and asks what happens to the distribution of wealth when the stock market booms. In particular, I examine the impact of the 1995 stock market boom on the wealth of families, by focusing on who won and who lost by demographic group. In this chapter, I also examine the role that housing and real estate ownership has played in wealth processes. Until recently, the family home accounted for the majority of the wealth of most Americans. The need for shelter has combined with tax incentives to create a nation of families whose largest asset has been a house. Recent research has speculated that housing no longer occupies this prominent position. I extend this literature by providing a detailed account of housing and real estate ownership patterns between 1962 and 1995, drawing on various data sources and the simulation model. In this chapter, I also use the simulation model to explain the relationship between federal estate tax rates (taxes paid by the wealthy at the time of death) and the distribution of wealth.

Chapter 8 focuses on the processes, at the level of individuals and families, that account for patterns of wealth accumulation and distribution. A question that has intrigued researchers for decades is: What happens to wealth over the life cycle? One common explanation of how people accumulate assets over their lives, the life-cycle hypothesis, suggests that people save until retirement and then dissave throughout the remainder of their lives. I extend literature in this tradition by examining asset and debt ownership over the entire life course of the same individuals. I explain trends in wealth mobility, and I also use the simulation model to examine the joint effect of educational attainment and race on wealth ownership.

In Chapter 9, I present estimates of wealth mobility patterns that span multiple decades. Because there is so little longitudinal data on wealth, it has been very difficult to study wealth mobility. For that reason, I draw almost exclusively on the simulation model in this chapter to estimate long-term patterns of wealth mobility and their causes. As is true of all of the simulated estimates in this volume, these are merely estimates. In earlier chapters, I compare short-term mobility estimates from the simulation model with comparable estimates from survey data (from panels of the Survey of Consumer Finances). I find that the simulated estimates are highly consistent with the survey data. Of course, long-term estimates are much more complex and the variance between the simulation model and the survey might be greater. The results tell an interesting and believable story that points to important facts about becoming rich, escaping poverty, and entering poverty over the life course.

The ability to estimate trends in mobility where data are scarce is one of the important advantages of the simulation model. Dynamic processes are, after all, at the heart of efforts to reduce problems associated with inequality. Finding ways to end poverty and to reduce inequality requires changes over the life course in the standing of certain individuals and families. Mobility is the process by which these changes occur. However, because I rely so heavily on the simulation model in Chapter 9, I must reiterate the caveat I mentioned in the preface to this book. I may discuss the simulated estimates as if they are fact, but I do that to avoid unnecessary complications in my language. Indeed, these are merely estimates. They are an approximation of the patterns we would likely find if we had long-term data on family wealth ownership. I do not intend for these estimates to replace survey data. Rather, I hope that my discussions in this book will raise questions about wealth inequality that could lead to the systematic collection of better data on these processes. I reiterate that point in my conclusion in Chapter 10.

# 2

# MEASURING TRENDS IN
# WEALTH INEQUALITY

In telling their stories, the rich are more novelist than liar. They may spin lofty tales, but they do so to make meaning rather than to mislead.

(Paul G. Schervish, *Gospels of Wealth*)

Weak data on the wealth holdings of top wealth holders is one of the primary reasons that accurate estimates of the size distribution of wealth in the United States have been difficult to obtain. The wealthy are generally underrepresented in surveys of household wealth, and those who are included are often unfamiliar with or unwilling to reveal the true size of their asset holdings. In surveys, unlike in in-depth interviews (such as those to which Schervish refers in the quote at the beginning of this chapter), the wealthy are unlikely to deliberately misrepresent themselves. Yet because the wealthy own the bulk of household assets in the United States, estimates of wealth distribution derived from surveys alone may, indeed, be misleading. My objective in this book is to synthesize data from various sources to present a detailed picture of household wealth distribution from 1962 to 1995 and to draw on a simulation model that allows me to investigate the processes that create this distribution. Lenski observed that it is difficult to measure the degree of inequality in any society because precise, quantitative data are difficult to obtain (Lenski 1966:Chap. 1). Lenski was convinced, however, that techniques such as using multiple data sources would make meaningful studies of inequality possible. Lenski's concern was with the more abstract concept of power and its distribution within society. However, his observations are also relevant to the study of wealth, perhaps a more precise measure of well-being than power, but one for which data are equally elusive.

My empirical strategy thus has two components. First, I draw on multiple basic data sources, including household survey data, estate tax data, and aggregate data on the total assets and debts of households, to re-create historical trends in wealth accumulation and distribution. Second, I use a simulation model to synthesize these basic data sources and produce unified estimates of historical trends in accumulation and distribution that are consistent with each basic source of wealth data. The simulated estimates fill gaps in our knowledge about trends in wealth accumulation and distribution, and at the same time, the model can be manipulated to examine how changes to basic processes affect wealth ownership and inequality. I begin this chapter with a more detailed discussion of the challenges of measuring wealth inequality and wealth distribution. I then introduce the three basic data sources that I use in the remaining chapters. I describe the merits and drawbacks of the survey data, estate tax data, and aggregate data in turn. I also briefly describe how I use each of the data sets in the simulation model. Finally, I introduce and describe the simulation model. Rather than provide a detailed, highly technical description of the building and functioning of the model, I concentrate instead on explaining the process by which I use the model to synthesize the basic data sources to produce unified, historically accurate estimates of patterns of accumulation and distribution. I provide more technical details in the Appendix.

## The Challenge of Measuring Wealth Inequality

Two central problems arise in attempts to empirically estimate the distribution of household sector wealth. First, in survey research on wealth ownership, convincing respondents to reveal how much wealth they have is difficult, particularly, as I mentioned briefly above, when the respondents are among the country's top wealth holders. As a result, detailed individual and family-level data on *income* have long been available to researchers, but similar data on the *wealth* of these families have simply not been adequate to produce a full picture of trends in wealth ownership. Existing data suggest that the ownership of wealth is highly concentrated, with the top 1 percent of wealth holders controlling approximately 30 percent of total wealth and the top 5 percent of wealth holders controlling up to 50 percent of total wealth (Wolff 1987b). Surveys include only a small portion of the group of families who own this wealth, however. Surveys, therefore, underestimate the extent of wealth ownership and, perhaps, wealth inequality in the United States. In the words of James Smith, "No matter whose research one examines, the distribution of personal wealth emerges as an incomplete pattern, the interpretation of which is more a vindication of Gestalt psychology than of economic empiricism" (Smith 1987:72).

In the 1980s and 1990s, the Federal Reserve Board's Survey of Consumer Finances (the SCF), one of the most thorough surveys of household wealth, deliberately oversampled high-income families in an effort to include more top wealth-holding families (Avery, Elliehausen, Canner, and Gustafson 1984b; Avery, Elliehausen, Canner, and Gustafson 1986; Avery, Elliehausen, Canner, Gustafson, and Springert 1986). The result was that the survey sample did indeed include more wealthy families. Yet the SCF was still far from perfect in its representation of the wealthy. As I mentioned in Chapter 1, household income is not a perfect predictor of household wealth. The relatively low correlation that is typically found between wealth and income suggests that using income to locate and sample the wealthy may still not produce enough top wealth holders (see discussion in Chapter 1; see also Lerman and Mikesell 1988:779). Moreover, even if top wealth holders are represented in a survey, they are unlikely to be fully informed about their wealth holdings. For both of these reasons, there are still gaps between SCF estimates of wealth ownership and true patterns. However, the SCF data are weighted to account for some of this difference, and the estimates from these data are widely considered the most reliable survey data available (Curtin, Juster, and Morgan 1989).

The second difficulty that arises in empirically estimating trends in household wealth distribution is obtaining adequate longitudinal coverage. Both the 1962 Survey of the Financial Characteristics of Consumers (SFCC) and the Surveys of Consumer Finances (SCF), two of the most widely used and accurate surveys of household wealth ownership, have provided cross-sectional portraits of family wealth holding. Yet even with these surveys, we are left with large gaps in our knowledge about trends in wealth distribution. We know, for instance, very little about what happened to wealth distribution in the 1960s and 1970s when the Survey of Consumer Finances was all but abandoned. We also know very little about the dynamics of wealth distribution and the dynamics of the accumulation processes underlying it. The recent panels of the SCF are beginning to rectify this situation, but these are efforts that cover only a handful of years at best. The SCF included panels for 1983–1986 and 1983–1989, but more recent surveys have been cross sections. It is possible to piece together information from the various cross sections of the SCF, but these tell us little about such basic processes as wealth mobility because we do not have the same families to observe over time. The Panel Study of Income

Dynamics (the PSID), a true longitudinal household survey, did include information about wealth between the mid-1980s and the mid-1990s. However, the PSID has wealth data for only a short time period and does not include details about the components of wealth. This limits questions that can be answered about such issues as mobility and the long-term processes underlying wealth accumulation.

## Sources of Basic Household Wealth Data

In order to overcome these obstacles, I use multiple sources and types of wealth data, including household survey data, estate tax data, and aggregate household wealth data, to piece together historical trends in household wealth accumulation and distribution. I also use a large-scale simulation model (specifically, a dynamic microsimulation model) to synthesize the information contained in these basic data sources in order to estimate historical trends. The estimates produced by the simulation model are synthetic, but they are consistent with patterns evident in each of the basic data sources. The synthetic estimates create a picture of wealth trends that is simply not apparent using a single basic data source in isolation or by piecing together information from the basic data sources in more crude ways. I discuss the basic data sources and the simulation methods in turn below.

### Household Survey Data

There are several household-level surveys that include information on wealth holdings. The principle advantage of household survey data is that it gives the researcher the greatest information on respondents and the greatest access to information asked of the respondents. The drawback is that the potential for reporting errors is likely greatest in surveys. The Survey of Income and Program Participation (the SIPP) and the Panel Study of Income Dynamics (the PSID) have both been used to estimate family wealth holdings. The most widely used source of survey information on household wealth holdings, however, is the Survey of Consumer Finances (the SCF).[1] The SCF is also the most comprehensive source of

---

[1] Curtin, Juster, and Morgan (1989) discussed the comparability of survey data sources containing information on wealth ownership. The SCF is the appropriate data source for this analysis because it includes the most comprehensive, current panel data on wealth

survey data on wealth ownership for three reasons. First, the SCF has the greatest breadth of coverage over time. The Federal Reserve Board first administered the SCF in 1960 and periodically conducted the same survey, with a hiatus in the 1970s, through 1995. The 1970s hiatus was broken in 1983 by the administration of the first wave of the 1983–1986 panel of the SCF.

Second, the SCF contains the greatest detail on the components of wealth. That is, the survey asked about ownership of stocks, bonds, mutual funds, certificates of deposit, money market accounts, checking and savings accounts, real estate, other financial assets, and so forth, in considerable detail. Likewise, the survey asked detailed questions about individual debts, such as credit card debt, student loans, car loans, mortgages, and even debts to family members. The alternative, an alternative that is common in many surveys, is to ask about net worth. There is reason to believe, however, that households accumulate different assets and debts in different ways. For example, the processes that account for the accumulation of housing assets and other real (or tangible) assets are likely to be different from the processes that account for the accumulation of stocks, bonds, and other financial assets. There is a good chance that asking about net worth also introduces bias into survey estimates because it requires respondents to do arithmetic before answering. To avoid these problems, rather than simply including information on household net worth, or household assets and debts from which net worth can be calculated, the SCF asked detailed information on the various assets and debts that comprise net worth.

A third advantage of the SCF is that it oversamples high-income households in order to capture more top wealth holders in the sample. As a result, when pieced together, the SCF can provide a relatively more accurate indicator of historical trends in wealth accumulation and distribution. Although studies indicate that response errors and nonresponse bias are greater among the wealthy, gains in accuracy in wealth concentration measures are considerable enough to justify oversampling. The SCF demonstrates a considerably higher concentration of wealth. The difference in the Gini coefficient (a measure of the concentration of wealth ownership) between the 1983 and 1989 Surveys of Consumer Finances and the 1984

holding. Kennickell and Shack-Marquez (1992) and Kennickell and Starr-McCluer (1994) discuss later versions of the SCF and the use of SCF data in general. Kennickell (1994a, 1994b) described the method used to impute missing values in the SCF.

and 1988 Surveys of Income and Program Participation demonstrates how much difference the choice of sampling frames makes (Wolff 1995a). The wealth Gini is 0.80 in the 1983 SCF and 0.69 in the 1984 SIPP. Similarly, it is 0.84 in the 1989 SCF and 0.69 in the 1988 SIPP. As Wolff (1995a:71) points out, this is not surprising: The greater the representation of those from upper wealth groups, the higher the degree of wealth concentration in the sample. The point is, however, that one must be at least somewhat suspicious of wealth concentration figures derived from representative samples such as the SIPP.

I draw on estimates from several years of the SCF, including 1962, 1983, 1986, 1989, 1992, and 1995.[2] Among these data sources, the most comprehensive surveys are the 1962 survey and those conducted in 1983 and beyond. The 1962 survey, the Survey of the Financial Characteristics of Consumers (SFCC) is also known as the Projector Survey, after Dorothy Projector, the principal investigator (Projector and Weiss 1966). The 1983 SCF was sponsored by the Federal Reserve Board and conducted by the Survey Research Center (SRC), which used an area probability method to select 3,824 representative families for the 1983 sample and federal tax returns to select 438 additional high-income families.

In the simulation model, I use the 1983–1986 SCF panel to produce microdynamic models (regression models with a lagged dependent variable; I refer to them as "micro" because they are family-level equations). The unit of analysis for the microdynamic models is the family. The SCF also uses the family (or household) as the unit of analysis. The SCF defines the family as all individuals related by blood, marriage, or adoption living in the same dwelling. A family can include single persons or multiperson households (Avery, Elliehausen, and Kennickell 1988; Avery and Kennickell 1988). This definition of a family differs slightly from the Bureau of the Census definition that labels single persons as "nonfamily households" or "secondary individuals" (Avery, Elliehausen, Canner, and Gustafson 1984a; Avery, Elliehausen, Canner, and Gustafson 1984b). In the microdynamic models, differences in wealth behavior between single persons and multi-

---

[2] I also used the 1970 and 1977 cross sections of the SCF. These panels of the survey were somewhat different from other years. They had corporate sponsors and thus included questions that were otherwise unrelated to the wealth survey. These unusual years also had less breadth in their coverage of wealth holdings than other years. Some researchers do not even consider these part of the full set of SCF data sets. As a compromise, I did use them to align the simulation model, but I do not rely heavily on the estimates generated from this part of the model.

person families is controlled for with a variable indicating marital status. The microsimulation model, discussed below, allows the behavior of individuals to vary separately from the behavior of families.

In the simulation, I used the 1983–1986 and the 1983–1989 panels of the SCF to age wealth values (see below for more detail). In 1986, the SRC re-interviewed 2,822 households from the 1983 survey. In my estimates, I use only households that were included in both the 1983 and 1986 samples in order to model changes in wealth holding. Moreover, the SRC interviewed only independent households; and because a significant portion of individuals age 24 or younger would be in school, in the military, or living with their parents, they would not have been considered in the selection of the sample in 1983. Because those young people who were included in the sample would not be representative of the population of their cohort living independently in 1986, I exclude all families whose head was age 24 or younger in 1983. For these reasons, the total sample size for the microdynamic models is 2,791 families.

## Estate Tax Data

Since wealth is highly concentrated, a representation of wealth accumulation and distribution must include accurate estimates of the wealth of top wealth-holding families. However, this has proven quite difficult. First, wealthy families are a small slice of the population and standard representative surveys pick up far too few such families for sampling accuracy. Second, wealthy families generally do not welcome queries about the extent of their wealth holdings, and even if they are willing to answer questions openly, they may not be well informed about the details of their portfolios. Hence quality problems are widespread in data about top holders. One solution to this problem is to consult historical data on the assets and debts of the wealthiest American families and incorporate these into estimates of wealth distribution. However, because the United States has no wealth tax, no administrative data are routinely collected on family asset and debt holdings that could be used to compensate for shortfalls in survey data.

This last point has one exception. When top wealth holders die, their survivors must file detailed estate tax returns, and these estate tax returns provide the best available glimpse of the detailed wealth portfolios of top wealth holders. There are, of course, many loopholes through which the wealthy can avoid paying these taxes and thus be absent from or misrepresented in estate tax data. Estate tax records are certainly not perfect. However, there is reason to believe that efforts to enforce accurate payment of estate taxes have reduced such avoidance and produced highly accurate estimates of the wealth of top wealth holders (Johnson 1994a, 1994b).

One of the first major sources of data on wealth holdings was estate tax data, that is, actual tax returns filed for probate (Wolff 1995a). Data from estate returns are collected by the Department of the Treasury on the asset and debt holdings of top wealth holders at the time of death. This data is largely regarded as the most reliable source of information on the wealth of the rich because estate tax returns are subject to audit by the state. As Wolff (1995a) notes, the primary difficulty with estate tax data is that the threshold for filing estate taxes is relatively high. Table 2–1 provides the net worth (in both current and constant 1990 dollars) level at which deceased individuals must file an estate tax return. Approximately 1

Table 2–1. *Federal Estate Tax Filing Requirements*

| Year | Net Worth (current dollars) | Net Worth (1990 dollars) |
|---|---|---|
| 1960 | $60,000 | $261,000 |
| 1977 | 100,000 | 202,000 |
| 1978 | 125,000 | 234,000 |
| 1979 | 150,000 | 259,000 |
| 1980 | 170,000 | 268,000 |
| 1981 | 180,000 | 258,000 |
| 1982 | 200,000 | 272,000 |
| 1983 | 250,000 | 324,000 |
| 1984 | 300,000 | 374,000 |
| 1985 | 375,000 | 450,000 |
| 1986 | 500,000 | 585,000 |
| 1987 | 600,000 | 680,000 |

*Note*: Filing requirements refer to the net worth level at which an individual is required to file an estate tax return upon death. The requirement remains unchanged from the previous figure in years for which no value is given. I used the CPI-U to adjust to 1990 dollars.

percent of the population files an estate tax return in any given year (Wolff 1995a). A second difficulty with these data is underreporting or nonfiling of returns. The value of fixed assets and assets such as cash, jewelry, and art are difficult to determine and are likely underreported. Likewise, the wealthy have incentives to underreport and disguise the value of their financial assets as well.

Finally, because estate tax data is on deceased individuals rather than living families, there is an added difficulty in using this data in estimating the meaning of the records for the living families that are of interest. "Estate tax multipliers" have been developed to address such problems. In order to incorporate the estate tax data into the simulation model (see below and the Appendix for details), I use a standard method here. The basic notion underlying the estate tax multiplier is that, controlling for wealth-based differences in mortality, the inverse of the mortality rate for a particular detailed demographic group can be used to estimate the number of living individuals represented by a given number of deceased taxpayers. I describe the technique I use in detail in the Appendix. While the assumptions of the multiplier affect the estimates derived from the estate tax data, again there is reason to believe that the estate tax data provide a reliable estimate of the wealth held by top wealth holders (Johnson and Woodburn 1994).

In the simulation model, I use estate tax data from every third year between 1962 and 1995 to benchmark and align the wealth of top wealth holders. I do not draw on the estate tax data to provide separate estimates of wealth ownership here, as others have provided extremely detailed descriptive statistics from these data (Johnson 1994a, 1994b; Johnson and Woodburn 1994). Rather, I rely on the estate tax estimates to adjust the simulation estimates. In incorporating the estate tax data into the simulation model, I drew on estimates of ownership and value of wealth components (including stocks, cash accounts, retirement accounts, bonds, mortgages, other debts, etc.) by detailed demographic group (including marital status, age, gender, year of death, and total net worth). I describe below and in the Appendix how I incorporated these data into the simulation model.

## Aggregate Household Wealth Data

The *Balance Sheets for the U.S. Economy* (also known as the flow of funds or FOF) is an economic time series of flows and levels (stocks) of aggregate wealth holdings for various sectors of the economy. The Board of Governors of the Federal Reserve System has prepared and published annual FOF estimates since 1945 and additional quarterly estimates since 1952. These accounts provide a broad estimate of investment activity by measuring the value of real assets and financial assets held and transferred throughout the U.S. economy and by simultaneously tracking the sources of funds used to acquire these assets. The purpose of the flow of funds is to produce estimates of total sources of funds moving among economic sectors, including the household sector and 26 other sectors such as state and local governments and nonfinancial corporations. These accounts also track each sector's use of the funds by estimating the movement of assets and liabilities among financial instruments.

Flow of funds data are taken from numerous private and public reports and publications and are constructed based on the principle that total sources of funds must equal total uses of funds. In other words, whatever funds leave one sector must enter another sector, and whatever funds leave one financial instrument must enter another financial instrument. As a result, flow of funds estimates are highly internally consistent. In addition, FOF estimates of national saving are reconciled with national income and product accounts data produced by the Bureau of Economic Analysis of the Department of Commerce. This ensures that increases in wealth represented by the FOF are also consistent with external sources of income and saving data (Federal Reserve System 1993). The estimates I discuss throughout the remainder of this book have been aligned to the aggregate figures following Antoniewicz (forthcoming). The Appendix identifies the actual flow of funds time series on which I rely; the following section describes in greater detail the use of the flow of funds in aligning the simulation model.

### Simulation Model

In this section, I introduce in stages the simulation modeling strategy and the actual model that I use. First, I describe in rather general terms the challenges of modeling multilevel social systems. Second, I discuss the objectives of microsimulation modeling, and third, I discuss my rationale for using this research design. My aim in the latter two sections is to explain how microsimulation modeling answers some of the challenges outlined in the first section. Fourth, I compare multiequation modeling strategies with single-equation strategies and describe why I chose to use

a multiequation model. Fifth, I discuss some of the basic principles underlying the microsimulation modeling strategy that I use. Sixth, I describe
the model that I use. In this section, I discuss the larger model to which
the wealth simulation is connected. Finally, I describe the wealth simulation component of the model.

The simulation modeling strategy that I use combines several of the
basic data sources described in the previous section to create joint estimates of wealth inequality. Unlike many models used for forecasting and
experimentation, the model I used is constructed of individuals and families, the fundamental units of the socioeconomic system that is being
modeled. Using the simulation model, I am able to generate life histories
for simulated families, including such behaviors and processes as birth,
marriage, divorce, widowhood, remarriage, education, earnings, transfer
payments, and wealth ownership. This type of model is stochastic rather
than deterministic: Random sampling from probability distributions is
used to determine which events occur to which families and to determine
when the events occur. Because it is dynamic, the model permits the probabilities to change over time. Dynamic microsimulation modeling is a
strategy for modeling the interacting behavior of decision makers (such as
individuals, families, and firms) within the context of a larger system. The
approach utilizes data on the characteristics of representative samples of
decision makers, with simplified models of behavior, to simulate the
population's evolution through time.

### The Challenges of Modeling Multilevel Systems

In addition to the challenges associated with modeling household wealth
ownership and accumulation that arise because of inadequacies in available basic data, there are additional challenges associated with modeling
multilevel social systems more generally. The estimation of wealth ownership and accumulation involves both microlevel (individual and family)
behaviors and processes and macrolevel (aggregate or group) behaviors and
processes. The issues fall into two main classes. The first set of issues has
to do with deriving the implications of knowledge at one level for knowledge at another level. The second set of issues has to do with creating
behavioral links across levels.

The first class of issues in multilevel modeling arises when we posit a
theory, specify a model, or empirically measure a relationship at one level
and ask if the resulting knowledge implies any corresponding knowledge

at another level. Four related questions arise from this first set of issues (Maddala 1977). First, given a certain microrelation, under what conditions can we justify estimation of a similar relation in macrovariables? For instance, given a linear additive microconsumption function, when can we estimate an aggregate consumption function, which is also linear additive? Second, what are the conditions on the microvariables that will justify a certain type of macrorelation? For example, what do we have to assume about individual firm behavior so that the production function at the aggregate level is of the Cobb-Douglas or CES form? Third, what is the relationship between the parameters of the macrorelations and the parameters of the microrelations? Finally, what are the gains or losses by aggregation when we have access to both microdata and macrodata?

It is evident that the aggregation questions identified by Maddala can be posed in either direction, from macroknowledge to microimplications, or from microknowledge to macroimplications. For the macro-to-micro case, given a theory or empirical data specifying relationships among *aggregated microbehaviors*, what theoretical or empirical information is implied about corresponding relationships among the microbehaviors themselves? Note that we limit the question to the domain of *aggregated* microbehaviors. For example, given an observed empirical (or a posited theoretical) relationship between national voting patterns and national employment levels, what is implied about the empirical (or theoretical) relationship between individual voting and individual employment status? Issues can be posed in the opposite direction as well. Given a theory or empirical data specifying relationships among microbehaviors, what theoretical or empirical information is implied about corresponding relationships among the aggregated microbehaviors? For example, if a *theory* posits that an individual's employment and wages influence the probability of regional out-migration, what is implied about the theoretical relationship between regional employment and wages to regional out-migration rates? The parallel *empirical* question would be: Given an empirical relationship between an individual's employment and wages and the probability of regional out-migration, what is implied about the empirical relationship between regional employment and wages and regional out-migration rates?

A second class of issues is related to creating theories and models that connect influences emanating from one level to outcomes occurring at another level. For example, the actions of individual people, acting alone or in concert, influence institutions and vice versa. Social science needs to be rich enough to invent theories and models with these multilevel behavioral links, and empirical methods need to be subtle enough to test and estimate multilevel theories and models. Finally, methods of derivation need to be powerful enough to derive the implications that flow from systems of multilevel relationships.

Ideally, a multilevel empirical model of social behavior would have several characteristics. It would be dynamic and would synthesize data from disparate sources. The model would represent actors at the level of the behaving unit, as well as at the level of aggregates of such units. One cannot learn about individual behavior from aggregate data unless the behavior of the individual actors is quite simple and follows simple laws. Since most microbehavior is quite complex, this is not possible. A multilevel empirical model would also incorporate elements of the social environment, the social context in which individual actors act, and would account for behavioral heterogeneity among actors. Finally, such a model would recognize that a great deal of behavior at the microlevel (e.g., family portfolio decisions rather than aggregate ownership patterns) involves choices among discrete options, rather than choices along a continuum. As models of discrete choice are intrinsically nonlinear, a great deal of microlevel behavior is intrinsically nonlinear and must be modeled as such. Microsimulation modeling aims to overcome these challenges.

## Objectives of Microsimulation Modeling

One of the primary objectives of microsimulation modeling is *using* knowledge that we have about individual and family behaviors and processes generated in scientific literature in conjunction with those specifically estimated from data. The goal is to knit together basic research results from a variety of sources. As a result, microsimulation modeling (like most large-scale modeling strategies) means *synthesis*, not analysis; that is, the goal of large-scale modeling is putting pieces of knowledge together, not creating pieces. Dynamic microanalytic models are used to synthesize data from multiple sources (including data at several levels of aggregation) and to synthesize fragments of knowledge to produce a more unified whole. Unlike other large-scale models, a microsimulation model represents *individual actors*, not aggregates of those actors, and locates the actors within *structural contexts*.

In addition, a dynamic microsimulation model uses samples and equations derived from actual data on the sample to represent initial condi-

## Text Box 2–1. Objectives of Microsimulation Modeling

---

- *use* existing knowledge to produce estimates of individual and family behavior and processes
- *synthesize* data from multiple sources
- *synthesize* isolated fragments of knowledge
- represent *individual actors*, not aggregates
- locate actors within *structural contexts*
- use *samples* to represent initial conditions
- represent evolution of system via *life paths* of actors in the system
- use numerical analysis to solve *complex systems*
- derive *aggregates* from individual outcomes

---

tions. The model represents evolution of the system via the *life paths* of the actors in the system. These life paths are again estimated from actual sample data or taken from existing scientific literature. The model uses numerical analysis to solve *complex systems*, allowing solutions to problems too complex to be solved by analytical analysis. Finally, dynamic microanalytic models derive estimates of *aggregate*, or system-level, outcomes from individual outcomes, rather than making inferences about microoutcomes from group outcomes as many other large-scale modeling methods attempt to do. Text Box 2–1 summarizes the objectives of dynamic microanalytic modeling.

## Rationale for Using Microsimulation Modeling

I use a microsimulation model for several reasons. This method allows me to move beyond the description of wealth inequality at the aggregate level to modeling the processes of ownership and accumulation at the level of individuals and families. An understanding of these processes will create basic scientific knowledge about the causal mechanisms underlying social stratification and will also suggest possible remedies to the problem of wealth inequality. I use a large-scale simulation model because of the complexity of the multiple processes interacting to create family wealth distributions. The large-scale model allows me to investigate and test the role numerous individual and family-level processes play in determining distributional wealth outcomes. Through experimentation, the model I use can explore questions concerning the interactions of multiple processes affecting family wealth through time, over the life course, and across the full population of families.

In addition, the model connects multiple processes that are interdependent in reality but are usually studied in isolation. In this way, diverse forms of knowledge can be synthesized, and the full complexity of the underlying social, economic, and demographic processes can be captured. Reciprocal feedbacks among behaviors can be included. Individuals and families can be embedded within contexts. Highly heterogeneous responses, endemic to humans, to an identical context are easily representable. Aggregation is possible by adding across each sample individual or family and weighting to population totals. Policy parameters can be connected to person and family outcomes. Moreover, longitudinal life paths are generated for each person and family incorporating simultaneous age-based, period-based, and cohort-based changes. Distributional analyses (descriptions of winners and losers and analyses of the processes that produce these differences) are easily carried out via detailed, flexible descriptions of persons and families. From a more methodological perspective, dynamic microsimulation exploits the testing and estimation power of the microdata that is becoming increasingly available. Finally, from the standpoint of a body of basic knowledge about social relations, dynamic microsimulation integrates and reconciles diverse bodies of data, pinpoints knowledge gaps, and helps establish research priorities.

## Multiequation Versus Single-Equation Social Models

Multiequation models, including dynamic microanalytic models, are distinct from the single-equation models that dominate current empirical research in the social sciences, including the literature on wealth accumulation and distribution. The single-equation model, such as a standard regression model, generally includes a single endogenous variable, although many equations might be used to estimate the model of the one variable.[3] In the single-equation model, all other variables are exogenous, by definition, and also, by definition, there is no causal chain or sequence involved in the estimation process. Validation of a single-equation model

---

[3] For example, it is possible to estimate separate equations for different demographic, economic, or social groups, or to use a more complex process, such as two- or three-stage least squares, to estimate the model.

is possible, if it occurs at all, in only two ways: in-sample or out-of-sample. That is, the model is validated against the data on which it is originally estimated, and it might also be fit to another data set as a secondary check of the consistency of the fit across samples.

The general class of multiequation models includes dynamic microanalytic models as well as such models as theoretical simulation models, macroeconometric models, and cell-based simulation models. Multiequation models are capable of estimating outcomes for multiple endogenous variables and include causal chains, either recursive or simultaneous, by definition. With multiequation models, additional types of validation are possible.[4] Moreover, multiequation models can be estimated with constraints imposed from historical data so that the estimates produced by the model are historically accurate. With multiequation models, it is also possible to conduct experiments in which the researcher alters an initial condition or some other aspect of the model, reruns the model, and compares the results with a run made prior to the change. Finally, multiequation models facilitate forecasting of trends, including forecasting for both basic science and policy purposes. Text Box 2–2 summarizes the characteristics of single-equation and multiequation models.

## Microsimulation Modeling: Some Basic Principles

A microsimulation model is composed of individual decision-making units (such as individuals, families, organizations, and governments), and each actor is separately represented. The characteristics of the actor are obtained from an initial sample, and the "life" of each actor is simulated, using coefficients from actual data, by the successive application of a set of behavioral modules, with each behavioral module updating a single attribute. For example, a schooling module might update an individual's schooling status by simulating school entrance, school progression, or school exit behavior. A migration module might update location by generating for each family in each year a probability of leaving its current location and then generating a destination for each family that is selected to leave. Using other behavioral modules, individuals are selected to enter the labor force, marry, have children, earn money, consume goods and services, become disabled, retire, pass on an inheritance, and so forth. A

---

[4] With multiequation models, in-sample, out-of-sample, out-of-type, and multiple module validation are possible (Orcutt, Greenberger, Korbel, and Rivlin 1961).

## Text Box 2–2. Types of Empirical Models

### Single-equation Models
Example: Standard Regression Models

- Single endogenous variable
- Other variables are exogenous
- No causal chain or sequence
- In-sample and out-of-sample validation possible

### Multiequation Models
Examples: Dynamic Microanalytic Models, Static Microanalytic Models, Cell-based Models, Macroeconometric Models

- Many endogenous variables
- Many or few exogenous variables
- Causal chains (recursive or simultaneous)
- In-sample, out-of-sample, out-of-type, multiple module validation possible
- Experimentation possible
- Forecasting possible

dynamic microanalytic model can be used to examine both aggregate and distributional outcomes. For example, one could use the model to estimate the aggregate and distributional effects of interregional migration on life-cycle patterns of family earnings and family asset accumulation.

Computationally, each individual or family in a population is sequentially read into memory In the first time period. Each variable characterizing the individual or family is either obtained from the initial data set (which is usually a census or a similar, inclusive data set that includes the basic demographic, social, and economic characteristics of the actor) or assigned from a supplementary data set. If the initial data set does not include an attribute needed by the model, that attribute is assigned to the actors using a separate data set. For example, a census might not include health characteristics, so a separate data set would assign the necessary characteristics to the actors, using stochastic equations to maintain a distribution of the characteristics, based on the known characteristics of the actor. A life history is created for each actor by the successive application of the behavioral modules that are composed of rules (as in rules that determine the individual's eligibility to receive social security benefits based on age, marital status, and earnings history) and stochastic equations (as in equations that determine the probability of such behaviors and processes as marriage, divorce, and death for each actor). This updated population then serves as an input for the next period in the model.

This complex method of aging each actor in small, successive increments in order to create detailed life histories is a defining characteristic of *dynamic* microanalytic models. The alternative, *static* aging, is much simpler but yields much less accurate results. In static models, aging occurs according to exogenously derived control totals. An entire group of actors is often aged simultaneously, and over long time periods, to reach a destination year. In contrast, dynamic microsimulation treats a historical sample as the outcome of a set of generating processes; the intent is to make the sample and its aging processes endogenous by modeling the generating processes as closely as possible. Static modelers are interested in data as an end in itself; dynamic modelers treat data as clues to underlying processes. In addition, static modelers are interested in whether a historical sample accurately represents the population at one point in time, not in the processes that generated the sample.

Dynamic modelers are interested in whether a historical sample accurately represents the population, but they are also interested in discovering the underlying processes generating a sample. Dynamic and static microsimulation both provide useful tools for policy analysis, though in different ways (Orcutt, Caldwell, and Wertheimer 1976; Zedlewski and Meyer 1989). Arguably, only dynamic microsimulation is useful for basic research, such as the research presented in this book as well as policy analysis, as both the process and the end result are of interest. Figure 2–1 illustrates the aging procedure of dynamic and static microsimulation models.

As the model is updated in small increments, it also repeatedly reestimates its parameters with constraints from additional, historical data. This procedure is often referred to as alignment because after the constraints are imposed, the predicted values from the model are consistent (or aligned) with the historical data. The purpose of the multistage estimation procedure is to rectify the discrepancies between the model's estimates and known historical values while incorporating multiple sources of knowledge into the model's estimates. Alignment is, therefore, analogous to optimizing subject to a constraint. The difference is that the output of

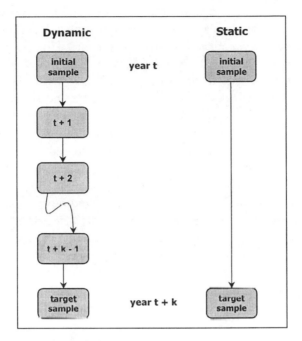

Figure 2–1. Dynamic vs. static aging.

the estimating equation is constrained rather than the constraint being incorporated in the actual estimation process. This difference is unavoidable because the model incorporates a very large number of equations, the output from which must be known and summed before the proportional adjustments can be made via comparison to the constraint.

There are numerous reasons that the model's predicted values might differ from historical values.[5] Consider as an example one demographic group: nonwhite females ages 70–74 in a microanalytic model of individ-

<hr/>

[5] Note that the expected values produced by *single-equation models* (such as standard regression models) are merely estimates of the true value of the dependent variable. These estimates do not reflect either the in-sample or out-of-sample value because of the error around the estimate. Likewise, the estimates produced by a multiequation model, such as a dynamic microanalytic model, are merely estimates. Thus the estimates from both single-equation and multiequation models differ from historical values. A key difference between single-equation and multiequation models is that multiequation models are often reestimated or aligned so that they are consistent with historical data. I supplement the comparisons in the text with additional validation tables in the Appendix (see Tables A–1, A–2, and A–3).

uals in the United States. When the microsimulation model is run from 1960 to 1990, the simulated group-level mortality rates generated by summing across the simulated individual-level mortality probabilities for this group do not equal the historical mortality rates published by the U.S. Office of Vital Statistics for nonwhite females 70–74. What factors give rise to these discrepancies? First, the values of the independent variables in the equations used to produce the model's estimates might be inaccurate, because the initial representation of the population is (almost always) a sample, and the sample joint distribution of independent variables is subject to random differences from the population joint distribution. Insofar as other equations in the model are imperfect in form or parameters they will generate inaccurate inputs to the mortality equation. Moreover, even if the equations are perfect fits to the initial data, outcomes in the model are subject to Monte Carlo variation. Hence, any given run will produce variations from the joint distribution observed in the real historical world.

The second reason that the model's estimates might differ from historical data is that the equations used to generate mortality at the microlevel might be misspecified. Violations of the following assumptions could cause misspecification: the assumption that parameters are constant in time, whereas the factors influencing mortality could be changing in magnitude in ways not captured by the equations; the assumption that period effects are absent or limited, whereas such historically specific impacts could be significant; and the assumption that there are no other specification flaws, whereas other specification flaws are inevitable. The microlevel mortality equations might be estimated from imperfect microdata on mortality. Imperfections in the mortality data could arise because the estimated parameters are subject to random variation around the population values; the data are drawn from a population whose definition is not necessarily identical to that of the population to which the historical statistics are meant to apply (e.g., in the treatment of the institutional population). Alternatively, the data could sample the historical period in question unevenly, an especially serious problem if the underlying parameters of a process have been changing over the time period.

A third reason that might account for discrepancies is that even if the mortality equations are population equations, they are stochastic processes, and hence any particular simulation will be subject to random variation in the mortality experience of different groups. Finally, flaws might actually be present in the official historical statistics themselves. Hence, even if the predicted probabilities are perfectly accurate, which is highly unlikely, flawed historical aggregates might generate discrepancies. Of course, given the complexity of a model of this sort, it is also possible that a programming error is accountable for the discrepancy between the model's estimate and historical data. In producing this sort of model, debugging code and validating estimates against survey estimates and other historical data occupies a considerable amount of the (already extensive) time involved in developing the model. In subsequent substantive chapters of this book (particularly the early substantive chapters) and in the Appendix, I include various comparisons of survey data with the simulation data to demonstrate that, after years of debugging and validation efforts, the model that I use produces estimates that are highly consistent with survey data.

## The Simulation Model

The specific simulation model I use includes a wealth module (or component) attached to a larger simulation model that produces estimates for multiple other behaviors and processes. The full model is called CORSIM (for CORnell SIMulation model) and was developed by Steven Caldwell and colleagues at Cornell University. The wealth simulation that I developed in conjunction with Caldwell is a single component of the larger model. Because of the detail it contains on the ownership and value of various wealth components, and because of the relatively complex alignment process, the wealth module is one of the largest components of the full simulation model. For simplicity, I refer to the simulation model in the remainder of the book, but my focus is almost exclusively on the wealth simulation.

The full model begins operation in 1960 using a representative 180,000-person sample drawn from the 1960 U.S. Census Public Use Microdata Sample (PUMS). Additional attributes that are needed by the model, but that are not available in the census, are assigned to the sample using data from alternative sources. Standard regression equations estimated on survey data are used to predict, for example, the probability of stock ownership as a function of characteristics of the family known from the census. For each family in the initial sample, a probability of stock ownership is calculated using this equation and a number is drawn from a probability distribution to determine whether the family will actually own stock. For those who are determined to own stock, the market value of the family's holdings is calculated in a similar manner (the next section provides a more complete description of the wealth model). Other attributes are assigned to individuals and families using this same method.

After creating an initial population with the desired characteristics, each characteristic is dynamically aged. Dynamic regression equations (e.g., including a lagged value), estimated from available survey data, are used to grow each characteristic forward (usually in one-year increments). Each individual (or family, depending on the behavior or process under consideration) is processed separately, but not necessarily independently. Changes in marital status and death, for example, would alter the probabilities of future events for the remaining partner. The model is also aligned with known historical values, such as data from estate tax records that is available only for somewhat aggregated subpopulation groups (divorced females of a certain age) but that is known to contain historically accurate information that is vital to the precision of the model's estimates. The model is aligned with historical data by changing the attribute of each member of the subpopulation group equally so that the total for that group matches the historical total. The result is a representative sample aged from 1960 to 1995 that is consistent with the most reliable data sources on each included process and that corresponds with historical estimates at the individual, family, and aggregate levels (Orcutt 1957; Orcutt, Greenberger, Korbel, and Rivlin 1961).

The model consists of thousands of distinct equations representing hundreds of equation-based processes, hundreds of deterministic algorithms, and well over thousands of parameters in both kinds of modules. Data used to test and estimate the separate equation-based modules are drawn from numerous, large national microdata files. Text Box 2–3 lists some of the major data sets used in the model. The model is partitioned into a series of modules, each responsible for a unique set of behaviors and processes. It includes such individual-level processes as fertility, mortality, age, schooling, leaving home, work, earnings, selected risk-factor behaviors, and most transfer payments. The full model also includes family-level processes such as family formation, assortative mating, family dissolution, immigration, most transfer payments, most kinds of taxation, savings, consumption, and, of course, wealth accumulation.

Each module, or section of the model, interacts either directly or indirectly with each other module, so that behaviors and processes represent the complexity of real-world economic and social processes. One process

Text Box 2–3. Data Used in the Microsimulation Model*

---

- Census
- Consumer Expenditure Survey
- Current Population Survey
- Flow of Funds
- Health Interview Survey
- High School and Beyond
- National Longitudinal Mortality Survey
- National Longitudinal Survey – Mature Women
- National Longitudinal Survey – Young Women
- National Longitudinal Survey – Youth
- National Health and Nutrition Survey
- Panel Study of Income Dynamics
- Survey of Consumer Finances
- Survey of the Financial Characteristics of Consumers
- Vital Statistics

---

* Not a comprehensive list.

might affect another directly if an outcome produced in one module is used as an input in another module. For example, earnings (a flow) and wealth (a stock) are produced in separate modules, but the earnings module directly affects wealth accumulation. Stochastic equations are used in the earnings module to determine an individual's weeks worked and earnings primarily as a function of demographic characteristics of the individual. The individual's earnings for the year are then used as an independent variable in a separate series of stochastic equations used to determine the likelihood that the family to which the individual belongs will hold certain assets and debts and the value of the assets and debts held. The indirect effect of one module on another occurs when the modules are not directly linked but the processes are interrelated. The mortality module, for example, affects all other modules because it determines the length of every individual's life. Other modules use only those people who survive in a given year in producing estimates of their unique processes.

The simulation model includes both primary and derived attributes. The primary attributes include person attributes (such as race), person links (such as ties between parents and children), family attributes (such as wealth), and family links (such as links between two families resulting from the marriage of two individuals). Of the primary attributes, kinship links are among the most consequential for social research and policy analysis. The derived attributes include all attributes that are calculated from basic information in the model. The derived attributes include such things as individual and family history attributes (such as earnings or health histories or the history of contributions to a pension plan).

The simulation model retains information linking all persons who have ever lived in the same family. Hence attributes for one person are often related to attributes of other persons linked by blood or marriage, as long as these ties were formalized by living together in families for at least one year. For example, children who no longer live with their fathers nevertheless can be tabulated by the income of fathers (though children who never lived with their fathers cannot). Similarly, the achievements of adults can be compared to those of their siblings, their parents, or any other individual for whom a kinship link exists. Kinship links include links with an actor's parents, grandparents, children, grandchildren, siblings, aunts, uncles, cousins, spouse, ex-spouses, in-laws, and former in-laws. Using kinship links, it is possible to track actual and potential resource flows through kinship networks and to study such processes as social and economic mobility (e.g., by comparing offspring's resources with the resources of their actual parents/grandparents at the same age).

## Simulating Wealth Inequality: The Wealth Module

The wealth simulation reconciles wealth data from multiple sources in order to (1) create a complete portrait of wealth distribution over the 1962–1995 period, (2) fully integrate existing knowledge about the way wealth ownership is distributed over distinct subsets of the population (including top wealth holders), and (3) accurately represent changes in ownership over time. The data sets that are used include: the 1962 Survey of the Financial Characteristics of Consumers (Projector and Weiss 1966); the 1983–1986 and 1983–1989 panels of the Survey of Consumer Finances (Avery and Kennickell 1988; Kennickell and Shack-Marquez 1992); cross-sectional estate tax records from the Department of the Treasury for eight years; cross sections of the Survey of Consumer Finances for eight years; cross sections of the Flow of Funds (FOF) or balance sheets for the U.S. Economy for 1962–1992 (Federal Reserve System 1993, 1995); cross sections of Department of Commerce data on real asset ownership for

Text Box 2-4. Data Synthesized by the Wealth Simulation

---

**Household Survey Data**
- Survey of Financial Characteristics of Consumers (SFCC), 1962
- Survey of Consumer Finances (SCF), 1983–1986 & 1983–1989 panels
- Survey of Consumer Finances (SCF), 1962, 1970, 1977, 1983, 1986, 1989, 1992, 1995

**Estate Tax Data, 1960–1992**

**Aggregate Data, 1960–1992**
- Flow of Funds (FOF)
- Department of Commerce Data on Fixed Asset Ownership

---

1962–1992; cross sections of Department of the Treasury data on the aggregate ownership of Individual Retirement and Keogh accounts for 1962–1992; the census of the population for 1960, 1970, 1980, and 1990; the 1980–1989 National Longitudinal Mortality Study (NLMS); the Dow Jones Industrial Average for the last business day for 1962–1995; and housing interest rates for 1962–1995. Text box 2–4 catalogs these data sets with details regarding the dates included.

In the simulation model, a family's net worth is the sum of 11 assets and 3 debts.[6] The real assets include the primary residence, other real estate, business assets, and vehicles. The financial assets include: stocks and mutual funds, bonds, checking and savings accounts, certificates of deposit and money market accounts, the cash value of whole life insurance, Individual Retirement and Keogh accounts, and a general category for other financial assets (such as trusts). The debts include: mortgages on the primary residence, mortgages on other real estate, and total other debt (such as vehicle loans, home improvement loans, credit card debt, and

---

[6] The most important omission from this definition of wealth is the present value of social security and private pension benefits. While these assets are not fungible, they are a central part of the savings of many households. The simulation model includes preliminary estimates of families' holdings of these assets, but the estimates were insufficient at the time this book was written to be included. The definition of wealth used here also omits the value of many consumer durables (the value of vehicles is included, but other durables are not). This omission was necessary because insufficient data exist to model household ownership of other consumer durables (Weicher 1997).

## Text Box 2–5. Assets and Debts in the Wealth Simulation

---

**Real Assets**
Home (primary residence)
Other real estate (including second homes)
Business assets
Vehicles

**Financial Assets**
Stocks and mutual funds
All bonds
Checking and savings accounts
Certificates of deposit
IRAs and Keogh accounts
Whole life insurance
Other financial assets

**Debts**
Mortgages on primary residence
Other mortgages
All other debt

---

education loans). Text Box 2–5 lists the assets and debts included in the simulation model's wealth module.

Using information about these basic assets and debts, it is possible to calculate additional measures of wealth, including such measures as net worth, gross assets, gross financial assets, gross debts, and home equity. Text Box 2–6 lists some of the additional wealth measures that can be calculated from the output of the wealth module.

The first step in the operation of the wealth module is invoking the initial sample. The model begins (as I mentioned above) with an 180,000-person (approximately 60,000-family) sample from the 1960 census (PUMS). The second step is to assign wealth values to this sample. Because the census does not include detailed information about family wealth holdings, I use the 1962 Survey of the Financial Characteristics of Consumers (SFCC) to assign ownership and initial values of each wealth type to each family. I use a series of stochastic equations, estimated on the 1962 SFCC

46

### Text Box 2–6. Calculated Wealth Measures in the Wealth Simulation

---

**Real assets** = value of primary residence + other real estate + business assets + vehicles

**Financial assets** = value of stocks and mutual funds + bonds + checking and savings + CDs + IRAs + whole life insurance + other financial assets

**Home equity** = value of the primary residence − mortgages on primary residence

**Equity in other real estate** = value of other real estate − mortgages on other real estate

**Gross assets** = value of real assets + financial assets

**Gross debts** = value of mortgages on primary residence + other mortgages + other debt

**Net Worth** = gross assets − gross debts

---

to assign ownership (yes/no) and value (dollar amount) for each of the 14 assets and debts to each family. Wealth ownership and value are aged in three-year increments using equations derived from the 1983–1986 panel of the Survey of Consumer Finances (SCF). I use the 1983–1986 panel of the SCF to estimate 28 dynamic (including a lagged value) regression equations. The first 14 equations (one for each asset and each debt) are logistic equations in which the dependent variable equals one if the family owned the asset or debt in 1986 and zero if the family did not own the asset or debt. The other 14 equations (again, one for each asset and each debt) are ordinary least squares equations, estimated only for those families who own the particular asset or debt. These equations are used to generate the first approximation of family wealth every three years.[7] I weight

---

[7] I have estimated the same equations on the 1983–1989 Survey of Consumer Finances and am able to substitute these equations for those estimated on the 1983–1986 SCF. Preliminary tests suggest that the model estimates are virtually unchanged as a result of the substitution. I use the 1983–1986 equations so that I have wealth estimates for every three, rather than every six, years.

all analyses in the current study to account for the inclusion of the high-income sample in the SCF data and to control for movement into and out of institutions, death, and changes in marital status.[8] The Appendix includes other details regarding the equations used in the wealth module.

Every three years, after the 1983–1986 SCF equations are used to produce an initial, updated estimate of wealth for each family, the model estimates are then reestimated with constraints imposed from historical data (i.e., the model is aligned with historical data). The alignment of the wealth module occurs in two stages. In the first stage, top wealth holders are separated from the remainder of the population and divided into 80 demographic groups based on gender, marital status, and age. I separate families into wealthy and nonwealthy groups for two reasons. First, the processes underlying wealth accumulation are different for wealthy and nonwealthy families; and second, existing sources of data on wealth ownership focus either on top wealth holders (e.g., estate tax data) or on nontop wealth holders (e.g., SFCC, SCF). In order to take advantage of the strengths of this data and to integrate the information included in this data into the wealth module, I need to consider families separately by whether they are top wealth holders or not. I apply the mortality multiplier to estate tax data to determine the proportion of the population that was wealthy in each year between 1962 and 1995 (Johnson and Woodburn 1994). See the Appendix for a more in-depth discussion of this process.

The wealth ownership (probability) and value of those in these detailed demographic groups are reestimated with constraints from either the estate tax data (for the wealthy, see description early in this chapter) or Survey of Consumer Finances (SCF) cross-sectional data (for the nonwealthy). The appropriate constraint is determined by estimating a separate stochastic equation on the estate tax or survey data and generating a predicted value for ownership or value, for each demographic group, for each year. The model estimate is then adjusted to adhere to this estimate for the group. Computationally, this is achieved by adjusting the intercept of the equa-

---

[8] I used the weight designed by the Federal Reserve Board for analyses of change in wealth between 1983 and 1986. See Kennickell and Woodburn (1992) and Avery and Kennickell (1988) for a more detailed account of the SCF and for descriptions of the design of SCF weights. Wolff and Marley (1989) reported that missing values in the SCF and adjustments designed to correct for missing values and sampling design did not drastically alter estimates of wealth inequality derived from the SCF.

tion for the linear (value) equations and through a multistage iterative process for the nonlinear (ownership) equations. I use estimates derived from these data as historical data with which I align the simulated port-folios of top wealth holder families in the simulation model. It is impor-tant to note that I do not simply introduce this mean value from the historical data at the outset because I want to preserve the wealth accu-mulation processes that occur at the microlevel. The data for wealthy fami-lies against which I align the model are composed of counts of people and the mean value of their wealth holdings within demographic groups and by wealth type within a given year. While this is extremely rich data, it groups families by demographic categories obscuring idiosyncrasies of individual households. Moreover, this data tells us nothing about how wealth holdings change over time. As a result, I chose to begin with dynamic, microlevel wealth estimates derived from the microdynamic regression equations and align the resulting wealth estimates to adjust for top wealth holding families. I provide a more detailed description of the methodology underlying these estimates below. See the Appendix for a detailed description of the equations used in this process.

The final stage of reestimation is designed to constrain the aggregate values for the entire population to agree with estimates of the aggregate wealth holdings of households. The historical estimates to which I align the model at this stage are yearly estimates produced by the Federal Reserve Board, the Department of Commerce, and the Department of the Treasury (Department of Commerce 1993; Federal Reserve System 1993, 1995; Internal Revenue Service 1975–1983) I draw on these estimates for each year in which the simulation model updates wealth values. See the Appendix for more discussion of the data used in this stage of reestima-tion. This final stage of alignment produces a set of estimates that corre-spond with historical estimates of aggregate stock holdings by households for every third year beginning in 1962. This stage of alignment ensures that the model produces historically consistent estimates of aggregate household wealth while retaining information about wealth ownership and accumulation at the level of households. Text Box 2–7 summarizes the steps involved in the operation of the wealth module.

One of the aims of dynamic microsimulation is to provide a platform within which "what if" experiments can be conducted. In carrying out an experiment, the model is run once using historically accurate equations, behavioral rules, and alignment data to produce "base run" output. Some aspect of the model is then altered, and the model is rerun to produce

## Text Box 2–7. Wealth Simulation Methods: Overview

---

**Step 1.** Initial sample (1960 Census)

**Step 2.** Assign initial wealth values

**Setp 3.** Assign initial aged values

**Step 4.** Three-phase reestimation of equations imposing constraints from:

    **A.** Estate Tax Data (for wealthy)
    **B.** SCF survey data (for nonwealthy)
    **C.** FOF and Commerce aggregate, household wealth data
       (for all families)

---

"experiment run" output. These two sets of output are compared, and any differences are attributed to the alteration made in the experimental run.

Three general types of experiments can be conducted using the wealth module in the simulation model. In the first type, the historical data against which wealth ownership and value are aligned would be altered. The stock boom experiment discussed in Chapter 9, in which the aggregate alignment data was altered to simulate the 1995 stock boom, is an example of this type of experiment. The second type of experiment that can be conducted using the wealth module is an experiment in which coefficients from the microdynamic equations (i.e., the equations that were derived from the 1983–1986 panel of the Survey of Consumer Finances and that produce initial/prealignment wealth estimates in the model) are altered. In this type of experiment, the microdynamic equations for one or more wealth component would be reestimated from the original SCF data, but the new specification of the equations would differ slightly from the original specification. The model would again be run twice. In the first run, the base run, the original microdynamic equations would be used to obtain the initial estimates of wealth ownership and value. In the second run, the experiment run, the new equations would be used. Again, all other parts of the model would be held constant so that any changes in wealth accumulation or distribution patterns could be attributed to the change in the specification of the microdynamic equations. I use experiments throughout the substantive chapters of this book to explore relationships between wealth and influences such as race, stock market booms, women's labor force participation, and federal estate tax policies.

The third type of experiment is a future scenario. This sort of experiment requires the researcher to make assumptions about the state of the world and allows adjustments to these assumptions in order to test the effects of alternative economic and social policies on potential future outcomes. In the future scenario reported here, the "alignment factors" (the numbers by which family wealth is adjusted when the model is aligned) for 1995 as calculated for each demographic group, and separately for top wealth holders and all other households, are held constant into the future. This allows aggregate wealth for each demographic group to change only in response to changes in the composition of each demographic group. Similarly, the alignment factors calculated from flow of funds data for national aggregates for each wealth type are also held constant. This again allows changes in wealth to occur only in response to changes in the composition of households. In effect, these are conservative experiments because real wealth increases only if the composition of the household sector becomes tilted toward households with characteristics that predict high wealth holding.

# Part II

## WEALTH DISTRIBUTION

# 3

# WHO OWNS WHAT? THE CHANGING
# DISTRIBUTION OF WEALTH

Men (in the United States) are nearer equality in wealth and mental endowments, or, in other words, more nearly equally powerful, than in any other country of the world or in any other age in recorded history.

(de Tocqueville, 1841)

Who owns what? How is the ownership of wealth distributed among families? Both basic research and practical concerns demand information about how many families are among the top wealth holders, how many families are truly asset-poor, and how many fall somewhere in the middle. Understanding wealth inequality also demands that we know how much these families own and how both levels of ownership and the extent of inequality have changed over time. What did the distribution of wealth look like in past decades, and what does it look like now? Few would expect wealth to be distributed evenly. Life-cycle patterns, baby booms, and other demographic trends affect the number of people earning income and accumulating assets at any time. Individual preferences for owning certain types of assets and debts vary over time as well as across generations at single points in time. Structural constraints limit the ability of entire groups of people to do the things necessary to accumulate assets and may even make them more likely to own debt. The availability of financial instruments varies over time, and laws regarding saving, investment, and related taxes affect the propensity of households to save. Of course, luck also plays an important role in distributing wealth unevenly. There is, of course, luck involved in even the most strategic stock investment decisions that can project some into the ranks of the top wealth holders and send others down to the bottom of the distribution.

Even if we accept some level of inequality as inevitable, it is disturb-

55

ing to find either very extreme levels of inequality or sharp rises in inequality in a short period of time. Clearly the first step in understanding how and why wealth inequality exists is to get a sense of how much inequality there is. Only once we understand the basic trends in the distribution of wealth can we begin to understand the economic and social processes that have accounted for these trends. In this chapter, I examine how wealth was distributed in the United States between 1962 and 1995. I identify the percentage of families that were among the richest wealth owners, how many had little or no wealth, and how many families were left somewhere in the middle. I use both survey data and the simulation model to explore the distribution of household wealth over these three decades. In the first section, I examine the mean and median household net worth. In the next sections, I use both survey data and simulated data to investigate the percentage of wealth held by households in various sections of the wealth distribution, and I examine changes in the composition of the typical family's net worth portfolio. I briefly discuss trends in wealth mobility, that is, trends in movement of families from one segment of the distribution to another over time. I address issues of mobility in greater detail in Chapter 9, but I introduce the concept here because it is vital to our understanding of intergenerational persistence in wealth inequality.

In addition to exploring trends in the distribution of wealth in this chapter, I also compare estimates of basic patterns from the survey data to those produced by the simulation model. The comparisons demonstrate that the simulation model is highly consistent with indicators of wealth ownership and accumulation that we obtain from standard data sources prior to any manipulations of the model. My intention is to demonstrate the model's abilities to re-create historical estimates while lending credibility to its postmanipulation estimates. In the final section of the chapter, I introduce the results of such a simulation experiment. Specifically the experiment simulates the distributional impact of a historic increase in middle-class stock ownership and finds some indication of a resulting increase in inequality.[1]

---

[1] I chose this experiment among many that I might have presented because portfolio behavior is relatively easily altered with policy changes and because middle-class stock ownership appears to have affected wealth distribution in the final years covered by this book. I might have presented the results of various other experiments, but I chose this because it is more practical (i.e., less abstract) than others.

## *Net Worth and Financial Wealth*

While levels of wealth ownership vary from year to year, long-term trends in mean and median holdings of net worth and financial assets are good indicators of the general level of household well-being. Looking at trends over long periods of time highlights the influence of short-term fluctuations in inflation, rates of return, levels of employment, and other economic indicators. Likewise, a long-term view accents the influence of demographic trends that affect the proportion of families that are in various stages of the life cycle. For example, we would expect levels of wealth ownership to vary as baby boomers move through the life cycle. Looking at both levels of net worth and financial wealth provides a more complete picture of well-being than either indicator alone. Net worth, total assets less total debts, is a good summary indicator of household finances; while financial wealth, total financial assets, indicates the savings that are immediately available to the household.

Historical data on aggregate household wealth and net worth suggest that aggregate levels of household wealth holdings have grown consistently since the early 1920s. Despite the methodological challenges that arise in collecting, synthesizing, and interpreting any data, particularly wealth data, over such long periods, Wolff and Marley (1989) were able to amass estimates of wealth ownership spanning the 1922–1983 period. Relying on both survey data and government estimates of aggregate wealth, they found that total household wealth per capita and net worth both grew dramatically in real terms over that period. Wolff and Marley used four separate definitions of wealth to investigate trends in wealth ownership. Because their concern was largely methodological, the use of separate definitions was sensible. In discussing their results, I refer to their first, basic definition of wealth, or total assets. There is little substantive difference in the trends that Wolff and Marley find across their different definitions. Ruggles and Ruggles (1982) used a similar methodology to estimate long-term historical trends in wealth ownership. While there are important differences in the findings of the two studies, the general trend in wealth ownership is the same in both. Wolff and Marley (1989:773) discussed the differences between the two studies in greater detail.

Between 1922 and 1983, real household per capita wealth and household net worth each increased more than three times (Wolff and Marley 1989). In the early 1920s, total household assets, or real wealth, was approximately $309 billion (in 1967 dollars).[2] By 1983, that number had increased to over $11 trillion. Similarly, total household net worth increased from $292 billion to nearly $9.4 trillion. Remarkably, while there are certainly downturns in this trend during difficult economic times, even during the worst times, only slight decreases are evident. During the 1930s, for example, both total wealth and net worth declined slightly, but the downturn appears as a minor jump in an otherwise steadily increasing trend. Wolff and Marley also used scattered survey and census data to estimate that these trends were evident across the components of total wealth as well. Their estimates of the value of owner-occupied housing from census data demonstrated that the value of the primary residence increased remarkably over the 1922–1983 period, with the greatest increases in the later years.

At the household level, there have also been dramatic increases in net worth and financial wealth historically. Between 1962 and 1995, the period for which survey data is available, mean and median household wealth increased markedly. Table 3–1 compares mean and median household net worth and financial wealth for 1962, 1983, 1989, 1992, and 1995. The survey estimates for 1962 are from the Survey of the Financial Characteristics of Consumers for 1962 (Wolff 1992). For the other years, the survey estimates are from the Surveys of Consumer Finances (Avery, Elliehausen, Canner, and Gustafson 1986; Kennickell and Shack-Marquez 1992; Kennickell and Starr-McCluer 1994; Wolff 1994, 1998). In these estimates, net worth refers to wealth that is marketable. That is, the current market value of all fungible assets less the current value of all debts. Assets include the value of the principle residence, other real estate, stocks and mutual funds, all bonds, cash accounts such as checking and savings accounts, certificates of deposit and money market accounts, Individual Retirement Accounts and Keogh accounts, other pension plans, the cash surrender value of whole life insurance, and trust accounts. Debts include all mortgage and non-mortgage liabilities held by the household. Financial wealth is defined as net worth less equity in owner-occupied housing. Financial wealth is a measure of a household's liquid assets and indicates resources available for immediate use. I use both measures for two reasons. First, while net worth is the standard measure of wealth, the financial wealth measure is a better indicator of available resources. Second, both are somewhat standard in the literature, allowing for relatively easy comparisons of my estimates with

---

[2] This is the sum of all assets owned by all families.

Table 3-1. *Household Net Worth and Financial Wealth, 1962–1995*

| | 1962 | | 1983 | | 1989 | | 1992 | | 1995 | |
|---|---|---|---|---|---|---|---|---|---|---|
| | Survey | Simulated | Survey | Simulated | Survey | Simulated | Survey | Simulated | Survey | Simulated |
| *Net worth* | | | | | | | | | | |
| Mean | 115,995 | 117,000 | 170,550 | 173,200 | 195,382 | 195,379 | 189,948 | 190,700 | 175,485 | 176,385 |
| Median | 30,996 | 35,218 | 43,801 | 48,700 | 46,881 | 47,181 | 39,995 | 40,721 | 39,146 | 41,000 |
| Percent with zero or negative | 11 | 12 | 16 | 17 | 18 | 19 | 18 | 19 | 19 | 19 |
| *Financial wealth* | | | | | | | | | | |
| Mean | 92,243 | 93,181 | 123,762 | 124,501 | 145,839 | 146,750 | 144,804 | 146,175 | 134,650 | 135,050 |
| Median | 8,358 | 8,200 | 9,453 | 9,580 | 11,166 | 11,212 | 9,366 | 9,418 | 8,537 | 8,613 |
| Percent with zero or negative | 21 | 22 | 25 | 27 | 27 | 27 | 28 | 29 | 29 | 29 |

*Note:* Survey estimates are author's calculations from the Survey of the Financial Characteristics of Consumers for 1962 and the Surveys of Consumer Finances for other years. Simulated results are from the simulation model. All values are adjusted to 1990 dollars, based on a standard CP-U.

other published estimates. The numbers in Table 3–1 are my own estimates, but they are consistent with other published estimates from these data sources (Wolff 1992, 1995b, 1998).

Mean net worth increased by more than 50 percent between 1962 and 1995, and while the general trend was a steady increase in mean net worth, the 1990s saw a downturn in this measure of wealth. In 1962, mean net worth was just under $116,000 (in 1990 dollars). By 1983 it had increased to more than $170,000, and the mean was nearly $200,000 by the end of the 1980s. In the early 1990s, however, mean net worth began to decline. By 1992, the mean was just under $190,000, and it fell to about $175,000 by 1995. Median net worth, of course, is much lower, one-quarter to one-fifth as large as mean net worth. However, the 1962–1995 trend in median values was similar to that of mean values. Median net worth increased from 1962 to 1983 and again from 1983 through 1989. But in the 1990s, median net worth also began to decline, although the decline was less than the decline in mean net worth in both absolute and relative terms. One reason for the decline in net worth during the 1990s is apparent from the table. That is, the percentage of households with zero or negative net worth rose steadily from 1962 through 1995, including during the 1990s.

Financial wealth also increased steadily between 1962 and 1989 and then started to decline. Mean financial wealth is, again, much greater than median financial wealth; in fact, it is 13 to 17 times greater. However, both mean and median financial wealth followed the same basic pattern that was evident in net worth values. Again, one of the reasons for this trend in wealth ownership was the increase in the number of families that had zero or negative financial wealth during the early 1990s. Between 1989 and 1995, the percentage of families with no financial wealth rose from 27 to 29 percent. What is perhaps most astonishing about the estimates included in this table is the magnitude of financial wealth that families owned during this period. That is, the median family had, at most, $11,000 of financial wealth at their disposal. In the worst years, the median was much less than this, as low as $8,300.

While the estimates from the Surveys of Consumer Finances (SCF) reported in this table suggest that most families had very little wealth, other sources of wealth data paint an even bleaker picture. For example, the Survey of Income and Program Participation (SIPP) estimates that household net worth for 1984 and 1988 was far less than estimates derived from the SCF (Wolff 1993). Moreover, according to the SIPP, mean household net worth grew much slower during the 1980s than SCF estimates indicate. The reason for the differences in these estimates likely originates with sampling methods. The SIPP is collected by the Bureau of the Census and is designed to gather information on income and household participation in government programs. The SIPP produces lower estimates of wealth ownership because it is based on a representative sample of the population, while the SCF oversamples high-income earners. Because this oversampled group contains many top wealth holders, the SCF sample includes more of the households that own the bulk of the country's wealth. The estimates I report in Table 3–1 are weighted by the Federal Reserve Board's weight that controls for the oversampling (Kennickell and Woodburn 1992).

One large gap in the information presented in Table 3–1 is the years between 1962 and 1983. I do not include estimates of net worth and financial wealth for those years because the Federal Reserve Board had essentially suspended the Survey of Consumer Finances during that period. There were other surveys of wealth information, but it is difficult to reconcile them with the SCF information. One method of estimating wealth during this gap is to use the estate tax data that I discussed in the previous chapter in my explanation of the simulation model. Smith (1987) used estate tax data and the estate multiplier method to estimate trends in wealth ownership between 1958 and 1976. His estimates indicate that total wealth ownership increased rather steadily during that period, consistent with the Wolff and Marley estimates discussed above. My own estimates of trends in net worth from the 1970 and 1977 Surveys of Consumer Finances (surveys that were scaled back from the primary years I discuss in this book and that are viewed as generally less reliable) indicate that mean and median net worth and financial wealth did, indeed, continue to increase during the 1962–1983 gap. However, the recessionary years of the 1970s slowed the growth of wealth considerably. Again, this trend can only be regarded as a preliminary finding as the data may be unreliable. At the same time, the estimates suggest that there was a rather interesting relation between aggregate growth and wealth during the 1970s.

Estimates of mean and median net worth and financial wealth from the simulation model that are also depicted in Table 3–1 are highly consistent with the survey estimates included in that table. The comparability of the survey and simulated estimates speaks to the ability of the model to produce historically consistent estimates of household wealth. Because the simulation model synthesizes survey data, estate tax data, and aggregate national balance sheets data, the model estimates are also consistent with historical estimates from each of these sources. The model estimates depict the same general trend in mean and median net worth over the 1962–1995 period. Both mean and median net worth increased from 1962 through 1989 and then began to decline. The difference between mean and median net worth is also substantial in the model estimates, and this difference is consistent in magnitude with the difference in the survey data. Likewise, the simulated estimates of trends in financial wealth and the percentage of households with zero or negative net worth and financial assets are also consistent with the survey estimates. One way in which the simulated estimates consistently diverge from the survey estimates is in magnitude. The simulation model consistently estimates moderately higher mean and median net worth and financial wealth than the survey. The differences are slight and not consistently statistically significant, but they are apparent. The slightly higher estimates are likely the result of alignment with the estate tax data, which tends to estimate higher wealth holdings for top wealth holders who are often not accurately represented in standard surveys. Interestingly, those who file estate taxes likely underreport their wealth even in their estate tax returns, so the true value of wealth holdings and the actual degree of wealth inequality may be greater than even the bleakest surveys indicate.

## Wealth Distribution

Historical evidence indicates that while the levels of inequality in the distribution of household wealth varied dramatically during the first part of the twentieth century, inequality in wealth ownership was consistently severe. Lampman (1962) was one of the first researchers to point to inequalities in wealth distribution as a source of social problems. Using estate tax data and the estate multiplier method, Lampman investigated trends in wealth ownership and inequality in the decades between 1920 and 1960. His findings indicated that between 1922 and 1953, the top 1 percent of wealth holders owned an average of 30 percent of total household sector wealth. While inequalities varied with macroeconomic trends during the decades Lampman studied, he provided convincing evidence that inequality was consistently extreme throughout that period.

Other historical estimates have produced similar evidence of inequality during the early twentieth century, even in the absence of systematic survey data. Wolff and Marley (1989) used various data sources, including Lampman's 1962 data and data compiled by Smith (1984, 1987), to study wealth inequality over the entire 1920–1990 period. For the early part of the century, their results are consistent with Lampman's findings. They demonstrate that the top 1 percent of wealth owners owned an average of 30 percent of total net worth between 1922 and the early 1950s. Between 1922 and the 1929 stock market crash, the share of wealth owned by the top 1 percent increased from about 29 percent to about 32 percent. During the 1930s and 1940s, the concentration of wealth declined, so that the top 1 percent owned less than 30 percent by the late 1940s. During the 1950s, economic prosperity brought with it increased wealth inequality, and by the late 1950s, estimates suggest that the top 1 percent of households owned nearly 35 percent of total wealth.

In 1962, the Survey of the Financial Characteristics of Consumers (SFCC) supplied a uniquely comprehensive look into the wealth holdings of Americans and contributed unequivocal evidence that wealth inequality was quite severe. The estimates in Table 3–2 demonstrate just how unequal the distribution of wealth was between 1962 and 1995. The table includes estimates of the percentage of total net worth and total financial wealth owned by households in various segments of the wealth distribution. The 1962 estimates in this table are from the SFCC and, again, the estimates for other years are from the Surveys of Consumer Finances (SCF). Net worth and financial wealth are defined as they were in table 3–1. This table also includes estimates of the wealth Gini coefficient, derived from the same survey data. The Gini coefficient is an indicator of the degree of inequality. It ranges from 0 to 1, with 0 indicating perfect equality and 1 indicating perfect inequality. Conceptually, if a single household were to own all wealth, the Gini coefficient would equal unity (Weicher 1995, 1997). The Gini coefficient is a convenient, single indicator of inequality that reflects changes in inequality in any segment of the distribution. As Weicher points out, however, the Gini's primary drawback is that it does not have an intuitive interpretation. For instance, a Gini of 0.5 does not mean that the distribution is halfway between equal and unequal, even if such a statement made any sense. Yet the coefficient has become widely used, as it is in the measurement of income inequality, as a single measure of the degree of inequality in the distribution of wealth. Thus I include estimates of it in the table.

From the estimates presented in Table 3–2, it is apparent that a very small portion of households has consistently owned the vast majority of

Table 3–2. *Distribution of Net Worth and Financial Wealth, 1962–1995: Survey Estimates*

| | Gini Coefficient | Top 1% | Next 4% | Next 5% | Next 10% | Top 20% | 2$^{nd}$ 20% | 3$^{rd}$ 20% | Bottom 40% |
|---|---|---|---|---|---|---|---|---|---|
| *Net Worth* | | | | | | | | | |
| 1962 | 0.80 | 33.5 | 21.2 | 12.5 | 14.0 | 81.2 | 13.5 | 5.0 | 0.3 |
| 1983 | 0.80 | 33.8 | 22.3 | 12.1 | 13.1 | 81.3 | 12.6 | 5.2 | 0.9 |
| 1989 | 0.85 | 37.4 | 21.6 | 11.6 | 13.0 | 83.6 | 12.3 | 4.8 | −0.7 |
| 1992 | 0.85 | 37.2 | 22.9 | 11.8 | 12.0 | 83.9 | 11.4 | 4.5 | 0.2 |
| 1995 | 0.87 | 38.5 | 21.8 | 11.5 | 12.1 | 83.9 | 11.4 | 4.5 | 0.2 |
| *Financial Wealth* | | | | | | | | | |
| 1962 | 0.88 | 40.3 | 23.8 | 12.8 | 12.7 | 89.6 | 9.6 | 2.1 | −1.4 |
| 1983 | 0.90 | 42.9 | 25.1 | 12.3 | 11.0 | 91.3 | 7.9 | 1.7 | −0.9 |
| 1989 | 0.93 | 46.9 | 23.9 | 11.6 | 10.9 | 93.4 | 7.4 | 1.7 | −2.4 |
| 1992 | 0.92 | 45.6 | 25.0 | 11.5 | 10.2 | 92.3 | 7.3 | 1.5 | −1.1 |
| 1995 | 0.94 | 47.2 | 24.6 | 11.2 | 10.1 | 93.0 | 6.9 | 1.4 | −1.3 |

*Note*: Author's estimates from Survey of the Characteristics of Consumers for 1962 and the Survey of Consumer Finances for other years. Cells indicate the percentage of net worth or financial wealth held by households in each segment of the distribution.

household wealth. In 1962, the top 1 percent of wealth owners owned 33.5 percent of total net worth. The next 4 percent owned an additional 21.2 percent, with the top quintile accounting for more than 80 percent of net worth holdings. The second quintile owned the next 13.5 percent, and the remaining 60 percent of the population shared only 5 percent of total net worth. The Gini coefficient for net worth in 1962 was 0.80, reflecting the story of extreme inequality that the distributional numbers in Table 3–2 tell. The distribution of financial wealth was even more unequal in 1962. The Gini coefficient was 0.88, and the top 1 percent of financial wealth holders owned more than 40 percent of total financial wealth. In 1962, the top quintile owned nearly 90 percent of total financial wealth, and the other 80 percent of the population shared the remaining 10 percent. The bottom 40 percent of the population actually owned negative financial wealth.

Wealth inequality remained unequally distributed but relatively constant between 1962 and the mid-1970s due to an extended stock market slump and the growth of welfare programs such as AFDC and Social Security (Smith 1987). Using estate tax data, Smith found evidence that after 1973 wealth inequality began to drop once again. Other researchers, using similar methodologies, have found that between 1972 and 1976, the share of total wealth owned by the top 1 percent of wealth owners declined from approximately 29 to about 19 percent of total wealth (Smith 1987; Wolff 1992). As with the estimates in Table 3–1, I do not include estimates of wealth distribution in Table 3–2 because there are not consistent sources of survey data from which to derive the estimates. Later in the book, however, I use the simulation model to discuss trends during the 1962–1983 period. The simulation model, which uses many of the same methods and data sources Smith and related researchers used to produce these estimates, produces similar results.

Wealth inequality began to rise considerably after 1979, a trend that continued throughout the 1980s. By 1983, wealth inequality had returned to and, indeed, surpassed, 1962 levels on some measures. By 1983, the Gini coefficient for net worth had returned to 0.80, and it was 0.90 for financial wealth. The share of wealth owned by the top 1 percent of wealth holders was 33.8 percent in 1983 and 37.4 percent by 1989. Real mean wealth grew at 3.4 percent annually during this six-year period, a rate that was nearly double the rate of wealth growth between 1962 and 1983. Others have found similar trends. Wolff (1993) found that mean family wealth increased 23 percent in real terms, but that median wealth grew by only 8 percent over that period. His research also suggested that the share of the top one-half of 1 percent of wealth owners rose 5 percent during this period, from 26.2 percent of total household sector wealth in 1983 to 31.4 percent in 1989. The wealth of the next half percent remained relatively constant at about 7.5 percent of total household wealth, but the share of the next 9 percent decreased from 34.4 percent in 1983 to 33.4 percent in 1989. Thus, the rich became richer and the poor became poorer.

Most striking is evidence of the decline in the wealth of the poorest 80 percent of households. The wealth of this group decreased by almost 3 percent, from 18.7 percent of total wealth in 1983 to 16.4 percent in 1989. Moreover, nearly all growth in real wealth between 1983 and 1989 was accumulated by the top 20 percent of wealth holders who gained 3.3 percent in their total wealth holdings. The second 20 percent lost 0.9 percent, the middle 20 percent lost 0.6 percent, the next 20 percent lost 0.4 percent, and the bottom group lost 0.9 percent. Wolff (1995b) found similar results in his examination of trends in wealth inequality. Existing research also indicates that in the 1980s, wealth inequality in the United States became severe relative to that found in European nations. Studies of wealth in the 1920s suggested that wealth was much more equally distributed in the United State than in Western European nations. By the late 1980s, however, research suggests that household sector wealth in the United States was considerably more concentrated than in Western Europe (Wolff 1995b).

While mean and median household net worth and financial wealth declined during the 1990s (Table 3–1), the distribution of wealth continued to worsen. By 1995, the Gini coefficient for net worth had increased to 0.87, an increase of 7 percent since 1962 and 2 percent since the late 1980s. Likewise, the Gini coefficient for financial wealth reached 0.94 by 1995, a steady increase from 0.88 in 1962. As a Gini coefficient of 1.0 would indicate perfect inequality, wealth ownership in the United States at that point was not far from being perfectly unequally distributed. The Gini coefficient accurately reflected trends in the distribution: As the estimates in Table 3–2 indicate, wealth ownership was highly concentrated by the mid-1990s. The top 1 percent of wealth owners owned 38.5 percent of net worth and 47.2 (nearly half!) of financial wealth. The next 4 percent owned 21.8 percent of net worth and nearly 25 percent of financial wealth. The extreme inequality that these numbers reflect is most evident in the proportion of total wealth owned by the top quintile: The top 20 percent of households owned nearly 84 percent of net worth and 93 percent of financial wealth in 1995. Of course, the most striking message these estimates convey is that the remaining 80 percent of households owned only 16 percent of net worth and only 7 percent of financial wealth.

Although these estimates are consistent with estimates from other research that relied on SCF data (Wolff 1995a, 1995b, 1998), other data sources produce considerably different estimates of wealth inequality. Wolff (1995b) compared the Gini coefficient for household wealth distribution obtained from the SCF and the Survey of Income and Program Participation (SIPP). He found that the SIPP estimate was considerably lower than that of the SCF (the number I report in Table 3–2). Consistent with the estimates I report in Table 3–2, Wolff found that the Gini from the SCF was 0.80 in 1983 and about 0.84 in 1989.[3] While both surveys indi-

---

[3] The estimate I report in Table 3–2 for 1989 is 0.85, slightly higher than Wolff's estimate and likely the result of rounding differences.

cate relatively high levels of wealth inequality, the SCF estimates are clearly more extreme than the SIPP estimates. The difference is, again, likely the result of the samples that are used in the two surveys. As Wolff pointed out (1995b:71), the greater the coverage of top wealth holders in a sample, the higher the degree of measured wealth inequality. The next logical conclusion is that surveys that rely on representative samples undoubtedly underestimate the degree of inequality, particularly inequality of household wealth, regardless of how it is measured.

The simulation model produced estimates of the distribution of household wealth that are comparable to the survey estimates. Table 3–3 includes simulated estimates of the distribution of total net worth across households between 1962 and 1995. The structure of the table is similar to that of Table 3–2 to facilitate comparison of the survey and simulation estimates. The longitudinal trends are consistent, as are the within-year estimates of distribution (Hurst, Luoh, and Stafford 1996; Wolff 1987b, 1993). The Gini coefficient calculated on the simulated output is also highly consistent in both magnitude and longitudinal pattern with the Gini coefficient estimated using the survey data (displayed in Table 3–2). One difference is that the simulation estimates suggest that wealth was more unequally distributed than is suggested by the survey estimates. As with the difference between the SCF and the SIPP, the SCF and the simulation are likely slightly different on this account because of the greater

Table 3–3. *Distribution of Net Worth, 1962–1995: Simulation Estimates*

| | Gini Coefficient | Top 1% | Next 4% | Next 5% | Next 10% | Top 20% | 2$^{nd}$ 20% | 3$^{rd}$ 20% | Bottom 40% |
|---|---|---|---|---|---|---|---|---|---|
| Net Worth | | | | | | | | | |
| 1962 | 0.81 | 34.2 | 21.5 | 12.4 | 13.7 | 81.8 | 12.9 | 5.1 | 0.2 |
| 1983 | 0.81 | 34.8 | 21.2 | 11.9 | 12.9 | 80.8 | 11.9 | 4.9 | 2.4 |
| 1989 | 0.86 | 38.5 | 22.6 | 11.7 | 11.5 | 84.3 | 12.4 | 4.1 | −0.8 |
| 1992 | 0.85 | 39.1 | 22.7 | 11.5 | 11.7 | 85.0 | 10.9 | 4.4 | −0.3 |
| 1995 | 0.87 | 39.1 | 22.6 | 11.1 | 11.9 | 84.7 | 11.1 | 4.4 | −0.2 |

*Note*: Author's simulated estimates. Cells indicate the percentage of net worth held by households in each segment of the distribution.

concentration of top wealth holders in the simulation. Remember that estimates of household wealth for top wealth holders in the simulation model are aligned with estate tax data and are typically increased slightly each year the model runs. As Table 3–2 indicated, mean and median net worth and financial wealth measures are thus slightly higher, and, not surprisingly, levels of wealth inequality are also higher in the simulation than in the Surveys of Consumer Finances.

## *Portfolio Composition*

What causes changes in the distribution of wealth over time? Part of the answer lies in the way Americans changed the type of assets and debts they owned. Portfolio behavior, decisions about which assets and debts to own and in what quantity, is one of the key means by which individual and family behavior affects wealth distribution. Table 3–4 decomposes wealth ownership into the assets that comprise it and displays the percentage of families owning each asset between 1962 and 1995. Consistent with the other tables in this chapter, the estimates in Table 3–4 are based on survey data from the 1962 SFCC and the Surveys of Consumer Finances for 1983, 1989, and 1995. The estimates indicate that the value of the primary residence, that is, the gross value of the household's owner-occupied principle residence, accounted for 26 percent of total assets owned by households in 1962. By 1983, the primary residence accounted for 30 percent of assets and was clearly the single most important asset in the typical household portfolio. This was unchanged through 1995. The second biggest asset in 1962 was stocks and mutual funds, followed by cash accounts (checking and savings accounts), then business assets, and bonds (including all federal, corporate, municipal, and international and other financial securities). By 1983, real estate other than the primary residence had become a more important component of household wealth, and stocks and mutual funds had declined considerably in significance. Cash accounts remained important through 1983 but the proportion of household assets accounted for by these highly liquid assets declined through the 1990s.

Various factors account for changes in the composition of household assets over time, including both aggregate economic and social trends as well as changes in household-level preferences for saving and investing. Likewise, the availability of assets and the ability of households to invest change over time. Patterns in the ownership of housing reflect both aggregate trends and household-level preferences. Housing is a unique asset

Table 3–4. *Composition of Household Gross Assets by Wealth Category, 1962–1995*

| | 1962 | 1983 | 1989 | 1995 |
|---|---|---|---|---|
| Primary residence | 26 | 30 | 29 | 30 |
| Other real estate | 6 | 15 | 13 | 11 |
| Business assets | 15 | 19 | 16 | 18 |
| Cash accounts | 17 | 15 | 14 | 7 |
| Stocks & mutual funds | 20 | 9 | 12 | 12 |
| Bonds | 8 | 4 | 6 | 4 |
| Whole life insurance | 1 | 2 | 2 | 3 |
| Pension assets | 2 | 2 | 3 | 9 |
| Personal trusts | 4 | 3 | 3 | 3 |
| Other assets | 1 | 1 | 2 | 3 |
| TOTAL ASSETS | 100 | 100 | 100 | 100 |

*Note*: Author's calculations from the Survey of the Financial Characteristics of Consumers for 1962 and from the Surveys of Consumer Finances for other years. Cells indicate the percentage of gross household assets in each of the wealth categories. Primary residence and other real estate are gross market value. Business assets include net equity in unincorporated farm and nonfarm businesses and other closely held corporations. Cash accounts include savings accounts, checking accounts, and certificates of deposit. Whole life insurance is cash surrender value. Pension accounts include IRAs, Keogh accounts, and other retirement accounts.

because it is not only typically a stable investment, but it also has current use-value. The family needs shelter, and the opportunity to fill the need for shelter while saving is appealing to many. Tax breaks for homeowners (it is in the interest of most societies to encourage home ownership) increase the appeal of this method of saving. Home ownership has other implications for families: The appeal of a secure place to raise children, a signal of stability, and membership in a community combine to further increase the attractiveness of home ownership. It is not surprising, then, that the value of the primary residence has been such a dominant part of the asset portfolio of households. Moreover, looking only at those in the bottom 80 percent of the wealth distribution, differences in patterns of home ownership across cohorts, racial groups, and income categories account for a substantial proportion of variation in wealth ownership. I address these differences in later chapters.

Compared to its central position in the portfolios of the nonwealthy, housing accounted for a smaller proportion of the assets of top wealth holders. The estimates in Table 3–4 indicate that housing assets consistently accounted for about 30 percent of the total assets of all families. In contrast, others using the same survey data have shown that housing accounted for only 6 percent of the assets of the top 1 percent of wealth holders and nearly 70 percent of the total assets of those in the bottom 80 percent of the distribution (see, e.g., Kennickell, Starr-McCluer, and Sunden 1997). The relative percent of total assets accounted for by any one asset changes over time, of course, as real estate markets, stock markets, and other economic forces fluctuate. Changes in the demographic composition of the population and household preferences for investing also change. In fact, in 1989, the primary residence accounted for a full 15 percent of the total assets of the top 1 percent of households. Yet while the exact percentage of wealth accounted for by housing does vary, housing wealth has consistently been an asset held primarily by the nonweathy. I address these patterns in more detail later in this book, particularly in Chapter 5, in which I examine the wealth of those who are not wealthy, and in Chapter 7 in which I discuss the impact of economic fluctuations on household wealth.

In contrast to housing, stocks were consistently an asset owned primarily by the wealthy. Because of the appeal of home ownership, many nonwealthy families first put savings into the family home. It is only after they have done this that they save or invest money in other ways. As a result, the middle class has traditionally not owned much more than their homes. The wealthy have been able to buy both houses and other investments, and stock ownership has been one of the ways they have consistently invested their savings. In 1995, stock ownership accounted for 30 percent of the total assets of the top 1 percent of wealth holders and only 5 percent of the wealth of those in the bottom 80 percent of the wealth distribution. As with housing, the relative importance of stock ownership has changed over time, but it has consistently dominated the portfolios of wealthy families. One important change that occurred starting in the late 1980s and early 1990s, in fact, was an increase in stock ownership among the nonwealthy. As the stock market soared and mutual funds became more accessible, the middle class began to buy stocks at record rates

(Norris 1996). By the end of 1995, stock ownership had become an important part of the portfolios of middle-class Americans, and academics and the popular press alike began to notice the presence of this group among stock owners (Sloane 1995; Thomas 1995; Wolff 1998). This change is apparent in the increase in the relative importance of stocks in the typical portfolio, and it might well have improved the distribution of wealth slightly. I discuss this change more in the next section and in subsequent chapters.

As stocks gained importance between 1983 and 1995, cash accounts declined in their relative share of the household wealth portfolio. Like housing, cash accounts tended to be owned primarily by the nonwealthy. More specifically, following housing ownership, checking accounts, savings accounts, and other demand deposits tend to dominate the portfolios of the middle and lower middle classes. The wealthy, of course, also own these assets, but their value tends to be overshadowed by more substantial investments in stocks, bonds, business assets, and real estate. At the other extreme, there are many in the very bottom of the wealth distribution who do not even own cash accounts. In any event, the relative importance of cash accounts in household wealth portfolios varies over time, but most of the change in the ownership of these assets typically reflects changes in the values of the stocks owned by the wealthy or the values of housing owned by the middle class. As markets boom, the importance of these other assets increases and cash accounts simply fall in relative importance. I discuss changes in ownership patterns of cash accounts, particularly among the truly poor, in more detail in Chapter 5.

## Middle-Class Investment and Wealth Distribution

What would have happened to the distribution of wealth if the middle class had begun to invest more heavily in the stock market early on? To explore possible answers to this question, I used the simulation model to conduct an experimental change in middle-class stock ownership and to examine the effect of this change on the distribution of wealth. In the experiment, I made two changes to historical patterns of middle-class stock ownership. First, I increased the probability of stock ownership among those in the second and third quintiles of wealth owners (by net worth) by 15 percent in 1962. To do this, I simply lowered the threshold above which a family in this part of the distribution became a stock holder. Second, I increased the value of stock holdings of all middle-class families (again those falling in the second and

third quintiles by net worth) by 15 percent in 1962. Subsequent stock ownership was a function of past ownership, that is, the equations in the model
that determine whether a family owns stock or other assets and the value of
the family's holdings contained a lagged dependent variable. Thus, the likelihood of stock ownership among middle-class families and the value of their
holdings increased throughout the 1962–1995 period, the period included
in the model.

To examine the effects of this change, I then reran the simulation model
and compared the distribution of wealth using the historically accurate
ownership and value patterns to the distribution of wealth using the experimental ownership and value patterns. The changes that appear after the
experiment reflect both (1) random variation and (2) the change from the
historical patterns of stock ownership to the experimentally imposed
patterns and random variation in the model. Because this simulation
model uses stochastic processes to determine things like ownership,
random variation appears when output is compared across runs of the
model.[4] Random variation is typically minimal and, by definition, it is
not systematic. What is left, then, is primarily differences that result from
the experiment.

The results from this experiment indicate that increasing both the likelihood of stock ownership and the value of stock holdings among the
middle class in 1962 and subsequent years took some time to have an
impact but eventually changed historical patterns in the distribution of
wealth. Table 3–5 presents the simulated estimates of household wealth
distribution before and after the experiment. The cells in the table indicate the percentage of net worth held by households in each segment of
the distribution before and after manipulation of the simulation model.
Estimates before the experiment correspond to simulated estimates of
wealth distribution in Table 3–3; however, the values in Table 3–5 are
rounded to the nearest percentage. In 1962, there was no change in the
distribution of wealth, as this was the first year of the change, and as with
most real changes in wealth ownership patterns, it takes time for the
changes to manifest themselves as distributional changes.

The experiment also had little effect on the distribution of wealth
during the 1960s and 1970s but became apparent by the 1980s. The

---

[4] The stochastic processes are incorporated into the model via the stochastic regression
equations predicting the likelihood of ownership and the value of holdings of families
in the model. See Chapter 2 and the Appendix for more detail.

Table 3–5. *Simulation Experiment: The Distributional Effects of Middle-Class Stock Ownership*

|  | Top 1% | | Top 20% | | 2nd 20% | | 3rd 20% | | Bottom 40% | |
|---|---|---|---|---|---|---|---|---|---|---|
|  | *Before* | *After* | *Before* | *After* | *Before* | *After* | *Before* | *After* | *Before* | *After* |
| 1962 | 34 | 34 | 81 | 81 | 12 | 12 | 5 | 5 | 0.2 | 0.2 |
| 1983 | 34 | 31 | 80 | 77 | 11 | 14 | 4 | 7 | 2.0 | 2.0 |
| 1989 | 38 | 31 | 84 | 78 | 12 | 16 | 4 | 7 | −0.8 | −1 |
| 1992 | 39 | 33 | 85 | 79 | 10 | 12 | 4 | 8 | −0.3 | −1 |
| 1995 | 39 | 33 | 84 | 78 | 11 | 15 | 4 | 7 | −0.2 | 0 |

*Note*: Author's simulated estimates. Cells indicate the percentage of net worth held by households in each segment of the distribution before and after manipulation of historical patterns of stock owner-ship among middle-class households. Estimates before the experiment correspond to simulated esti-mates of wealth distribution in Table 3–3. Values in this table are rounded to the nearest percentage with the exception of absolute values between zero and unity. The experimental conditions involved increasing the likelihood that middle-class families (those falling in the second and third quintiles by net worth) owned stocks in 1962 and subsequent years and increasing the value of stock ownership of all middle-class families over the same decades. See text for details.

impact of the experimental change was minor during those years for two reasons. First, changes in portfolio behavior take time to be realized as changes in distributional outcomes; and second, during the 1970s, the stock market was also quite sluggish, and stock ownership had a relatively minor impact on wealth distribution. Because the changes during the 1962–1980 period were negligible, I did not include them in Table 3–5. By 1983, however, the stock market had begun to rise, and the distribu-tional impact of the experiment had become apparent. As the estimates included in Table 3–5 indicate, the share of wealth owned by the top 1 percent of the distribution declined from 34 percent using the historical stock ownership patterns (before the experiment) to 31 percent in the model based on the experimental conditions. Indeed the share of wealth owned by the entire top quintile was reduced in the experiment from 80 percent of total net worth to 77 percent. Correspondingly, the share of wealth owned by those in the second and third quintiles had risen by 1983.

The second quintile owned about 11 percent of wealth historically and 14 percent after the experiment. The third quintile's share rose from 4 percent historically to 7 percent after the experiment.

During the 1980s and 1990s, the experimental change had an even bigger impact on the distribution of household wealth. The top 1 percent lost 8 percent of their share in 1989 and 6 percent of their share in 1992 and 1995 as a result of the experiment. The equalizing effect of the experiment was also evident across the entire top quintile. Six percent of the wealth that this quintile owned historically was redistributed to the middle class in each 1989, 1992, and 1995 as a result of the experiment. Again, the gains were apparent in the share of household wealth owned by middle-class households. Those in this segment of the distribution consistently gained wealth over the 1989–1995 period as a result of the experimental increase in their stock holdings. Because the experiment held their portfolio behavior constant, the bottom 40 percent of households did not share in the redistribution of wealth. The changes that appear in their wealth holdings are minor and reflect random changes that occur in a simulation model across trials rather than any actual change in wealth ownership. The lesson to be drawn from the experiment is that portfolio behavior matters. It matters for the well-being of families, and it matters for patterns of the distribution of wealth across families. In particular, this experiment demonstrates that middle-class investment patterns, particularly middle-class investment in stocks can impact the overall distribution of wealth. Of course, as the lack of change in the distribution of wealth in the 1970s in the experiment attests, market conditions must also be favorable and distributional effects take time to accrue.

### *Wealth Mobility*

Not only was the distribution of wealth highly unequal between 1962 and 1995, but there was also a tendency for families to remain in the same segment of the wealth distribution over time. Income mobility has been shown to be minimal, and wealth mobility appears to be equally rare. The estimates in Table 3–6 suggest just how much persistence there is in placement in the distribution of wealth. The survey estimates in this table are from the 1983–1989 panel of the Survey of Consumer Finances. The simulated estimates, like the others presented in this chapter, are from the simulation model that I discussed in Chapter 2. The cells in the table indi-

Table 3–6. *Wealth Mobility, 1983–1989*

| | 1989 Net Worth Percentile | | | | | | | | |
|---|---|---|---|---|---|---|---|---|---|
| | Bottom 25 | | 25–74 | | 75–94 | | Top 5 | | |
| 1983 Percentile | Survey | Simulated | Survey | Simulated | Survey | Simulated | Survey | Simulated | Total |
| Bottom 25 | 67 | 65 | 31 | 30 | 2 | 5 | 0 | 0 | 100 |
| 25–49 | 25 | 25 | 69 | 70 | 6 | 5 | 0 | 0 | 100 |
| 50–74 | 7 | 7 | 66 | 67 | 25 | 24 | 2 | 2 | 100 |
| 75–89 | 1 | 1 | 42 | 41 | 52 | 54 | 5 | 4 | 100 |
| 90–94 | 3 | 3 | 31 | 30 | 50 | 51 | 16 | 16 | 100 |
| Top 2–5 | 0 | 0 | 23 | 22 | 26 | 26 | 51 | 52 | 100 |
| Top 1 | 0 | 0 | 5 | 4 | 11 | 9 | 84 | 87 | 100 |

*Note*: Survey estimates are author's calculations from the 1983–1989 panel of the Survey of Consumer Finances. Simulated results are from the simulation model. Cells are the percentage of households that were in the specified row percentile in 1983 and the corresponding column percentile in 1989. The final column indicates that the other columns, both the survey and simulated columns, sum to 100 percent.

cate the percentage of households that were in the specified row percentile in 1983 and the corresponding column percentile in 1989. For example, if a household was in the bottom 25 percent of the wealth distribution in both 1983 and 1989, it would be among the 67 percent of households that were in the bottom 25 percent in both years. Because the table includes only endpoints of the 1983–1989 time period, a household's movement in the interim is not intelligible from the table. For instance, if the hypothetical household that was in the bottom 25 percent of the distribution in 1983 moved up to another percentile by 1985, but then returned to the bottom 25 percent by 1989, the household would still be counted among the 67 percent in the first cell. The final column in the table indicates that the other columns, both the survey and simulated columns, sum to 100 percent. That is, the estimates in the table account for each household that was included in both the 1983 and 1989 waves of the data. These estimates are consistent with other estimates of wealth mobility from the 1983–1989 SCF wave (Kennickell and Starr-McCluer 1997).

Between 1983 and 1989, 67 percent of wealth owners who were in the bottom quartile of the wealth distribution remained in the bottom. Thirty-one percent of those who started out in the bottom moved up to either the second or third quartile, and only 2 percent moved farther. The estimates in Table 3–6 suggest that this pattern was typical throughout the distribution: Families tended to be in the same segment of the distribution in both periods, with some relatively small amount of movement, either higher or lower, out of that segment. There was no movement from one extreme of the distribution to another (e.g., between the bottom quartile and the top 5 percent), and very little movement occurred between near extremes (e.g., between the second quartile and the top quartile). Even the movement that does seem to be apparent in the table might be deceptive. It might be that the wealth owner just moved a small amount. In many cases, movement between two quintiles may have meant only a slight increase in wealth, one that carried a person from the top of one quintile to the bottom of the next highest quintile.

Mobility patterns were similar for families that experienced some sort of structural disruption during the 1983–1989 period. Kennickell and Starr-McCluer (1997:390) used the 1983–1989 SCF panel to estimate separately the mobility patterns of stable households, that is, households that did not change appreciably between 1983 and 1989 due to marriage, divorce, separation, or the death of a spouse. Their estimates for these households were quite similar to their own estimates on the full sample (and those displayed in Table 3–6). The estimates on the stable households indicate slightly more persistence in wealth standing for those in the bottom quartile of the distribution and somewhat less for those in the top 1 percent of households. They note that some of this difference likely appears because the sample weights that are designed to account for over-sampling of high-income households do not address the difference between stable and nonstable households. If the estimates are correct, the difference might be interpreted as reflecting the negative consequences that are generally associated with major changes in household structure. Because the interpretation of estimates on stable households is uncertain, I do not make this distinction in my analyses.

Simulated estimates of wealth mobility between 1983 and 1989 were comparable to the survey estimates. Table 3–6 compares simulated and survey estimates, and the results indicate that while there was slightly less persistence in the bottom of the distribution in the simulated estimates, the general patterns were quite similar to patterns in the survey estimates. For example, estimates from the survey data suggest that a full 67 percent of households that started in the bottom quartile in 1983 remained there in 1989. The simulated estimate for the same families was 65 percent. At the other end of the distribution, the survey estimates revealed that 51 percent of those households that started in the top 5 percent of the distribution finished in the top 5 percent. In the simulated results, 52 percent of households were in the top 5 percent in 1983 and in the top 5 percent in 1989. Indeed, in most cells in the mobility table, Table 3–6, the simulated estimate is within 1 to 2 percent of the survey estimate. The slight differences are likely the result of alignment of the simulation model with estate tax data or small changes in wealth that changed a household's position in one data source and not the other. In any event, the differences are quite minor.

There are many reasons that families tend to remain in the same segment of the wealth distribution. Social reproduction, the notion that power and privilege are reproduced from one generation to the next, usually enters into sociological discussions of explanations of mobility. Much sociological literature on inequality has observed that among the many indicators of individual and family well-being, there tends to be little mobility. Research in the status-attainment tradition argues that education plays a fundamental role in preventing or enabling mobility, thereby emphasizing the notion that opportunities exist and mobility is possible if the individual makes certain decisions (Blau and Duncan 1967; Kerckhoff 1976). Others contend that schools teach students to behave in ways that restrict them to certain social classes or, more precisely, that inculcate certain personality traits that restrict people to certain classes (Willis 1981). Still others argue that social connections, again often acquired through schools, enable certain individuals to get ahead and constrain others (Persell and Cookson 1986). Whatever the cause, social structure most likely does play a role in enhancing or restricting mobility, wealth mobility as well as income and educational mobility. However, the time period reflected in Table 3–6 is rather short. Indeed, it is unlikely that many factors other than minor portfolio changes at the household level or market fluctuations (including the rather significant increases in the stock market that occurred between 1983 and 1989) influenced the movement that is visible in the estimates included in the table.

While short-term trends in wealth mobility are important, long-term trends are more consequential and more indicative of true patterns of stratification. Unfortunately, long-term trends are also much more difficult to estimate than short-term trends (which themselves are extremely difficult, given the absence of true longitudinal wealth data). Here a long-term trend would be a trend over a period greater than a decade, preferably over at least 20 years, which indicates actual lifetime mobility patterns. After all, mobility analyses are designed to answer questions about life chances, that is, the likelihood of movement through social strata over the life course. Moreover, wealth accumulation is a long-term process. It would be surprising to see much movement in short periods of time as few people really do get rich quickly. Likewise, it is rare to lose enough wealth over a short period of time to move considerably within the wealth distribution. However, it is difficult to measure long-term wealth mobility, again because of the lack of longitudinal data on wealth ownership.

In the absence of adequate survey data, simulation modeling can be used to begin to fill gaps in our understanding of long-term mobility patterns. To answer questions about lifetime mobility, a data source would need to follow the same individuals over long portions of their lives and, at the same time, include adequate information about both the wealth of their families of origin and their own wealth in adulthood to allow analysis of changes in position in the wealth distribution. Early mobility analyses used cross-sectional data sets that contained information about respondents and their parents (usually their occupations) to determine patterns of social change (Blau and Duncan 1967). Existing data sources on wealth do not have such information, and, if they did, this information would still be inadequate to ask questions about changes the respondent experienced over his or her own life. The Panel Study of Income Dynamics (PSID) truly is longitudinal data. However, even though the PSID respondents have been followed since the 1960s, the survey did not include questions about wealth until the 1980s. The simulation model I use is consistent with short-term patterns in mobility (Table 3–6). It is also consistent with our understanding of historical patterns of wealth ownership (Table 3–1) and distribution (Tables 3–2 and 3–3). While none of these demonstrate that the simulation's estimates of long-term mobility will be exact, the estimates are likely to be relatively reliable indicators of the general patterns of mobility.

Long-term trends in wealth mobility appear to mirror short-term

Table 3–7. *Wealth Mobility, 1975–1995: Simulated Estimates*

| 1975 Percentile | 1995 Net Worth Percentile | | | | | | |
|---|---|---|---|---|---|---|---|
| | *Bottom 25* | *25–49* | *50–74* | *75–89* | *90–94* | *Top 5* | *Total* |
| Bottom 25 | 60 | 21 | 12 | 6 | 1 | 0 | 100 |
| 25–49 | 19 | 48 | 21 | 11 | 1 | 0 | 100 |
| 50–74 | 5 | 20 | 52 | 18 | 4 | 1 | 100 |
| 75–89 | 2 | 9 | 31 | 38 | 15 | 5 | 100 |
| 90–94 | 0 | 8 | 26 | 29 | 25 | 12 | 100 |
| Top 5 | 0 | 0 | 2 | 9 | 35 | 54 | 100 |

*Note*: Author's simulated estimates. Cells are the percentage of households that were in the specified row percentile in 1975 and the corresponding column percentile in 1995.

trends. Table 3–7 contains simulated estimates of wealth mobility over the 1975–1995 period. This 20-year period covers large portions of the lives of the modeled households and the individuals that comprise them. Because households are not stable over such long periods, the estimates in Table 3–7 use the individual as the unit of analysis and take the net worth of the individual's household as the relevant measure of wealth. The Table contains the same type of information contained in Table 3–6, but Table 3–7 maps transitions from 1975 to 1995. The results indicate that there was little movement among wealth percentiles, even over a 20-year period. Sixty percent of those who started in the bottom 25 percent in 1975 were in the bottom 25 percent of wealth owners in 1995. Only 21 percent had moved to the second quartile, and 12 percent had moved to the third quartile. There was no movement over these 20 years from the bottom of the distribution to the very top, among these households. Downward movement was also rare. Most of those starting in the top of the wealth distribution remained there, with a few sliding down marginally. The patterns that Table 3–7 depicts are quite similar to the 1983–1989 mobility patterns evident in Table 3–6. I discuss mobility in more detail in Chapter 9.

## *Summary and Conclusions*

In this chapter, I explored patterns of the distribution of household wealth in the United States between 1962 and 1995. I used existing research to briefly discuss patterns that existed prior to 1962, but the bulk of the chapter used survey data and simulated estimates to examine 1962–1995 patterns. I first examined patterns of ownership of wealth. Using data from the 1962 Survey of the Financial Characteristics of Consumers and the 1983, 1989, 1992, and 1995 cross sections of the Surveys of Consumer Finances, I explored patterns in the mean and median net worth and financial wealth of households. I also compared simulated estimates to the survey estimates in this section. The simulated estimates varied slightly but were largely consistent with the survey-derived estimates. These analyses revealed that mean and median household wealth increased between 1962 and the late 1980s, but then started to decline. The results suggested that increases during the 1990s in the percentage of households with zero or negative wealth (measured both as net worth and financial wealth) accounted for some of this decline.

I also used both survey and simulated data to examine patterns in the distribution of wealth among families over the 1962–1995 period. The results revealed remarkable degrees of inequality, with Gini coefficients ranging from 0.80 to 0.94. The results also suggested that inequality steadily increased over the three decades included in this investigation. Some of the changes that were apparent in the distribution of wealth resulted from changes in the composition of household wealth portfolios and differences between wealthy and nonwealthy households in saving and investment behavior. I used the simulation model to explore the distributional impact of an increase in middle-class stock ownership. The results revealed that, while increasing middle-class stock ownership as early as the 1960s did not immediately affect the distribution of household wealth, long-term inequality was less severe as a result of this change in investment behavior. Finally, I explored both short-term mobility patterns (using both survey data and the simulation model) and long-term mobility patterns (using the simulation model alone). The results revealed considerable persistence in household percentile position in the wealth distribution even over long periods of time.

Wealth inequality is disturbing because it is so extreme and because of the implications for those who have little or no wealth. To think that wealth would be equally distributed is unrealistic. Yet even if inequality is inevitable, it is startling to discover inequality as extreme as the results of this chapter revealed. It is also disturbing to find that the likelihood that an individual will significantly improve his or her position in this structure is quite low. Such findings are certainly at odds with notions of equality of opportunity. In the next chapter, I continue to investigate patterns in the distribution of wealth by examining segments of the distribution in more detail. I start with the top percentiles of the wealth distribution because it is these households that control the majority of household wealth.

# 4

# THE RICH AND THEIR WEALTH

Wealth is not without its advantages and the case to the contrary, although it has often been made, has never proved widely persuasive.

(J. K. Galbraith, 1958)

In the past, we have known little about the wealthy because data on these families has been scarce at best. Truly wealthy families are not represented well in surveys because there are so few of them and, moreover, many of the wealthy either do not know or are not willing to reveal details about their wealth. Fred Lennon is an example of a wealthy man who prefers not to be noticed. Called "The Shiest Billionaire" by *Forbes* magazine, Fred Lennon controls 70 percent of the Crawford Fitting Company that, in 1995, had between $700 million and $1 billion in revenues, net profit margins over 10 percent, and no debt (Lane and Johnson 1995). *Forbes* estimates Lennon's personal worth at $1 billion. However, unlike the more visible rich, such as David Rockefeller or Bill Gates, Fred Lennon's name is not widely recognized. Like many of America's wealthy, Fred Lennon prefers to keep the details of his fortune a secret. According to *Forbes*, Lennon lives in a modest home in a secluded housing development in Hunting Valley, Ohio. His home is more than a mile from the nearest public road and his mailbox is not labeled with his name. Lennon has also taken great pains in the business that produced his fortune, a tube and valve fitting company, to ensure his anonymity. He has separated the company into dozens of independent firms and scattered them across the country. When Lennon buys a new factory, he even occasionally leaves the factory's old sign on the building to reduce attention in hopes of ensuring his anonymity. Yet the secrecy that Lennon tries so desperately to maintain accounts for much of the appeal of the *Forbes* article on the shy billionaire. As with most of America's wealthy, there is a great deal of curiosity about Fred Lennon's lifestyle, and deliberate efforts to conceal these details feed our curiosity.

Research reports occasionally suggest that they are going to provide insight into who the wealthy are, but these reports are generally disappointing either because they look at those with high incomes (rather than wealth) or because they tell us about only a few really wealthy individuals. In their volume *How Rich Is Too Rich?* (1992), for example, Inhaber and Carroll deal primarily with income inequality rather than wealth inequality. While details about earnings and income inequality are certainly important, they address only part of the inequality problem. As they have been for centuries, the truly rich are still separated by their wealth rather than their income. Moreover, as I mentioned in the introduction to this book, there is only a modest relationship between total income and wealth. In another example, Schervish, Coutsoukis, and Lewis do deal with wealth and wealth ownership in *Gospels of Wealth* (1994). While Schervish and his coauthors actually look at the truly wealthy, they focus on a relatively small sample of the rich and look at how the rich portray themselves. Both the Inhaber and Carroll and Schervish et al. works are typical of existing research that focuses on the wealthy, and neither work provides a clear picture of who the wealthy actually are or how they got that way.

In this chapter, I continue to discuss the distribution of household wealth in America. Rather than examining trends and patterns in the entire wealth distribution, however, I focus on part of the distribution: top wealth holders including the top 1 percent, top 5 percent, and top 20 percent of households by wealth ownership. Understanding trends among top wealth holders is clearly an important part of understanding major patterns of wealth accumulation and distribution because it has been those at the very top of the distribution who have controlled the vast majority of household wealth for decades.

This chapter is divided into five parts. In the first section, I examine trends in the mean net worth and financial wealth of the wealthy between 1962 and 1995. In part two, I begin to investigate the factors that separate the wealthy from everyone else. I explore the assets and debts that these households own and examine what fraction of total assets and debts in each category are controlled by the wealthy. In the third section, I present the characteristics of the wealthiest households. In the final two sections, I present the results of a simulation experiment designed to explore the effects of race on wealth accumulation and distribution. In this experiment, I force white and minority families to accumulate wealth in the same way, beginning in the early 1960s, and examine the impact on wealth distribution three decades later. In other words, I remove the effect of race on wealth accumulation processes in one decade and look at its effects after several decades of wealth accumulation.

### Net Worth of the Wealthy

The well-being of the rich is something that typically receives little attention. After all, the rich, by definition, are doing relatively well. Yet an understanding of inequality necessitates an understanding of how much wealth the truly rich control, whether that wealth increases or decreases over time, the causes of these changes, and, of course, a sense of whether the nonwealthy have experienced similar trends. In *The Affluent Society*, Galbraith (1958) pointed out that wealth of the kind experienced by Europeans and Americans in recent decades was unheard of throughout most of history. Galbraith noted: "As with individuals, so with nations. And the experience of nations with well-being is exceedingly brief. Nearly all throughout history have been very poor. The exception, almost insignificant in the whole span of human existence, has been the last few generations in the comparatively small corner of the world populated by Europeans. Here, and especially in the United States, there has been great and quite unprecedented affluence" (Galbraith 1958:1). Only a handful of relatively recent generations have known well-being, and only a handful of persons and families within those generations have enjoyed the utter prosperity that America's wealthy have enjoyed in the twentieth century. Just how rich are America's wealthy?

Table 4–1 isolates top wealth holders and compares their wealth within segments of the distribution from 1962 through 1995. The survey estimates in this table are from the 1962 Survey of the Financial Characteristics of Consumers and the 1983, 1989, and 1995 Surveys of Consumer Finances. Just looking across the top 1 percent, the next 4 percent, and the next 5 percent of wealth holders, it is apparent that the bulk of wealth was in the hands of the very wealthy over these decades. In 1962, while the mean net worth of the top 1 percent was over $3.2 million (1990 dollars), the mean net worth of the next 4 percent of households was only $647,000. Of course this is still a considerable amount of wealth, but the decline from the top 1 percent to the next 4 percent was a full 80 percent in 1962. In 1983 and 1989, the wealth of the top 1 percent was also about 80 percent greater than that of the mean for the next 4 percent of

Table 4-1. *Mean Wealth of the Wealthy 1962–1995*

| | Top 1% | | Next 4% | | Next 5% | | Next 10% | | Top 20% | | All households | |
|---|---|---|---|---|---|---|---|---|---|---|---|---|
| | Survey | Simulated | Survey | Simulated | Survey | Simulated | Survey | Simulated | Survey | Simulated | Survey | Simulated |
| *Net worth* | | | | | | | | | | | | |
| 1962 | 3,233 | 3,321 | 647 | 711 | 280 | 315 | 162 | 172 | 49 | 58 | 116 | 117 |
| 1983 | 4,755 | 4,888 | 952 | 969 | 413 | 421 | 223 | 235 | 693 | 711 | 170 | 173 |
| 1989 | 5,172 | 5,202 | 1,161 | 1,177 | 504 | 565 | 255 | 295 | 883 | 892 | 195 | 195 |
| 1995 | 6,756 | 6,781 | 956 | 1,001 | 404 | 458 | 211 | 226 | 736 | 778 | 175 | 176 |
| *Financial wealth* | | | | | | | | | | | | |
| 1962 | 3,874 | 3,968 | 547 | 556 | 225 | 236 | 117 | 125 | 414 | 424 | 92 | 93 |
| 1983 | 5,308 | 5,411 | 777 | 798 | 304 | 331 | 137 | 145 | 564 | 555 | 124 | 125 |
| 1989 | 7,077 | 7,090 | 1,058 | 1,115 | 380 | 401 | 162 | 172 | 749 | 785 | 146 | 147 |
| 1995 | 6,394 | 6,491 | 826 | 911 | 302 | 315 | 136 | 144 | 626 | 637 | 135 | 135 |

*Note:* In thousands. Survey estimates are author's calculations from the Survey of the Financial Characteristics of Consumers for 1962 and the Surveys of Consumer Finances for other years. Simulated results are from the simulation model. All values are adjusted to 1995 dollars, based on a standard CPI-U.

households. By 1995, the difference between the top 1 percent and the next 4 percent of households was not as dramatic as the distribution became more equal.

If the richest 1 percent of wealth holders seem rich, the affluence of the richest 0.5 percent is astounding. The majority of the wealth owned by households in the top 1 percent, that is, the majority of the net worth and financial wealth depicted in Table 4–1 as owned by these families, was actually owned by only a fraction of the families in the top 1 percent. However, for many of the same reasons that it is difficult to collect consistent and accurate data on the wealth of the top 1 percent, it is even more difficult to gather information on the top 0.5 percent. Sampling, confidentiality, and individuals' knowledge about their wealth holdings combine to make this a difficult group to study. Smith (1987) used estate tax data to make some inroads into understanding how wealthy the very rich (or the super-rich, as they are often called) actually are. Smith's estimates suggest that in 1962, the top 0.5 percent of households owned 22.2 percent of total household net worth, and the next 0.5 percent owned only an additional 6.0 percent. Smith shows that although the proportion of wealth owned by the super-rich declined somewhat into the mid-1970s, it remained a significant portion of total household wealth. I summarize Smith's estimates in Table 4–2.

Indeed, the very rich dominated the ownership of wealth throughout the entire 1962 to 1995 period. Turning back to Table 4–1, we see that the net worth of the top 1 percent was consistently many times greater than that of even the next 4 percent of the distribution. In 1962, the mean net worth of the top 1 percent was $3.2 million, nearly five times greater than the mean of $647,000 that the second 4 percent owned. Likewise, in 1983, the top 1 percent owned approximately five times as much wealth as the second 4 percent. This difference decreased to about 4.4 percent in 1989, but by 1995, the survey data suggest that the net worth of the top 1 percent was 7 times as large as the net worth of the second 4 percent of households. Remarkably, the average net worth of the top 1 percent increased consistently from 1962 through 1995. This group owned $3.2 million in net worth in 1962, but their average net worth had increased to $6.7 million by 1995. It is important to note that these are in constant (1990) dollars, so the effects of inflation have already been removed from these estimates. Further, while the wealth of this group appears to increase steadily between 1962 and 1995, there is evidence from estate tax data (Smith 1987) that during the 1970s the wealth of the very wealthy

The Rich and Their Wealth

Table 4–2. *The Wealth of the Super-Rich, 1962–1976*

|      | Top 0.5% | Next 0.5% | Top 1% |
| ---- | -------- | --------- | ------ |
| 1962 | 22.2     | 6.0       | 28.2   |
| 1965 | 25.4     | 5.9       | 31.3   |
| 1969 | 21.8     | 5.6       | 27.4   |
| 1972 | 21.9     | 5.8       | 27.7   |
| 1976 | 14.4     | 4.8       | 19.2   |

*Note:* Smith's estimates from estate tax data (Smith 1987).

declined. This is not surprising. We would expect the wealth of the upper segments of the distribution to fluctuate with trends in inflation, real estate market trends, and the movement of the stock market. I will discuss this in greater depth in Chapter 7, but it is important to note that the trends that are evident in Table 4–1 document that wealth inequality is correlated with general economic trends.

The affluence of America's richest households is even more dramatic if wealth is defined as financial wealth, rather than liquid wealth. In addition to estimates of mean net worth, Table 4–1 includes estimates of mean financial wealth. The financial wealth of the top 1 percent of households was greater in each year with the exception of 1995. In 1962, the net worth of the top 1 percent of wealth owners was 83 percent of their financial wealth (net worth was $3.2 million and financial wealth was $3.8 million). By 1983, the net worth of these families was 89 percent of their financial wealth. By 1995, the Survey of Consumer Finances indicates that finan cial wealth for top wealth holders was less than their net worth. Again, there were years, particularly during the 1970s, when increased inflation and declining stock and real estate values eroded the financial wealth of these households, but generally the wealthiest households have been even more affluent when wealth is measured as financial wealth. Even when values of financial worth declined, however, the magnitude of the wealth of the rich was astounding. Mean financial wealth was $3.8 million in 1962. It had increased to $5.3 million by 1983 and was more than $7 million in 1989. Even in 1995, when net worth was greater than financial wealth, the financial wealth of the rich averaged more than $6 million. In contrast to the top 1 percent of households, those farther down the distribution owned little financial wealth. The financial wealth of even the next 4 percent of the distribution was less than $1 million in each year included in the table, with the exception of 1989. For those even farther down the distribution, financial wealth was rarely greater than $500,000. The dramatic differences in the wealth ownership of the rich and the rest of the population are evident in this table, but when this group is compared to the wealth of households below the top 20 percent, the differences are even more startling. I take up this topic in more detail in the next chapter.

For comparison, Table 4–1 also includes simulated estimates of mean net worth and financial wealth for top wealth holders. I include both estimates for two reasons. First, I report both estimates to provide some validity to the simulated estimates. The simulated estimates are consistent with the survey estimates both cross-sectionally and over time. This indicates that the simulation model is able to produce historically accurate estimates of wealth ownership in multiple forms. The survey estimates included in the table are not unusual estimates of unique groups. Rather, these estimates are consistent with other published estimates of wealth ownership (see Wolff 1998 for comparison). Second, I provide both sets of estimates because the differences in the simulated estimates suggest that the wealth ownership of the rich is greater than we deduce from survey estimates alone. The largest discrepancies between the simulated estimates and the survey estimates are in the top 1 percent of the distribution, the segment of the distribution that would be most affected by alignment with estate tax data. In this case, the simulated estimates are consistently greater than the survey estimates indicating that once the survey is aligned with estate tax information, the magnitude of wealth owned by the top 1 percent is even greater than indicated by survey data. For example, the survey estimates suggest that the top 1 percent of wealth owners owned an average of $3.2 million in net worth in 1962, while the simulated estimates suggest that this number was actually $3.3 million. Similarly, the survey estimate suggests that the top 1 percent had $6.3 million in financial wealth in 1995, while the simulated estimate indicates that this number was closer to $6.5 million.

Increasing affluence in the United States during the 1980s and 1990s was evident in what Robert Frank deemed *Luxury Fever* (Frank 1999). Frank documented spectacular increases in spending patterns among

American households that involved such extravagant endeavors as the building of a lavish, medieval-style castle in Long Island's Hamptons by a Jersey City banker and his brother. Building the castle cost $10 million, and the banker told the *New York Times* that he undertook this extreme project simply for the sake of building. When the reporter asked whether there was any toy that the banker might still like to add to his new home (a house that already included an underwater sound system in the indoor swimming pool, a tennis court, and six suits of armor), the banker replied that if there had been anything else he had wanted, he would have included it originally. The banker was 32 years old (Frank 1999:3). In addition to new luxury homes and improvements to existing homes, Frank documented that many of the super-rich spent similarly extravagant sums of money on luxury items. While the economy boomed and their wealth expanded, the rich spent lavishly on automobiles, boats, home appliances, jewelry and watches, and cosmetic surgery. This lavish spending also began to include premiums for amenities such as a view or a desirable location in the purchase of a home, or premiums for sought-after wines and cigars (Frank 1999).

Extreme and increasing levels of affluence in America during the 1980s and 1990s also affected inequality relative to other countries. Wolff (1995b) cautioned that comparing wealth distribution patterns across countries is difficult because of differences in accounting conventions. Yet, recent evidence from Wolff himself and others suggests that wealth inequality in the United States during the last part of the twentieth century became much more severe than in developed European countries. In the early 1900s, wealth inequality was much lower in the United States than in the developed European countries. The starkest contrast is between the United States, the United Kingdom, and Sweden. Wolff (1995b) estimated that the top 1 percent of wealth holders in the United Kingdom owned nearly 60 percent of total net worth in the 1920s. By 1970, this percentage had decreased to about 20 percent and changed little through the 1990s. In Sweden, there was also a dramatic decline in wealth inequality between 1920 and the mid-1970s. In this country, the share of net worth owned by the top 1 percent declined from about 40 percent in 1920 to just under 20 percent in 1975. In Sweden, as in the United States, there was a sharp increase in inequality between 1985 and 1990. As Wolff noted, it is surprising that inequality in the United States and Sweden increased in the late 1980s and 1990s but changed little in the United Kingdom during that period, because the United States and the United Kingdom both followed similar and rather conservative economic policies during that period. In contrast, Sweden directly taxed wealth ownership and followed somewhat more liberal economic policies. This suggests that while economic trends are important determinants of wealth distribution, policy alone is not responsible for producing inequality.

Inheritance also plays a role in producing and perpetuating wealth inequality, and some argue that inheritance inevitably leads to increases in the wealth ownership of top wealth holders (McNamee and Miller 1998). There was a time when opportunities for upward mobility in a single lifetime were abundant enough to make the American dream possible. The tag line to the 1950 movie *The Jackie Robinson Story* was that America is a land "where every child has the opportunity to become president or play baseball for the Brooklyn Dodgers" (Kuttner 1987). This idea was grounded in a fair amount of realism. In the nineteenth century, wealth was primarily realized as land ownership, and land was available in abundance from the government to homesteaders. In the early to mid twentieth century, with the exception of the years during the Great Depression, many working-class Americans moved into the middle and upper classes by taking advantage of relatively cheap housing prices, expanding educational opportunities, and extended bouts of economic growth (Kuttner 1987).

In contrast, in the latter part of the twentieth century, there was evidence that mobility was more difficult and that family of origin was more important than it had been even a couple of decades before. John D. Rockefeller once purportedly claimed: "I was born into it and there was nothing I could do about it. It was there, like air or food or any other element. The only question with wealth was what to do with it." McNamee and Miller pointed out that inheritance provides those from privileged backgrounds a combination of advantages ranging from political power to cultural capital to social contacts and, of course, economic advantage. Of course, inheritance also affords the privileged the opportunity to maintain these advantages from generation to generation. As a result, laws protecting the rights of the wealthy to pass along their assets to following generations not only protect the well-being of those fortunate enough to be born into wealthy households but also lead to increases in inequality as the same families amass greater and greater amounts of wealth over repeated generations. Unfortunately, inheritance is as difficult to study as it is to change. Few data exist on the degree to which the wealthy pass along their assets. Estate tax data provide some insight, and I discuss these in later chapters, but more complete data are not available. McNamee and Miller also correctly observed that it is difficult to make changes to inheritance laws and practices because of the political influence that comes with wealth ownership. Wolff (1995b) advocated a more severe wealth tax as a partial remedy to inheritance leading to increasingly greater inequality, and his findings support this policy recommendation. Yet Wolff's finding that Sweden's more liberal (versus the United States' and the United Kingdom's) economic policies had only a limited impact on inequality outcomes suggests that this is only a partial solution.

Of course, some households accumulate wealth by saving, a process that has received considerably more attention from economists as well as from sociologists but that remains at least a partial mystery to researchers in both fields. Many of those who save do so with retirement in mind. In fact, estimates from the 1989 and 1992 Surveys of Consumer Finances suggest that 23.8 percent of families saved primarily because they wanted to have money for retirement. Similarly, in 1992, 26.6 percent saved for retirement (Kennickell and Starr-McCluer 1994). More often, if families save at all, they do so for more immediate reasons. Among all the families included in the 1989 and 1992 Surveys of Consumer Finances, current liquidity was an important reason that families saved. According to the same study, 41.4 percent of families cited liquidity as the most important reason for saving, and 42 percent had the same reply in 1992 (Kennickell and Starr-McCluer 1994).

Other reasons that families saved included planned purchases, buying a home, and education. Families seldom cited investment as the number one reason they saved. In fact, only about 10 percent of families in either 1989 or 1992 listed investment as the main reason they saved. Naturally, among the wealthy, reasons for saving are quite different. Estimates from the same surveys indicate that investment was a primary reason for saving for most of those in the top 1 percent of wealth owners. Does this suggest that top wealth owners are fundamentally different from other families? Perhaps so, but primarily in the resources to which they have access. As I will discuss in the next chapter, investment and wealth accumulation are goals that, for most families, can only be pursued after immediate needs are met. Thus, while some families will become wealthy by saving, most will not be able to spare enough current income for this purpose. By contrast, the wealthy have the resources to meet short-term consumption needs while investing for long-term gain. Revisiting the discussion of inheritance, the intergenerational transmission of wealth undoubtedly exacerbates this difference.

## The Assets and Debts of the Rich

We know that the rich are different from the rest of the population because they have more overall wealth, but how are they different in terms of the assets they own? Are there some assets that the rich are more likely than others to own? And what about debt? Do the wealthy have debt? Portfolio behavior, that is, decisions about which assets to own and which debts to hold, is one of the keys to understanding the processes underlying wealth accumulation and distribution, particularly because at least some degree of wealth is created by increases in market values of assets enjoyed by all owners. As we saw in the previous chapter, if the middle class had begun investing in stocks prior to the dramatic increases in the market that occurred in the 1980s and 1990s, their share of total wealth would likely have been greater in the mid-1990s. Table 4–3 includes survey and simulated estimates of the 1995 portfolio composition of the wealthy compared to all households. That is, the table includes estimates of the percentage of the total portfolio of these families held in select assets in 1995. The estimates indicate that the rich kept much more of their wealth in high-risk, high-return assets, such as stocks and bonds, as opposed to housing and other real assets. One of the most striking differences in the wealthy is the percentage of their total assets accounted for by the primary residence. Families in the top 1 percent of wealth owners held only 6 percent in the primary residence, while all families together held 30 percent of their assets in housing. Like tendencies to save, this number likely reflects the fact that most families can only afford to invest in necessities like housing.

In contrast, the wealthy were able to keep a larger percentage of their assets in more high-risk, high-payoff investments because they have resources in excess of those needed for current expenditures. The estimates in Table 4–3 suggest that top wealth owners had 11 percent of their gross assets invested in real estate (other than their primary residence) in 1995 and a full 37 percent in business assets. These families also had 30 percent of their assets in stocks and bonds. Each of these assets is likely to increase in value much more quickly than low-risk investments such as cash accounts. Surprisingly, cash accounts comprised comparable percentages of the total assets of the wealthy and nonwealthy. Looking at all households together, Americans had 7 percent of their assets in cash accounts such as checking and savings accounts and other highly liquid assets, while top wealth holders kept 8 percent of their assets in cash accounts. The wealthy

Table 4–3. *Portfolio Composition of the Wealthy, 1995*

|  | All Households | | Top 1% | |
|---|---|---|---|---|
|  | *Survey* | *Simulated* | *Survey* | *Simulated* |
| Primary residence | 30 | 30 | 6 | 6 |
| Other real estate | 11 | 12 | 11 | 11 |
| Business assets | 18 | 18 | 37 | 38 |
| Cash accounts | 7 | 7 | 8 | 8 |
| Stocks & bonds | 16 | 15 | 30 | 31 |
| Pension assets | 9 | 10 | 5 | 5 |

*Note*: Author's calculations from the Survey of the Financial Characteristics of Consumers for 1962 and from the Surveys of Consumer Finances for other years. Simulated estimates are from the
simulation model. Cells indicate the percentage of gross household
assets in each of the wealth categories. Primary residence and other
real estate are gross market value; business assets include net equity
in unincorporated farm and nonfarm businesses and other closely
held corporations; cash accounts include savings accounts, checking accounts, certificates of deposit; whole life insurance is cash surrender value; pension accounts include IRAs, Keogh accounts, and
other retirement accounts.

were different, however, in their use of electronic means of accessing their
cash accounts. In addition to information on wealth, the 1995 Survey of
Consumer Finances collected detailed information on the use of electronic
media for financial transactions and decision making. Kennickell and
Kwast (1997) analyzed the SCF questions on use of electronic banking and
found that wealthier households, particularly those with greater financial
assets, were much more likely to use electronic banking – direct deposit,
credit and debit cards, automatic teller machines, internet banking, tele-
phone transfers, and other electronic transfers.

Because of their tendency and ability to invest in different assets, the
wealthy tended to control the majority of total assets of certain types.
Figure 4–1 isolates 1995 and compares the percentage of total assets and
debts owned by the top 1 percent of wealth owners to the share owned by

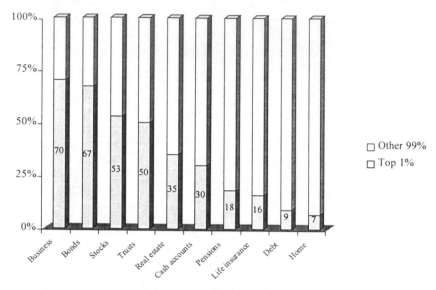

Figure 4–1. Percentage of total assets and debts owned by the top 1 percent, 1995. *Note:* Author's calculations from the 1995 Survey of Consumer Finances. Bars indicate the percentage of gross household assets in each of the wealth categories owned by households in the top 1 percent of wealth owners. Primary residence and other real estate are gross market value; business assets include net equity in unincorporated farm and nonfarm businesses and other closely held corporations; cash accounts include savings accounts, checking accounts, and certificates of deposit; whole life insurance is cash surrender value; and pension accounts include IRAs, Keogh accounts, and other retirement accounts.

the remaining 99 percent. The figure indicates that the top 1 percent of wealth owners controlled 70 percent of total business assets in 1995. This would not surprise Domhoff who has argued for two decades that America's firms are controlled by a power elite of the wealthiest families (Domhoff 1970, 1990). Others would argue that entrepreneurship is a certain way to enter the ranks of the wealthy and that as a result the wealthy own a disproportionate share of business assets.

Market trends also accounted, to some degree, for the types of assets controlled primarily by the wealthy. Rises in stock values in the 1980s and 1990s injected value into the portfolios of those who owned stocks, and as Table 4–3 demonstrates, the wealthy were certainly stock owners. By 1995, Figure 4–1 indicates that the top 1 percent of households owned 53 percent of stocks. Many of the wealthy were fortunate enough to also enjoy real estate windfalls in the 1960s and 1970s and consequently had large amounts of wealth in their homes and other real estate by the mid-1990s. As Figure 4–1 indicates, however, because the middle and lower classes also invest in the primary residence, the share of principal residence assets owned by the wealthy was minimal (7 percent of the total) in 1995. In contrast, the top 1 percent owned 35 percent of other real estate such as vacation homes, other second homes, and investment real estate. The figure does not include simulated estimates, but the estimates from the simulation are comparable to the survey estimates.

While the wealthy held only a small minority of debt in 1995 (and other earlier years), Figure 4–1 indicates that they did, indeed, have some debt. Between 1962 and 1995, American households incurred vast sums of debt, including mortgages, automobile loans, credit card debt, student loans, home improvement loans, and various other liabilities that, for some families, grew much more rapidly than their incomes (Canner, Kennickell, and Luckett 1995). Estimates from the 1983, 1989, and 1992 Surveys of Consumer Finances indicate that for most households, the ratio of debt payments to total income increased from approximately 10 to about 15 (Canner, Kennickell, and Luckett 1995). The wealthy did own debt, and in many cases their debt burden was greater than their income. However, the ratio of debt to income was not as severe as that of less wealthy households (less than 9 in 1983, 1989, and 1992 for high-income and high-wealth groups), and it did not increase much over the 1983–1992 period. One reason for this difference is that consumer debt increased much more quickly than other types of debt, and the wealthy were unlikely to have heavy consumer debt burdens. Likewise, demographically, minorities and young households accrued the greatest amounts of debt during the 1980s and 1990s, and as the next section will indicate, these families were unlikely to be wealthy.

### Profile of the Top Wealth Holders

It is fairly widely known that a small proportion of families owned the great majority of wealth in America throughout the twentieth century. What is not quite so widely known is what the families in the various segments of the distribution of wealth look like. In this section, I present estimates of the demographic characteristics of the very wealthiest families. Table 4–4 compares the age, race, and education levels of those in the top 1 percent of wealth owners to all households. The demographics refer to the household head. The table presents the demographic breakdowns

Table 4-4. *Profile of the Wealthy, 1983–1995 (percent)*

| | 1983 | | | | 1989 | | | | 1995 | | | |
|---|---|---|---|---|---|---|---|---|---|---|---|---|
| | All Households | | Top 1% | | All Households | | Top 1% | | All Households | | Top 1% | |
| | Survey | Simulated | Survey | Simulated | Survey | Simulated | Survey | Simulated | Survey | Simulated | Survey | Simulated |
| *Age* | | | | | | | | | | | | |
| Under 35 | 30 | 30 | 1 | 1 | 26 | 28 | 1 | 1 | 25 | 25 | 2 | 2 |
| 35–44 | 20 | 19 | 9 | 10 | 23 | 25 | 16 | 15 | 23 | 23 | 21 | 21 |
| 45–74 | 43 | 44 | 84 | 85 | 42 | 40 | 71 | 72 | 42 | 41 | 72 | 73 |
| 75 and older | 7 | 7 | 6 | 4 | 9 | 7 | 12 | 12 | 10 | 11 | 5 | 4 |
| *Race* | | | | | | | | | | | | |
| White (non-Hispanic) | 81 | 81 | 98 | 98 | 75 | 77 | 95 | 97 | 78 | 82 | 95 | 96 |
| Black (non-Hispanic) | 12 | 11 | 0.5 | 0 | 13 | 14 | 0.7 | 0 | 12 | 10 | 1 | 0 |
| Hispanic | 4 | 4 | 0.0 | 0 | 8 | 5 | 1.0 | 0 | 6 | 4 | 0 | 0 |
| Asians and others | 3 | 4 | 1.5 | 2 | 4 | 4 | 3.3 | 3 | 4 | 4 | 4 | 4 |
| *Education* | | | | | | | | | | | | |
| High school graduate or less | 59 | 58 | 13 | 13 | 57 | 57 | 13 | 14 | 50 | 52 | 14 | 15 |
| Some college | 20 | 20 | 12 | 12 | 20 | 20 | 14 | 15 | 24 | 26 | 17 | 17 |
| College graduate or more | 20 | 22 | 75 | 75 | 23 | 23 | 73 | 71 | 26 | 22 | 69 | 68 |

*Note:* Author's calculations from the Survey of the Financial Characteristics of Consumers for 1962 and from the Surveys of Consumer Finances for other years. Simulated estimates are from the simulation model. Cells indicate the percentage of gross household assets in each of the wealth categories. See text for details.

for 1983, 1989, and 1995 and includes simulated estimates along with estimates from survey data.

According to the estimates in Table 4–4, America's top wealth holders were predominantly middle aged, but getting younger. In 1983, 84 percent of those in the top 1 percent were between the ages of 45 and 74, while only 43 percent of all households were in that age bracket. Only 1 percent of the top 1 percent were younger than 35, 9 percent were between 35 and 44, and 6 percent were older than 75. In contrast, the age distribution across all households was much more even. In that year, 30 percent of all households were under 35, 20 percent were 35–44, and 7 percent were older than 75. By 1989, only 71 percent of those in the top 1 percent were middle aged (or 45–74 years old). By that time, 16 percent of the wealthiest families were headed by someone age 35–44, a marked increase in young wealthy. In 1989, there is also evidence of a simple aging of the former middle-aged wealthy from the previous time period: In 1989, 12 percent of the wealthy were 75 and older. By 1995, the young accounted for a much larger segment of the top 1 percent. Indeed, in that year, 35- to 44-year-olds accounted for more than 20 percent of the top 1 percent of wealth holders. This trend perhaps captures one of the phenomena that Frank addressed, albeit indirectly, in his discussion of luxury fever. An increasing number of those who had the money to indulge their extravagant tastes during the 1980s and 1990s were young people. Often, much like the banker who built the castle in the Hamptons, the young wealthy were those who made it big in financial dealings during the economic booms that characterized these decades.

The top 1 percent of wealth owners were typically highly educated, although those with less than a college education were more predominant among the wealthy in 1995 than in prior years. In 1983, 75 percent of those in the top 1 percent of wealth owners had at least a college education, while only 20 percent of those in the general population had attained this degree of advanced education. An additional 12 percent of the top 1 percent of wealth owners had some college, while only 13 percent had never attended college. Among all households, a much higher 59 percent were high school graduates or less. These breakdowns were virtually unchanged in 1989, but by 1995 there had been a noticeable decline in the percentage of the top 1 percent that had a household head who had attained at least a college education. By the mid-1990s, only 69 percent of those in the top 1 percent of wealth holders had graduated from college or completed more higher education, while 17 percent of this top group had just attended some college. At the same time, there were declines in the percentage of all households that had a high school education or less. Two factors likely accounted for this trend. First, increased middle-class investment in the stock market accompanied by economic booms likely propelled some families from the middle to the upper class; and second, real estate busts that affected many of the wealthy more heavily than the middle class, likely pushed some wealthy families down from the ranks of top wealth holders. The combined effect was the slight readjustment of the education-wealth profile that is evident in Table 4–4.

Not surprisingly, when we look at the race of the rich, we see that the top wealth holders in America are an extremely homogeneous group racially. Oliver and Shapiro (1995) demonstrated that there was extreme racially based wealth inequality in the early 1990s. The estimates in Table 4–4 provide support for Oliver and Shapiro's findings. These estimates suggest that nearly all top wealth holders in the 1980s and 1990s were white, and that minorities were beginning to enter the top of the wealth distribution. However, the estimates in this table suggest that the entry of minorities into the wealthiest classes was slow, of only minor magnitude, and dominated by Asians. In 1983, 98 percent of the top 1 percent were white families; this declined to 95 percent by 1989 and remained there through 1995. At the same time, the percentage of blacks in the top 1 percent grew slightly from 0.5 in 1983 to 0.7 in 1989 and to 1 percent by 1995. There were a few more Asians in the top 1 percent. In fact, Asians accounted for 4 percent of the top 1 percent by 1995. Although there were 2.6 times as many Asians in the top 1 percent in 1995 as there had been in 1983, 4 percent is an exceedingly small percentage of families. The estimates of race composition in Table 4–4 indicate that there was clear racial inequality of enormous proportions in the 1980s and 1990s. As Oliver and Shapiro (1995) argued extremely eloquently in *Black Wealth/White Wealth*, this is a problem that deserves not only research attention but immediate policy attention as well.

### What If Race Did Not Matter?

Racial inequality in socioeconomic well-being, in general, has been documented extensively in the social sciences. Evidence that blacks, in particular, have not kept pace with whites emerges in research that highlights differences in such indicators as earnings (Cancio, Evans, and Maume 1996), labor force participation, and labor force outcomes (Browne 1997;

Petterson 1997), and quality of living conditions (Henretta 1979; Massey, Condron, and Denton 1987). The estimates in the last section suggested that the relationship between race and wealth ownership is rather clear: Families with white heads constitute the majority of the wealthy class. Part of the reason for this difference is disparities in the process by which whites and blacks accumulate assets. But what if race did not matter? That is, what if blacks and whites accumulated assets in the same way? In this section, I use the simulation model to separate the effects of asset ownership from the effects of racial differences in family wealth history, earnings, education, marital behavior, fertility, and other influences on wealth accumulation starting in the early 1960s and then examine the distributional impact in the 1980s and 1990s. My objective is to examine the role that asset ownership plays in creating and maintaining the racial differences that are evident in the profile of the wealthy. I do not intend to imply that families freely select the combination of assets that they own. Clearly, a variety of factors influence a family's ability and willingness to own each of the components of net worth.

The direct relationship between economic booms and wealth inequality has largely been a function of stock market movement and the distribution of stock ownership across families (and, to a lesser degree, the ownership of other relatively risky investments such as bonds). The value of stocks has increased during booms, and owners have prospered. Those who have not owned stocks have fallen in relative standings. Long-term trends in the stock market and wealth inequality indicate that the two have largely followed the same pattern of ups and downs for decades (Wolff 1995b). The relationship between the stock market and wealth inequality was particularly evident in the early to mid 1990s. Before that time, most Americans, and particularly most black Americans, kept the majority of their wealth in the family home or in checking and savings accounts. Tax incentives (and, of course, the need for shelter) encouraged families to first build equity in housing and to use only excess savings to make other investments. Moreover, the risk associated with buying stocks was so great that most families were not willing to risk losing the little excess savings they had. The result was that only the wealthiest Americans, those who had sufficient excess capital available to invest, as well as funds to pay professional investors, owned stocks (Wolff 1995b).

As the estimates in Table 4–3 indicate, the largest single component of total wealth for most families has been the primary residence (Holloway 1991; Levy and Michel 1991). In the 1980s and 1990s, market growth changed this somewhat. An increasing number of Americans began putting their savings into stocks and stock-based mutual funds (including Individual Retirement Accounts and pension plans), hoping to reap some of the benefits of a stock market that experienced record increases in the eight consecutive years between 1988 and 1995 (Norris 1996). Moreover, the increasing availability of mutual funds in the 1980s and early 1990s made stock ownership more feasible for more people, and by the mid-1990s stocks surpassed housing wealth as the largest component of Americans' portfolios (Sloane 1995). While the stock market spiraled upward, the housing market topped out, making real estate investments less appealing and stock investments more appealing. Because increased numbers of households were investing in stocks, stock market booms in the 1990s had a less dramatic effect on inequality than they had had in the past.

The relationship between stock ownership and wealth inequality suggests that the combination of assets owned affects wealth distribution, but how might asset ownership be linked to racial differences in becoming rich? There is nothing unique about stock ownership. In fact, any wealth component whose value increases relative to other components would have the same effect. However, certain wealth components, such as stocks, because they involve higher relative risks tend to have a more noticeable effect on wealth distribution. What matters is that if families of different races tend to make different decisions about which assets to own or, more importantly, if structural constraints restrict ownership in systematic ways, the link would be unambiguous. Prior research suggests that there is reason to suspect that there are indeed systematic variations between blacks and whites in asset ownership for various reasons (Oliver and Shapiro 1995). Economists explain differences in asset ownership by resorting to discussion of differences in preferences to save, that is, differences in willingness to postpone consumption (Brimmer 1988; Lawrence 1991). While there may indeed be black-white differences in willingness to postpone consumption, structural factors lead to even greater racial differences in portfolio decisions than would be expected from a pure postponed-consumption argument.

Opportunities to make investments vary systematically because income varies systematically by race and affects ability to save. A more detailed discussion of reasons that income varies systematically with race is beyond the scope of this book. However, whether such differences result from discrimination in hiring and promotion or differences in labor force participation and career preferences, the implications for wealth ownership are the same. In addition, the socioeconomic well-being of the family of origin varies systematically by race. Blacks tend to start out in families that are less well off and experience lower rates of upward mobility than whites (Oliver and Shapiro 1995). This directly affects portfolio behavior. If a family does not have savings available initially, it will be unable to invest in risky assets. As a result, the family will not enjoy high returns on savings, and it will not be able to make high-risk investments in subsequent time periods.

In addition to demographics and family background, other direct structural differences are likely to influence the portfolio behavior of black and white families differently. In particular, discrimination in lending and interest rate differences experienced by families of different races also make some assets less attractive or unreachable to some groups of people or in some regions of the United States. Opportunities to invest (determined by such factors as the location of banks) are structurally constrained and thus also systematically influence the types of assets families own (Oliver and Shapiro 1995). Not only do investment opportunities vary systematically by race, but the ability to even save money that might be invested varies systematically because families without savings must often pay more than other families for basic financial services (Caskey 1994). As Caskey points out in his work on fringe banking, a household that does not have savings is much less likely to begin saving simply because the cost is too high. In addition, families with little or no savings are often forced to assume additional credit and are unable to improve their debt to income ratios sufficiently to gain access to mainstream financial instruments, including both assets and liabilities. Caskey demonstrates that these conditions became much worse during the 1980s and 1990s, exacerbating increases in inequality that originated with stock market booms and the stagnation of the housing market.

Oliver and Shapiro (1995, especially Chap. 7) have suggested that the types of assets a family owns affect the relationship between race and wealth. They point to the ownership of housing, the ownership of business assets, and (to a lesser degree) the ownership of stocks as being important influences on wealth and inequality. They do not, however, model or discuss directly the accumulation of the components of net worth. This is not surprising, as most data sets, including the Survey of Income and Program Participation (SIPP) on which Oliver and Shapiro rely for much of their empirical support, do not include detailed enough data to identify differences in asset ownership among families. Brimmer (1988) does directly deal with racial differences in asset ownership, but he encounters a second major problem with this type of research. Even if racial differences can be identified using standard data sets, the effects of asset ownership cannot easily be separated from other effects (i.e., marriage, fertility behavior, earnings) on wealth accumulation. Because education, marriage, fertility, and earnings affect portfolio behavior and because race affects each of these behaviors and processes, race affects asset ownership both directly and indirectly. Using only standard regression techniques, it is difficult to separate these effects.

In order to separate the effects of asset ownership from the effects of racial differences in family wealth history, earnings, education, marital behavior, fertility, and other behaviors and processes that also affect wealth accumulation, I use the simulation model. In order to examine the impact that asset ownership has on the distribution of wealth, I run the simulation model once using historically accurate regression equations and alignment data. This produces output that resembles (and, in fact, is typically indistinguishable from) historical estimates (this is true of estimates of wealth ownership and accumulation as well as of other behaviors and processes that are included in the simulation model). I then set the coefficients indicating the race of the family (based on the race of the household head) in the logistic and GLS regression equations (those estimated using the 1983–1986 SCF) to zero and run the model again holding all else constant. This experiment is equivalent to asking: "What would the distribution of wealth look like if there were no racial differences in asset ownership?" I present estimates of the percent of top wealth holders who are white and those who are minorities before and after the experiment. I also present estimates of the distribution of wealth before and after the experiment. The only difference in the estimates is that I produced the "after" estimates with the race coefficients equal to zero. The compounding effect of the removal of these coefficients is significant, because, in the simulation model, prior wealth affects the ownership and value of each net worth component in the current period.

Table 4–5 includes estimates labeled "before" and "after." The "before" estimates refer to estimates of the distribution of wealth from the simulation model when the model is run with historically accurate inputs. Therefore, the "before" estimates are consistent with several data sources including survey data from various years, estate tax data for the wealthy, and aggregate government estimates of total outstanding household wealth.

The Rich and Their Wealth

Table 4–5. *Simulation Experiment: Race and the Top 1%, 1983–1995 (percent)*

|  | 1983 | | 1989 | | 1995 | |
| --- | --- | --- | --- | --- | --- | --- |
|  | *Before* | *After* | *Before* | *After* | *Before* | *After* |
| White (non Hispanic) | 98 | 91 | 97 | 89 | 96 | 85 |
| Black (non-Hispanic) | 0 | 3 | 0 | 4 | 0 | 5 |
| Hispanic | 0 | 1 | 0 | 1 | 0 | 1 |
| Asians and others | 2 | 5 | 3 | 6 | 4 | 9 |

*Note.* Simulated estimates before and after simulation experiment removing effects of race on wealth accumulation processes. Cells indicate the percentage of households in the top 1 percent that were of the specified races in the years indicated. "Before" and "After" labels refer to estimates before and after the simulation experiment that removed the effects of race on wealth accumulation processes. See text for details.

The "after" estimates are postexperiment estimates. In 1983, the percentage of the top 1 percent that were non-Hispanic whites declined from 98 before the experiment to 91 after the experiment. The decline was even more marked by 1989 and 1995. In the historical (before) conditions, 97 percent of the top 1 percent of household wealth owners in 1989 were white, but only 89 percent were white after I imposed the experimental conditions. Similarly, 96 percent of the families in the top 1 percent were white in 1995 historically, but only 85 percent were white in the simulation experiment. As a result of the experiment, an increasing percentage of minorities entered the top 1 percent through the 1980s and 1990s. Historically, there were no black families in the top 1 percent through 1995, but as a result of the experiment, 3 percent of this richest wealth class were black in 1983, 4 percent were black in 1989, and 5 percent were black in 1995. There was only a slight change in the proportion of these families that were Hispanic, but Asians captured a dramatic percentage of this segment.

Removing the direct effect of race on asset ownership also had a consistent equalizing effect on the distribution of wealth. The estimates in Table 4–6 compare the percentage of total wealth owned by the top 1 percent and that owned by the top quintile of household wealth holders

Table 4–6. *Simulation Experiment: The Distributional Effects of Racial Differences in Wealth Accumulation*

|      | Top 1% | | Top 20% | |
| --- | --- | --- | --- | --- |
|      | *Before* | *After* | *Before* | *After* |
| 1962 | 34 | 32 | 81 | 79 |
| 1983 | 34 | 31 | 80 | 76 |
| 1989 | 38 | 30 | 84 | 78 |
| 1992 | 39 | 32 | 85 | 79 |
| 1995 | 39 | 31 | 84 | 78 |

*Note*: Author's simulated estimates. Cells indicate the percentage of net worth held by households in each segment of the distribution. Estimates before the experiment correspond to simulated estimates of wealth distribution in Table 3–3. Values in this table are rounded to the nearest percentage with the exception of absolute values between zero and unity. "Before" and "After" labels refer to estimates before and after the simulation experiment that removed the effects of race on wealth accumulation processes. See text for details.

between 1962 and 1995. The percentage of household wealth owned by these families declined rather consistently over this three-decade period, with the exception of a minor increase in the early 1990s that is consistent with historical trends. What is perhaps most startling initially, however, is that despite the removal of the effects of race on asset ownership for the 33 years (1962–1995) represented in the table, dramatic racial differences in wealth inequality remain. What causes this persistence in racial differences in wealth ownership? Indirect effects of race on wealth ownership and accumulation patterns are the most likely explanation. I have said that the simulation model allows me to separate the effects of asset ownership from other effects (such as marital behavior, fertility, earnings, etc.) on wealth ownership. These tables demonstrate that ability. The remaining racial differences in wealth ownership evident in Tables 4–5 and 4–6 do not reflect the direct effects of asset ownership, but rather they reflect the indirect effects of these other factors. The bottom line result of the experiment is that asset ownership does have an important and dramatic effect on racial differences in wealth ownership. However, changing asset ownership alone will not end racial inequality in wealth ownership. Rather, wealth will be unequally distributed until black and white families become more equal on an entire spectrum of behaviors and processes.

Social scientists have documented the existence of racial inequality in socioeconomic well-being. When wealth is considered part of the equation, racial disparities in well-being are more considerable than what research on income, education, and other indicators of well-being suggests they are; indeed, the truly rich are still separated by net worth rather than income or other status indicators. The results presented in Tables 4–5 and 4–6 indicate that differences in asset ownership play a central role in perpetuating these differences. Clearly racial differences in wealth ownership are influenced by many forces, but these results indicate that decisions about how families save are important. The results suggest that efforts to improve understanding of different methods of savings as well as efforts to remove structural and policy barriers to investment might lessen wealth inequality. Eliminating wealth inequality, however, is not as easy. Persistent inequality in wealth ownership is deeply embedded in inequality in earnings, education, and other behaviors and processes that indirectly affect wealth ownership. Not until these disparities are eliminated will racial differences in asset ownership be erased completely.

The conclusion of this experiment is not that asset ownership alone explains inequalities in wealth ownership or that structural factors do not lead to the staggering levels of wealth inequality that have been present in this country for decades. Rather, the results of this study suggest that while numerous factors contribute to the creation of wealth inequality, much of the existing disparity could be alleviated by policies that encourage blacks to own assets that are likely to increase their net worth. Making high-risk asset ownership accessible to black families would not end wealth inequality, but it would clearly reduce the current dramatic disparities that are perpetuated by black-white differences in asset ownership. As Caskey (1994) notes, our society devotes very few resources to monitoring and regulating fringe banking. We devote considerable resources to protect consumers in the middle- and upper-income brackets, but almost nothing to protect low-income consumers of financial services. Not only would additional protection be desirable, but the evidence reported here suggests that if we provided opportunities and incentives to low-income, low-wealth households to save and to invest in more long-term, sound financial instruments, we could go a long way toward reducing wealth inequality.

## Summary and Conclusions

In this chapter, I examined the distribution of wealth among families more closely than in the previous chapter by examining the wealth holdings and wealth accumulation patterns of the rich. The data presented here provided a detailed account of the wealthiest Americans over the past three decades. I began by asking how much wealth the wealthy own and discovered that not only do both survey and simulation estimates indicate astonishing levels of wealth ownership among these households, but that the general trend in wealth ownership was increasing through the mid-1990s. Investigation of portfolio behavior indicated that the rich were likely to keep a large portion of their assets in relatively risky investments such as stocks and bonds and that they, therefore, controlled large proportions of such assets.

I presented estimates of the demographic characteristics of the rich that indicated that this group is largely middle aged, highly educated, and white. Finally, I presented the results of an experiment designed to isolate the effects of racial differences in wealth accumulation on distributional and other outcomes. This experiment, which removed racial differences in asset ownership from the simulation model, suggested that wealth ownership declined considerably over the three decades included in the model (specifically 1962 through 1995). The simulation also indicated, however, that remaining, and quite stark, racial differences in earnings, education, fertility, marriage behavior, etc., allowed quite substantial racial inequality in wealth ownership that persisted despite the absence of racial differences in asset ownership.

# 5

## THE REST OF THE DISTRIBUTION:
## THE MIDDLE CLASS AND POOR

In class society, everyone lives as a member of a particular class and every kind of thinking, without exception, is stamped with the brand of class.

(Mao Zedong)

Having profiled the richest Americans in the previous chapter, I now turn my attention to the rest of the distribution: the middle class and the poor. First, the middle class. While the middle class does not control anything like the amount of wealth that those in the top wealth-holding categories do, the sheer size of this class makes it important for both basic research and policy issues. Indeed, it is because the middle class is so large and relatively wealth-poor that there is reason for both interest and concern. Numerically, the middle class is roughly the group of households that comprise the second and third quintiles of the wealth distribution. Substantively, the term *middle class* means much more than the people who fall between the rich and the poor. When asked to what class they belong, a disproportionate percentage of people claim to be numbers of the middle class. The middle class is the median class, the class that is thought to be average.

As we saw in the previous chapter, a small fraction of the rich controls the bulk of wealth in the United States. Clearly the behavior of the rich can affect the distribution of wealth. Yet because there are so many families in the middle class, their behavior can also have a significant impact on the distribution of wealth. A recent example is the increase in the tendency of the middle class to invest in stocks and mutual funds. The increasing ease of investing in mutual funds has enticed the average middle-class family to begin keeping more of their assets in stocks and mutual funds and to consequently invest less of their savings in housing assets (Norris 1996). As a result, stock market booms and busts that once disproportionately affected the wealthy may now also impact the middle class. It is likely that this change in the savings behavior of the middle class has already impacted the distribution of wealth, though researchers are only beginning to explore the consequences of this change. In this chapter, I examine the wealth accumulation patterns of the middle class and begin to explore how these patterns affect the distribution of wealth among all families.

In this chapter, I also investigate patterns of wealth accumulation among the poor, that is, the wealth-poor. As I do throughout this book, I argue that while income is an important determinant of well-being, it is wealth that really separates the rich and the poor. Thus, I devote attention in this chapter to the group of people at the very bottom of the distribution of wealth, the truly poor, who may have income but have extremely little wealth. In many cases, the families that fall at the bottom of the wealth distribution have more debt than they do assets, yielding negative net worth. I begin this chapter by examining the amount of wealth that the bottom 80 percent owns. I separate these households by quintiles and examine trends in the value of the wealth of the middle class and poor as separate groups between 1962 and 1995. I then discuss the portfolio behavior of these families. I ask whether they keep their assets in checking and savings accounts or whether they are able to invest in assets with more favorable returns. I also examine the debt holdings of these families and discuss reasons for increases in the 1980s and 1990s in the propensity to assume liabilities. Finally, I use the simulation model to explore two areas: First, I examine the relationship between the debt burden of middle- and lower-class families and the distribution of wealth; second, I explore the relationship between family composition and the distribution of wealth. The results of the experiment lend support for the idea that both portfolio behavior and other family processes contribute to patterns in the distribution of households' wealth.

## The Bottom 80 Percent

In *Out of Place in America*, Schrag described the middle class as the working class: "He does all the right things, obeys the law, goes to church and insists – usually – that his kids get a better education than he had. But the right things don't seem to be paying off" (Schrag 1970: 16). The middle class is also the forgotten class. "While he is making more than he ever made – perhaps more than he'd ever dreamed – he's still struggling while a lot of others – 'them' (on welfare, in demonstrations, in the ghettos) – are getting more of the attention. 'I'm working my ass off,' a guy tells you on a stoop in South Boston. 'My kids don't have a place to swim, my parks are full of glass, and I'm supposed to bleed for a bunch of people on relief'" (Schrag 1970: 16). The middle class is neither rich enough nor poor enough to warrant much attention until an election is imminent because its numerical domination is significant enough to determine the election's outcome. Usually, the working class is considered part of the lower class, but when the middle class is divided into its upper and lower segments, there is little difference between middle and poor. This is particularly true when households are divided by wealth. Those in the bottom 80 percent of the wealth distribution own little enough wealth that it is sensible to examine them as a single category.

There are certainly households who own so little they are clearly among the wealth-poor. Schrag pointed out in the same book: "Wealth is visible and so, now, is poverty. Both have become intimidating clichés. But the rest? A vast, complex, and disregarded world that was once – in belief, and in fact – the American middle: Greyhound and Trailways bus terminals in little cities at midnight, each of them with its neon lights and its cardboard hamburgers; acres of tarpaper beach bungalows in places like Revere and Rockaway; the hair curlers in the supermarket on Saturday, and the little girls in the communion dress the next morning" (1970: 24). There have been changes in the wealth ownership of the middle class in recent decades and, as I discuss below, the general trend has been increases in the mean and median amounts of wealth that this group of families owns. At the same time, however, both the debt burden (Canner, Kennickell, and Luckett 1995) and spending (Frank 1999) grew among these households raising questions about whether they realized much improvement in well-being.

If we look even farther down the distribution of wealth, we find a group of people who own nearly nothing. While he was generally quite insightful in his observations of conditions in America, de Tocqueville was rather misguided when he referred to the United States as one of the most equal societies in the world (de Tocqueville 1841 [1966]). Take New York City as an example. Kerbo (1991) documented that some zip codes in New York have average incomes higher than any other place in the United States, perhaps the world. Yet New York also has the greatest number of welfare recipients per capita in the country. Some of the world's richest and poorest people live within a few short city blocks of each other. The wealthy pass scores of homeless, the truly poor, on their way home to apartments that cost millions of dollars. One estimate suggested that New York might also have the greatest concentration of homeless people with more than 30,000 people in 1981 having no place to sleep other than city park benches and sidewalks. Another estimate suggested that this number was as high as 50,000 in 1983 (Kerbo 1991). Clearly there is inequality in America. Clearly there is a class of people with almost no possessions, the poor.

Unlike the middle class, the poor are not forgotten. Unfortunately, though, these families often receive attention for negative reasons. When we talk about the poor, it is often because they are a burden, receiving public assistance or otherwise needing to be supported. When we talk about the poor, they are usually identified by their incomes, the flow of money they receive (or do not receive) over a certain period of time. We refer to families that are living "below the poverty line." The poverty line is a simple number indicating the amount of income a family would need to meet the most basic living expenses. In 1984, for a family of three the poverty line was about $8,300 and for a family of four it was about $10,600. Median family income that year was just over $31,000 (Ellwood 1988). The purpose of the poverty line is to allow us to count the number of families who are poor, and it serves this purpose fairly well. But the poverty line is based on income, and income tells us little about the material hardships faced by a family. And it is material hardship, the ability to afford shelter and other necessities, that concerns most people about the poor (Mayer and Jencks 1989). Wealth is a much better indicator of hardship for both the poor and the middle class.

### The Wealth of the Middle Class and Poor

### The Middle Class

How much wealth did the middle class own between 1962 and 1995? Table 5-1 compares the mean net worth of families in the middle class (those in the second and third quintiles of the wealth distribution) to the mean net worth of both the wealthy and the poor (those in the top quintile and the bottom two quintiles) and to the wealth of all families combined. The table includes estimates for both mean net worth and financial wealth for 1962, 1983, 1989, and 1995 and also includes estimates from the simulation model. Mean net worth for those in the second quintile was consistently only 15 to 20 percent of mean net worth for the top quintile.

Table 5–1. *Mean Wealth by Quintile, 1962–1995*

| | Top 20% | | Second 20% | | Third 20% | | Bottom 40% | | All households | |
|---|---|---|---|---|---|---|---|---|---|---|
| | *Survey* | *Simulated* | *Survey* | *Simulated* | *Survey* | *Simulated* | *Survey* | *Simulated* | *Survey* | *Simulated* |
| *Net worth* | | | | | | | | | | |
| 1962 | 348 | 352 | 78 | 79 | 32 | 30 | 2 | 2 | 116 | 117 |
| 1983 | 693 | 711 | 107 | 111 | 47 | 45 | 2 | 2 | 170 | 173 |
| 1989 | 883 | 892 | 120 | 127 | 47 | 45 | 1 | 1 | 193 | 195 |
| 1995 | 736 | 778 | 100 | 102 | 40 | 42 | 1 | 1 | 175 | 176 |
| *Financial wealth* | | | | | | | | | | |
| 1962 | 414 | 424 | 44 | 46 | 9 | 10 | −4 | −3 | 92 | 93 |
| 1983 | 564 | 555 | 49 | 54 | 10 | 9 | −5 | −5 | 124 | 125 |
| 1989 | 749 | 785 | 55 | 52 | 12 | 13 | −11 | −10 | 146 | 147 |
| 1995 | 626 | 637 | 46 | 45 | 9 | 11 | −9 | −9 | 135 | 135 |

*Note*: In thousands. Survey estimates are author's calculations from the Survey of the Financial Characteristics of Consumers for 1962 and the Surveys of Consumer Finances for other years. Simulated results are from the simulation model. All values are adjusted to 1990 dollars, based on a standard CPI-U.

In 1962, for instance, families in the second quintile had, on average, $78,000 in net worth, while those in the top 20 percent had nearly $350,000 in net worth. Similarly, in subsequent years, the gulf between these two segments of the distribution remained quite large. The gulf between the third quintile and the top quintile was even larger, of course, and the size of the gulf is quite dramatic. In each year depicted in the table, mean net worth for families in the third quintile was less than 10 percent of that held by families in the top quintile.

The difference between the financial wealth holdings of middle-class and wealthy families was even more dramatic. In each year depicted in the table, mean financial wealth for families in the second quintile was only 10 percent or less of that held by those in the top quintile. Even more startling, families in the third quintile had very little financial wealth. In fact, in 1995, the mean financial wealth for families in the third quintile was only 1 percent as large as that of top wealth holders. Median net worth was lower for both segments of the distribution, but because these estimates are broken down by quintile, there is not as much skew in the estimates as there would be if the wealth of the entire distribution were estimated simultaneously.

As a percentage of all households, middle-class wealth was still quite low. The mean for all households is positively skewed by the wealth of the top quintile, but middle-class wealth as a percentage of the wealth of all households was still surprisingly low. For the years depicted in the table, the mean net worth of the second quintile was about 60 percent that of all the mean net worth for all households. The proportion of total household net worth accounted for by the second quintile ranged from about 67 percent in 1962 to about 57 percent in 1995. The percentage of financial wealth accounted for by the second quintile was even smaller, ranging from about 47 percent to about 33 percent. The third quintile accounted for even less of total net worth and financial wealth. In 1962, the third quintile had an average of $32,000 in net worth and $9,000 in financial wealth. The net worth for all households for that year was approximately $116,000 and the financial wealth for all households was $92,000. Thus, the third quintile accounted for only 27 percent of net worth in that year and a mere 9 percent of financial wealth. The percent of net worth and financial wealth accounted for by the third quintile was equally low in the other years included in the table. Table 5–1 also includes estimates from the simulation model of net worth and financial wealth by quintile. Because I use the Survey of Consumer Finances, in part, to produce and scale the simulated estimates, it is not surprising that they are highly consistent with the wealth estimates displayed in the table that are derived directly from the survey data.

Both the net worth and financial wealth of middle-class families increased through the late 1980s but then decreased in the early 1990s. At the same time, however, middle-class wealth relative to the wealth of the top 20 percent declined. Between 1962 and 1983, wealth grew at a fairly rapid rate, and it grew even faster after that. Indeed, mean net worth grew almost twice as fast between 1983 and 1989, so that by 1989, mean wealth for all families was nearly $200,000, a 70 percent increase over 1962 wealth. Net worth growth was also rapid among middle-class families. Between 1962 and 1983, net worth grew from $78,000 to $107,000 for the second quintile and from $32,000 to $47,000 for the third quintile. While the second quintile did enjoy some of the rapid growth in household wealth during the 1980s, the wealth of the third quintile stayed constant. In fact, nearly all of the wealth gain that occurred during the 1980s was enjoyed by the top quintile.

When we look at financial wealth, the story is much the same, although the magnitude of the wealth portfolios of the middle class is considerably smaller. Financial wealth for all families grew a considerable 1.34 times between 1962 and 1983. During that time, the financial wealth of both the second and third quintiles increased by 1.11 percent, while the wealth of the top quintile grew 1.36 percent. Like net worth, financial wealth increased rapidly during the 1980s as well. For all families, financial wealth increased 1.17 percent from $124,000 to $146,000. While the top quintile enjoyed much of this increase, the middle class did not fare badly. The financial wealth of the second quintile grew 1.12 percent, and that of the third quintile grew 1.2 percent. In sum, between 1962 and 1983, the wealth of the middle class increased, but it increased at a slower pace than the wealth of the top quintile. By the 1990s, this trend had reversed and the middle class began to lose wealth.

The vigorous growth of mean wealth depicted in Table 5-1 masks some of the changes that occurred in the distribution of wealth. Wolff (1995b) discussed how median wealth differed from mean wealth over this same period. Unlike mean net worth, median net worth grew faster between 1962 and 1983 than it did during the 1980s. From 1983 to 1989, mean wealth increased by about 23 percent, but median wealth grew by only 8 percent. This difference reflects the fact that the majority of wealth gains during the 1980s were accrued by top wealth holders. There is also some chance that mean estimates are distorted because they reflect both actual increases in wealth and changes in the number of households in the particular groups. For instance, if the mean wealth of the middle class did not increase over a certain period of years, but the number of households in that group increased during the period, the mean would indicate a decline in mean wealth. There is not a simple way to distinguish from the means the effects of actual wealth growth from population growth. However, holding the number of households in each quintile constant over time can help distinguish these effects. The results of such analyses indicate that overall wealth grew even more rapidly than the estimates in Table 5-1 indicate and that, particularly during the 1980s, the amount of wealth accrued by the top quintile was greater than the estimates based on the raw survey data. This finding is consistent with the estimates that others have produced using similar data sets (Wolff 1993, 1994).

Average household income increased more rapidly than average household financial wealth but not as rapidly as average net worth between 1962 and 1983. In fact, Wolff (1993) used the Surveys of Consumer Finances, the same data sets from which I obtained the wealth means included in Table 5–1, to estimate that average net worth for all families increased 46.5 percent and financial wealth increased 33.7 percent between 1962 and 1983. In contrast, mean income for all families increased 36.4 percent during that period. During the 1980s, growth in both net worth and financial wealth surpassed average income growth. On each of these measures of well-being, the majority of total real growth accrued to the top quintile (Wolff 1993). Between 1962 and 1983, the top quintile gained 82 percent of net worth increases, 96 percent of financial wealth increases, and 68 percent of income increases. During that same period, only 11 percent of net worth increases, 10 percent of financial wealth increases, and 15 percent of income increases accrued to the second quintile. The third quintile faired even worse, gaining less than 10 percent of increases in each category. On each measure, the top quintile made the greatest gains again during the 1980s.

These trends in wealth accumulation and inequality began, in the late 1980s and early 1990s, to cause researchers and policy analysts alike to question whether the middle class was diminishing. In their article aptly titled "W(h)ither the Middle Class?" Duncan, Smeeding, and Rodgers (1993) used data from the Panel Study of Income Dynamics (PSID) to ask whether there was a trend toward fewer and fewer middle-class families. Typically, the PSID produces somewhat less reliable estimates of wealth ownership because, unlike the Surveys of Consumer Finances, it does not include a high-income sample. Moreover, the PSID only covered wealth in later years, and even then coverage of wealth ownership was less complete than coverage in the PSID. However, one particularly important advantage of the PSID is that it is longitudinal data and thus provides information about changes over time.

Duncan et al. took advantage of this to analyze trends in the transitions of what they called "prime age" adults (those aged 25–54 years) into and out of the middle class. They found that the middle of the income distribution had indeed withered during the 1980s. Specifically, their analyses indicated that a middle-income adult's chances of falling from the middle of the distribution to the bottom increasingly exceeded their chances of moving from the middle to the top during the 1980s. They extrapolated their findings to predict that if the trends they found were to continue through the 1990s, the middle-income group would constitute less than 65 percent, and perhaps closer to 60 percent, of the population. They also found that changes in wealth ownership during the 1980s intensified the changes they found using income alone. That is, the size of the middle class was declining because adults were more likely to experience (and not recover from) downward mobility rather than upward mobility.

Perhaps because they were more likely to experience downward mobility than upward mobility during the 1980s, the middle class also increased the amount of time they spent at their jobs. In *The Overworked American*, Schor examined trends in the amount of time Americans worked during the 1970s and 1980s, in an attempt to understand why we did not experience the increase in leisure time that earlier forecasts predicted would result from increasing mechanization of work (Schor 1991). As Schor pointed out, the rise in work time was unexpected, as hours had declined for nearly a hundred years prior to the 1950s. Since 1948, productivity in the United States increased consistently (failing to rise in only five years between 1948 and 1990). In Schor's words, "the market for free time hardly existed" by the late 1980s. But not all of this increase in work can be explained by declining shares of wealth and income. In the 1970s and 1980s, spending increased dramatically in the United States in all classes (Frank 1999; Schor 1991). Both Schor and Frank (in *Luxury Fever*) noted that the result of this spending spree was that Americans had a much higher quality of life than at most other times in recorded history. Another potential result was that Americans, particularly the middle class who had little financial wealth to begin with, depleted their savings and contributed to some of the distributional changes that occurred during the 1980s and 1990s.

Why do families save? Economists argue that households solve an intertemporal maximization problem to determine their consumption (Attanasio 1993; Goldsmith 1956; Modigliani and Ando 1957). That is, the household calculates the amount of money it will need for consumption in the next time period and saves that amount in the current time period. Realistically, however, few households behave this way. Perhaps more realistic are arguments that "keeping up with the Jones" motivates much of the saving and consumption behavior of Americans (Frank 1999). Frank's examination of spending behavior provided evidence that the saving and consumption behavior of Americans was, to a large extent, determined by the behavior of those with whom they have contact. While Frank is an economist, his argument is more consistent with sociological theories of saving.

While sociologists share the assumption of resource scarcity with economists, the sociologist typically affords demand a less central place in theory. Indeed, sociological theory centers on structure and sees saving and consumption as by-products of the groups in which the individual actor is embedded (Frenzen, Hirsch, and Zerrillo 1994).

Empirically, saving behavior has received more attention from economists than from sociologists. Recent evidence indicates that saving behavior varies considerably within classes, as well as by demographic characteristics of the household. In the early 1990s, the middle class was more likely than top wealth holders to spend as much as they earned and to save little (Kennickell 1995). The same report indicated that the middle class was less likely than the wealthy to have some type of plan for saving their money. These patterns naturally varied demographically as well, with more young households and more households with mid-level incomes planning their savings. A related study examined differences in saving and financial planning. The study used focus groups both to examine the process by which families developed personal financial plans and to understand differences in saving and consumption behavior.

The study began with the observation that financial planning is extremely complex. The ideal financial plan accounts for earnings, growth in earnings, assets, rates of returns, pension contributions and benefits, social security benefits, special needs such as education and large one-time expenditures, insurance rates, changes in household composition, and tax laws. Even more, the ideal financial plan considers mortality probabilities, disability probabilities, and the probability that household composition will change. The authors noted that it is unrealistic to think that most families are able to consider even most of these factors in planning their savings, and they asked how, in reality, families make saving-related decisions. Most of the focus group respondents were indeed saving money, and most of the people in the study regularly put away money each month. While these findings are generally consistent with survey estimates, there are some important differences. The nonrepresentative group of individuals who were included in the focus group each claimed to have some sort of financial plan, whereas of the 1992 SCF respondents, nearly 25 percent reported having no plan. Similarly, while 75 percent of the focus group reported saving regularly, only 54 percent of those in the 1992 SCF made a similar report.

Despite the differences between the focus group results and the survey results, there are important lessons contained in the discussions with the more qualitative focus group method. In particular, the focus group study examined *why and how* households save. The results indicated that the primary reason the respondents saved money was for retirement. The second most important reason was for emergencies, and the third most important reason was for major purchases. The emphasis that the focus group respondents placed on retirement saving was particularly interesting. As evidence of increases in luxury spending indicate, an important obstacle to middle-class wealth accumulation is spending. Concern with having assets for retirement is something that policy makers could draw on to both decrease luxury spending and increase saving. In particular, tax incentives designed to encourage retirement saving might be an effective means of decreasing luxury consumption and increasing savings.

Individual Retirement Accounts have been designed for this purpose. In 1974, a federal law created IRAs as a means of tax-deferred retirement saving for those not covered by employee pensions plans. The 1981 Economic Recovery Tax Act made IRAs available to everyone, but actual contributions to IRAs were concentrated at high-income levels suggesting that those who did contribute to IRAs were not increasing their saving rate but rather were simply transferring existing assets to IRAs as tax shelters. Because one of the primary goals of IRAs was to increase saving, the Tax Reform Act of 1986 restricted the benefits of IRAs by preventing those in high-income brackets from receiving the initial tax deduction previously enjoyed by all contributors to IRAs. Some empirical studies argued that the early IRAs were not very effective in increasing middle-class saving (Avery and Kennickell 1990; Bovenberg and Evans 1990; Bovenberg 1989; Hendershott and Peck 1989; Japan 1989). While others have provided evidence that IRAs do encourage saving (Gravelle 1991; O'Neil and Thompson 1987; Venti and Wise 1993). A third group of research concluded that IRAs only affect decisions to transfer assets from other non–tax-deferred instruments to IRAs (Collins and Wykoff 1988; Feenberg and Skinner 1989). Despite continued disagreements about how and why IRAs are effective, continued increases in luxury spending and simultaneous increases in concern about retirement saving suggest that there is indeed a need for a financial instrument like the IRA. Since the IRA was first introduced in the mid-1980s, regulations regarding use of this means of saving have changed, in part, in an effort to improve the effectiveness with which they encourage savings. The introduction of the Roth IRA in the late 1990s was one of the more drastic changes and allowed investors to pay taxes on their IRA contributions and then enjoy the benefits tax-free after retirement. Continued research is needed to determine the effectiveness of such legislation, but there is reason to believe that IRAs and similar financial instruments do encourage saving, particularly among middle-class households.

## The Bottom 40 Percent

While wealthy and middle-class families enjoyed increases in their wealth holdings over much of the 1962–1995 period, a full 40 percent of the population had almost no wealth at any point during this period. Indeed the wealth holdings of the families in the bottom two quintiles of the wealth distribution got markedly worse between the early 1960s and the early 1990s. Referring back to Table 5–1, we see that the mean net worth for those in the bottom two quintiles of the wealth distribution was $2,000 in 1962 and had not increased appreciably by 1983. Through the 1980s and early 1990s, the mean net worth of these families declined to about $1,000. When we look at financial wealth, the picture is even more dismal for families in the bottom two quintiles. In each year included in Table 5–1, the mean financial wealth of the bottom 40 percent of families was negative. Remember that net worth is the current value of all marketable (fungible) assets less the current value of all liabilities. In contrast, I define financial wealth as net worth less net equity in owner-occupied housing. This is consistent with definitions of wealth used in the literature. The estimates in Table 5–1 are also consistent with the estimates that others have produced using the same data sets (Wolff 1995a, 1995b, 1998).

Financial wealth can be negative either if net worth is negative or if net equity in owner-occupied housing exceeds net worth. Financial wealth is an important indicator of well-being not only because it captures a considerable amount of information about portfolio differences between the rich and the poor (e.g., the greater amounts of debt held by the poor) but also because it reflects more precisely the liquid portion of the wealth that families do own. Between 1962 and 1983, the financial wealth of the poorest 40 percent of families declined slightly from negative $4,000 to negative $5,000. During the 1980s, however, the financial wealth of these families declined dramatically to negative $11,000. The situation of the poorest families improved slightly in the 1990s, but it is almost comical to refer to a mean financial wealth of negative $9,000 as an improvement. The proportion of total household net worth accounted for by these families was only 2 percent at its peak in 1962 and declined to less than 0.5 percent in the 1990s. The percentage of average financial wealth accounted for by the poorest families was, of course, consistently negative.

Why was wealth so scarce in the 1980s? The longest economic expansion in the history of the United States occurred during the 1960s, and during that period the term "trickle down" was coined to refer to the positive effect economic growth has on poverty (Blank 1993). Blank pointed out that between the fourth quarter of 1982 and the fourth quarter of 1990, the United States experienced its second longest economic expansion. Yet, as the estimates in Table 5–1 indicate, poverty rates increased during that same period. Blank documented that the poverty rate (for income) exceeded 15 percent after the recession of 1981–1982 and declined during the remainder of the 1980s, but poverty was still at 12.8 percent in 1989. One reason for these extremes in poverty was changing wage structures during the 1980s. Blank argued that the lower responsiveness of poverty to economic expansion during the 1980s had little to do with labor market responsiveness during that decade. Rather she argued that labor market involvement was actually more responsive than in previous decades. She provided evidence that unemployment declined more rapidly than in previous periods and that earners in the bottom quintile of the earnings distribution increased their work efforts more sharply in the 1980s than in the 1960s or 1970s. What was different about the 1980s was that real wages declined notably. Blank argued that the lower responsiveness of the income of low income households to economic expansion during the 1980s was entirely due to declining real wages, resulting in slower income growth.

What are the implications of this pattern in real wages for wealth accumulation and distribution patterns? Lower real wages, which primarily affected those in the bottom segments of the income distribution, decreased saving among low-income households. Lower real wages also gradually increased the debt that these families held, particularly credit card debt and other liabilities that are intended to be short-term debt. Low-income families already typically pay disproportionately high interest rates for credit (Caskey 1994), and when this is combined with high rates on credit card debt that is difficult to control if it is allowed to accumulate, liabilities can quickly become quite extensive. Simultaneously, those who owned stocks and other higher-risk investments enjoyed considerable increases in the value of their portfolios as the stock market soared and largely avoided debt. The result of each of these patterns was that the wealth of the poor steadily declined, and wealth was largely redistributed away from low-income, low-wealth households toward the rich.

There were also occupational reasons for the increases in poverty that occurred during the 1980s. Two trends in particular that began in the 1960s and 1970s and then intensified in the 1980s were at least partially responsible for increasing wage inequality by occupation during the 1980s (Galbraith 1998). The first trend was in technological advances. For decades prior to the 1970s, technological advances occurred without increasing inequality. But in the late 1960s and the 1970s, the benefit of technological progress was disproportionately enjoyed by those in high-skilled, "information" sector jobs at the expense of those in unskilled service occupations. The result, as Galbraith argued in his examination of trends in wages during the 1980s, was increased inequality in earnings between skilled and unskilled occupations (Galbraith 1998). Braun (1997) presented similar findings in his examination of increases in inequality in the United States and throughout the world. According to Braun, low-skilled workers and, indeed, entire regions that were predominantly low-skill regions suffered increases in poverty as a result of technological advances during the 1980s.

At the same time, increasing globalization also impacted the wages of the blue-collar workers, particularly those with the lowest skill levels. Trade between the United States and other countries expanded steadily between the late 1960s and the 1980s, and imports of manufactures grew dramatically, particularly during the 1980s. Galbraith pointed out that it is unlikely that these increases impacted the wages of U.S. workers as much as some extremists argue, but it is true that there was some impact. Again, low-skilled service workers suffered the most from these changes, while the earnings of those in information-related occupations continued to improve. Braun (1997:224) used census data to document that between 1982 and 1992, the earnings of executives, on average, increased 2.2 percent, and the earnings of professionals increased 8.1 percent. At the same time, the earnings of sales and clerical workers declined by 4.2 percent, the earnings of laborers declined by 3.9 percent, and the earnings of production and craft workers declined by a full 7.8 percent.[1] The result

---

[1] Braun also documented, however, that the wages of farming, forestry, and fishing workers increased a dramatic 51.2 percent between 1982 and 1992. The reasons for this difference are not directly relevant to the discussion in this chapter. See Braun, Chapter 5, p. 224, for details.

was, again, decreased earnings power among those in low-skilled occupations that leads to increases in the debt burden and decreases in the saving of those who can least afford it.

In addition to declines in real wages and increases in occupation-based wage inequality, growing wealth inequality during the 1980s also had roots in differences in wealth ownership patterns and earnings patterns among different types of households. While I do not intend to examine the relationship between demographic characteristics of families and their wealth accumulation patterns in much depth until Chapter 8, it is important to note that a disproportionate percentage of families in the bottom 40 percent of the wealth distribution between 1962 and 1995 were nonwhite. In their excellent portrayal of black/white differences in wealth ownership, Oliver and Shapiro (1995) argued that to talk about middle class and poor as consistent classes without regard to race is inaccurate. In reality, there are two middle classes and two poor classes. The difference derives from racial differences in asset ownership.

Using the 1992 Survey of Income and Program Participation, Oliver and Shapiro estimated that middle-class blacks earned 70 cents for every dollar earned by middle-class whites, but that blacks possess only 15 cents for every dollar of wealth held by middle-class whites. My estimates in Chapter 8 indicate that perhaps this difference is even greater, and I conclude, as Oliver and Shapiro did, that claims of the emergence of a black middle class are, thus, exaggerated by emphasis on income. Racial differences in earnings, education, and saving behavior contribute to the disproportionate representation of blacks in the lower segments of the wealth distribution, but discrimination and other structural constraints continued to impact race-based inequality into the 1990s. The experiment that I presented in Chapter 4 demonstrated that changing racial differences in wealth accumulation patterns would affect race-based differences in wealth distribution considerably. But even in that experiment, other factors appeared to be operative in addition to race. I discuss these patterns in more detail in Chapter 8.

## The Assets and Debts of the Middle Class and Poor

Another factor that contributes to patterns in wealth ownership and inequality is family portfolio behavior, that is, the combinations and amounts of assets that families own and debts that they hold. A family that invests primarily in stocks when there is a stock boom is likely to fare better financially than a family that uses a low-interest, low-risk savings account to store money. Likewise, those who amass considerable long-term credit card debt are likely to fare more poorly than those who hold a large amount of mortgage debt. The latter, of course, are using a liability to create home equity, while the former are likely doing little other than consuming. Just as numerous factors affect a family's propensity to save, numerous factors contribute to the types of assets and debts the family acquires. Ability to save, given earnings and necessary expenses, combined with propensities to consume, of course, matter. There is also evidence that saving varies demographically; class, race, occupation, education, age, family background, and multiple other factors combine to produce a family's propensities to save and to consume. In the same way, these factors affect portfolio behavior.

Class differences in portfolio behavior, resulting from differences in income, education, family background, and other factors, are usually evident in comparisons of the savings of the wealthy and the nonwealthy. The estimates in Table 5–2 illustrate typical differences by comparing the portfolio composition of the bottom 80 percent of the wealth distribution, middle-class and poor households, with overall household wealth portfolio composition for 1995. The story that this table tells is one that flavors most discussions of middle- and lower-class saving behavior: Compared to the wealthy, middle- and lower-class households tend to own the primary residence and some cash. They tend not to own high-risk investments, although pension plans and stocks became more common, especially among the middle class, in the late 1980s and the 1990s. The estimates in this table indicate that those in the bottom 80 percent of the wealth distribution held 66 percent of their assets in the primary residence and divided their other assets among several other areas.

The second most popular form of saving for the vast majority of Americans was cash accounts; families in the bottom 80 percent of the distribution kept 11 percent of their assets in checking and savings accounts and other highly liquid financial instruments. When the top 20 percent of wealth holders were added in, the percent of total assets kept in housing dropped to 30 percent, and the percentage allocated to other high-risk accounts (such as stocks and bonds, business assets, and investment real estate) increased. The simulated estimates included in this table indicate that the simulation model consistently produced similar estimates of portfolio composition in that year. Simulated estimates of portfolio composition were consistent for other years as well. Families have also varied

Table 5–2. *Portfolio Composition of the Middle Class and Poor, 1995*

| | All Households | | Bottom 80% | |
|---|---|---|---|---|
| | *Survey* | *Simulated* | *Survey* | *Simulated* |
| Primary residence | 30 | 30 | 66 | 64 |
| Other real estate | 11 | 12 | 5 | 5 |
| Business assets | 18 | 18 | 3 | 5 |
| Cash accounts | 7 | 7 | 11 | 11 |
| Stocks and bonds | 16 | 15 | 4 | 4 |
| Pension assets | 9 | 10 | 9 | 10 |

*Note.* Author's calculations from the Survey of the Financial Characteristics of Consumers for 1962 and from the Surveys of Consumer Finances for other years. Cells indicate the percentage of gross household assets in each of the wealth categories. Primary residence and other real estate are gross market value; business assets include net equity in unincorporated farm and nonfarm businesses and other closely held corporations; cash accounts include savings accounts, checking accounts, and certificates of deposit; whole life insurance is cash surrender value; and pension accounts include IRAs, Keogh accounts, and other retirement accounts.

demographically in their tendency to own certain assets. A majority of families own their primary residence. In 1992, for example, 63.9 percent of all families owned the house they lived in, and 64.7 percent owned their homes in 1995 (Kennickell, Starr-McCluer, and Sunden 1997). Higher income households, of course, were more likely to be homeowners, although more than 50 percent of families even in the $10,000–$24,999 income bracket (in 1995 dollars) owned their homes.

Similarly, home ownership was most likely among those who were middle aged (with a peak of 82 percent of owners between the ages of 55 and 64) and white (69.4 percent versus 48 percent for nonwhites). There were also occupational differences in the propensity to own a home. Those in professional and managerial occupations as well as the self-employed were more likely to be homeowners than those in lower-skilled and service occupations. Similar trends were evident in the ownership of investment real estate and business assets, although the patterns were more exaggerated (i.e., high-income, white professionals were much more likely to own these nonfinancial assets). Similar patterns were also evident in 1995 in the ownership of financial assets. High-income, middle-aged, white professionals were likely to own high-risk investments such as stocks, bonds, and other high-risk assets. Cash accounts, savings bonds, and relatively low-risk investments were more common among other households. Kennickell, Starr-McCluer, and Sunden (1997) examined these patterns in considerable detail for 1992 and 1995. Comparing this report with Kennickell and Starr-McCluer (1994), it is apparent that these trends were consistent throughout the 1980s and 1990s.

As a result of these patterns, middle-class and poor families controlled a majority of primary residence assets and cash account assets in 1995. Figure 5–1 compares the percent of total assets in several categories controlled by the bottom 90 percent of the wealth distribution to the percent controlled by the remainder of the distribution in 1995. Not surprisingly, the bottom 90 percent owned 68 percent of primary residence assets, 55 percent of whole life insurance assets, and 38 percent of assets kept in cash accounts. The share of higher-risk assets, such as stocks, bonds, and business assets, owned by these families was considerably smaller. Because most of these patterns were consistent for many years, I included only 1995 estimates in the figure.

One change that is apparent in an examination of portfolio behavior over time is a marked increase in the propensity of middle-class families to own stocks, starting in the late 1980s and growing through the 1990s. Kennickell, Starr-McCluer, and Sunden (1997) commented on this pattern and used the 1989, 1992, and 1995 Surveys of Consumer Finances to estimate the proportion of families that owned some sort of stock in each of the three years. They show that in 1989, 31.7 percent of all families had direct or indirect (through pensions) stock holdings. By 1992, 37.2 percent owned stock, and by 1995, 41.1 percent were stock owners. Kennickell et al. also showed that the value of stock ownership increased over this same time period. In 1989, the median stock portfolio was valued at $10,400; by 1992, the median value had increased to $11,500; and the 1995 value was $13,500 (in 1995 dollars). What was most interesting about this trend was that changes in portfolio behavior occurred primarily in relatively low-net-worth, low-income households. I explore these changes, the factors that motivated them, and their impact on wealth distribution in more detail in Chapter 7.

While there were some positive changes in family portfolio behavior

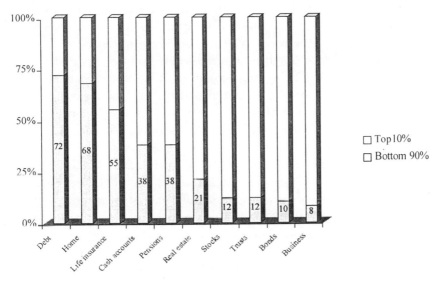

Figure 5–1. Percentage of total assets and debts owned by the bottom 90 percent, 1995. *Note:* Author's calculations from the 1995 Survey of Consumer Finances. Bars indicate the percentage of gross household assets in each of the wealth categories owned by households in the top 10 percent of wealth owners. Primary residence and other real estate are gross market value; business assets include net equity in unincorporated farm and nonfarm businesses and other closely held corporations; cash accounts include savings accounts, checking accounts, and certificates of deposit; whole life insurance is cash surrender value; and pension accounts include IRAs, Keogh accounts, and other retirement accounts.

during the 1980s and 1990s, two problems related to portfolio behavior remained. First, while many middle-class and poor families kept much of their savings in checking and savings accounts, large numbers of families did not even own cash accounts. The proportion of families with no type of cash account (checking, savings, money market, etc.) was approximately 13 percent in both 1992 and 1995, a relatively large number, but a number that does reflect a decline from about 15 percent in 1989 (Kennickell, Starr-McCluer, and Sunden 1997). As Caskey (1994) pointed out in his work *Fringe Banking*, not having a checking account makes families vulnerable to many abuses in the relatively unregulated secondary financial market. Unscrupulous owners and operators of pawnshops and check cashing outlets routinely take advantage of those who are often unable to even cash a paycheck in a bank because they do not have an account with assets great enough to cover the value of the check. Those who use secondary, or fringe, banking institutions often pay exorbitant fees for basic check-cashing services that those using banks in the primary financial market do not pay. The result is that those who can least afford it often pay the highest prices for banking privileges. Families reported several reasons for not having a checking account (Kennickell and Starr-McCluer 1994; Kennickell, Starr-McCluer, and Sunden 1997) and for using fringe banking establishments (Caskey 1994). Not having enough money to open an account and high minimum balances are important reasons that families go without cash accounts. At the same time, however, these families also report in both the SCF (Kennickell and Starr-McCluer 1994; Kennickell, Starr-McCluer and Sunden 1997) and in Caskey's (1994) analysis that convenience is an important influence. Many report not liking the way they are treated by banks, but many simply say that they prefer to use fringe banking establishments.

A second significant problem in the portfolios of many middle-class and poor families was debt ownership. As Figure 5–1 indicates, the middle class and poor owned the majority of outstanding household debt in 1995, and the same was true for the preceding decades. Debt holdings would be less detrimental if the majority of the debt were mortgage debt. In reality, many middle-class and poor families assumed large amounts of credit card debt, debt that they held for extended periods of time during the 1980s and 1990s. Debt ownership was one reason that the poor got poorer during the 1980s and 1990s. As Medoff and Harless argued in *The Indebted Society* (1996), slowed growth and stagnant wages in the 1970s forced more Americans into greater debt. As a result, according to Medoff and Harless, Americans accumulated massive amounts of debt on multiple credit cards in the 1980s and 1990s in order to maintain and improve a standard of living that might not have been feasible given wage levels at the time. In 1983, 62.5 percent of households had consumer debt (primarily credit card debt); and in both 1989 and 1992, approximately 65.0 percent had consumer debt (Canner, Kennickell, and Luckett 1995). More striking is the amount of income the typical family spent on paying off their credit card debt each month. In 1983, the median monthly credit card payment for all families was $134 (in 1986 dollars); by 1986, the median payment had increased to $145 (Avery, Elliehausen, and Kennickell 1987). Not surprisingly, low-income, nonwhite families held the majority of this debt and made the greatest payments (Canner, Kennickell, and Luckett 1995). I explore the relationship between debt and wealth distribution in the next section and in Chapter 8.

## Debt and the Distribution of Wealth

What would happen to the distribution of wealth if the middle and lower classes had incurred fewer liabilities during the 1980s and early 1990s? Would, for example, the distribution of wealth have been less unequal by the mid-1990s? During the economic expansion of the 1980s, the household sector amassed large amounts of mortgage and consumer liabilities. Household sector debt grew considerably faster than income, and aggregate outstanding household debt as a ratio of total personal disposable income increased from 0.56 to 0.78 between 1983 and 1989. As Canner, Kennickell, and Luckett (1995) noted, that was a record high at that time. In the early 1990s, the accumulation of debt slowed as the economy passed through a recession. By 1993, however, families again began to incur debt rapidly. By the end of 1994, the ratio of debt to disposable income had risen to an astounding 0.81. Some of the increase in the debt to-income ratio was attributable to slow wage growth, but household borrowing was definitely rising as well. At the end of 1994, aggregate mortgage debt on the primary residence was $3.15 trillion and consumer installment credit debt was greater than $900 billion (Canner, Kennickell, and Luckett 1995). The large amounts of debt that households amassed raised concerns about repayment problems, the potential for mass increases in household sector bankruptcy, and the general financial well-being of the household sector.

In addition to its effect on household financial well-being, household sector borrowing has the potential to contribute to inequalities in the distribution of wealth. Because those at or near the bottom of the distribution seldom have substantial assets, accumulating debt can quickly result in zero or negative values of net worth. At the other end of the spectrum, the wealthy typically have asset portfolios that are substantial even after debt values are subtracted. Thus when household debt increases, all households will suffer, but those at the bottom will appear worse off more quickly. If the middle class and poor were to accumulate debt more quickly than the wealthy, there would certainly be an actual shift in the distribution of wealth toward the wealthy. If, on the other hand, the pace at which the nonwealthy accumulate debt were to decrease, it is likely that the distribution of wealth would shift toward the middle class and poor (regardless of the saving and investment behavior of the lower classes).

Was there a relationship between this increase in debt accumulation and the increasing wealth inequality that occurred during the 1980s and early 1990s? In Chapter 3, I discussed trends in the distribution of net worth and documented that wealth inequality increased at the same time that debt accumulation was on the rise. There is also evidence that the household sector's financial condition had begun to improve by the mid-1990s, at the same time that inequality appeared to have eased slightly. Ratios of debt payments to income declined after 1989 and delinquency rates on mortgages and consumer debt declined considerably (Canner, Kennickell, and Luckett 1995). In order to examine the relationship between household consumer debt and the distribution of wealth, I used the simulation model to decrease the surge in borrowing that occurred during the 1980s and 1990s. Specifically, beginning in 1980, I reduced holdings of total debt by 15 percent for those in the middle and lower classes each year included in the model. I did not change the liabilities held by the wealthy during that period, nor did I make any other changes to the portfolios of the middle class and poor. I then reran the simulation model and reestimated the distribution of wealth. In this experiment, I do not address the *causes* of household consumer debt. Rather, I concentrate solely on the distributional *consequences* of a particular, historical increase in household sector borrowing, that is, the borrowing increase that began in the 1980s and extended through the early 1990s.

Of course, there are important differences between consumer debt and other debt such as mortgage debt. Mortgage debt has the potential to create home equity, which is a type of wealth. In contrast, consumer debt has no such benefit. Payments on mortgage debt are investments, while payments on consumer debt are nothing more than consumption. Other liabilities such as student loans are an investment of a different sort, as there is evidence that wealth ownership increases with education even net of income. However, student loans are generally indistinguishable from credit card debt and other consumer liabilities in a household's wealth portfolio. In the short run, consumer debt and mortgage debt are likely to affect the distribution of wealth in a similar way, even though there may be important long-run differences. Because the long run in this context is generally beyond several years, I do not distinguish between mortgage debt and other debt. In addition, because the simulation model does not distinguish nonmortgage debt such as student loans from non-mortgage debt such as credit card debt, I would not be able to isolate consumer debt from other types of nonmortgage liabilities. For these reasons, in the experiment I simulate a historic change in the total liabilities of middle-class and poor households.

The impact of the simulated decrease in household sector borrowing during the 1980s and 1990s was a considerable readjustment of the distribution of wealth in favor of families in the middle and lower classes. Table 5–3 includes estimates of the percentage of net worth held by households in several segments of the distribution before and after the experiment. Estimates of the percentage of total net worth owned by the top 1 percent of the distribution are included along with estimates of the share owned by quintile. The estimates marked "before" are the historically accurate estimates from the simulation model; these estimates correspond to the simulated estimates of wealth distribution in Table 3–3 and are consistent with the estimates from the Surveys of Consumer Finances included in Table 3–2. The "after" estimates in Table 5–3 are those from the model in which middle- and lower-class debt burdens had been reduced. The estimates in the table indicate that in each year after the experiment was initiated, the bottom 40 percent of wealth owners gained in the share of total net worth they owned. Before the experiment, the bottom two quintiles owned only 2 percent of total net worth, and they owned 3 percent

Table 5–3. *Simulation Experiment: Consumer Debt and the Distribution of Household Wealth*

|  | Top 1% | | Top 20% | | 2$^{nd}$ 20% | | 3$^{rd}$ 20% | | Bottom 40% | |
|---|---|---|---|---|---|---|---|---|---|---|
|  | *Before* | *After* | *Before* | *After* | *Before* | *After* | *Before* | *After* | *Before* | *After* |
| 1983 | 35 | 30 | 81 | 75 | 12 | 15 | 5 | 7 | 2 | 3 |
| 1989 | 39 | 33 | 84 | 76 | 12 | 16 | 4 | 8 | −1 | 0 |
| 1992 | 39 | 32 | 85 | 75 | 11 | 15 | 4 | 10 | 0 | 0 |
| 1995 | 39 | 32 | 85 | 75 | 11 | 15 | 4 | 9 | 0 | 1 |

*Note*: Author's simulated estimates. Cells indicate the percentage of net worth held by households in each segment of the distribution before and after manipulation of middle- and lower-class consumer debt holdings in the 1980s. Estimates before the experiment correspond to simulated estimates of wealth distribution in Table 3–3 and are consistent with survey estimates in Table 3–2. Values in this table are rounded to the nearest percentage with the exception of absolute values between zero and unity. The experimental conditions involved decreasing middle- and lower-class holdings of consumer debt in 1980 and subsequent years. See text for details.

after the experiment. Similarly, the share of this group increased by one percent in 1989 and 1995. The share of the bottom 40 percent was unchanged in 1992, the recessionary period.

While the experimental increases may appear minimal, they are indeed substantial as wealth has a tendency to stay in the same hands. Moreover, the changes that are evident after the experiment happened quickly. Nearly as soon as the experimental change was implemented, there was a change in the distribution of wealth. Of course, some of the changes that are apparent in Table 5–3 had to occur by definition. By definition, if the debt burden of entire segments of the distribution decline, their share of net worth will increase. This is evident in the table, particularly in 1983, the earliest year in which the experiment could have had an effect on wealth distribution. What is neither obvious nor trivial is the cumulative effect of these changes. That is, decreased debt affects the distribution of wealth not only in the current year, but also in future periods. Because debt ownership (like asset ownership) is in part a function of prior ownership, the amount of debt owned by households in the current period affects the amount owned in subsequent periods. The method of modeling this is quite simple, a lagged dependent variable on either a logistic ownership or linear value equation, but the effect is rather realistic. In reality, debt that is not paid off in one period cumulates and has a bigger effect in subsequent periods. The cumulative effect of the experimental condition is particularly evident in Table 5–3 in the continued redistribution of wealth in the later years included in the table.

## Household Composition and the Distribution of Wealth

The discussions earlier in this chapter also suggested that family demographics contribute to patterns in household wealth distribution. There is evidence that female-headed households, single-person households, and elderly households have a higher propensity to be poor (Bane 1986). Thus family structure often enters debates about how to alleviate poverty and improve welfare programs (Epstein 1997). Researchers have also demonstrated that children, that is, the number, age, and birth spacing of children, also affect family well-being (Bane 1986). This is not particularly surprising, as children are expensive. Households with children have higher expenses than those without children, and the more children in a household, in general, the greater the expenses. Of course, as expenses increase, saving decreases by definition. What is particularly relevant in understanding wealth distribution is that family size tends to be higher among those in the middle and lower segments of the wealth distribution. The question I ask in this section is: If households in the middle and lower classes (by wealth) had a lower propensity to have children, would wealth inequality lessen?

To explore the relationship between family composition (i.e., number of children in the household) and the distribution of wealth, I again turn to the simulation model. Specifically, I designed an experiment in which I reduced the propensity to have children for middle-class and poor households (single and married) by 10 percent every year from 1980 through 1995. The simulation model that I use is particularly useful for exploring questions such as this because the wealth simulation is embedded within a larger set of simulations of various individual and family processes. Each of the processes is aligned to relevant historical estimates and allowed to interact with other processes where relevant. In the case of household size, simulated actors in the model have a stochastically determined probability of having children in each year the model runs. This probability is a function of various pertinent demographic characteristics such as age, gender, marital status, income, and education. The probability is also aligned where possible to census, vital statistics, and other data that are available and considered accurate. The number of children in each household, in turn, affects the accumulation of each of the 14 assets and debts modeled (first by propensity to own, then by amount owned) in the wealth module.

In the experiment, I decreased the propensities of the middle class and poor (by wealth) to have children, starting in 1980. The distributional results are depicted in Table 5–4. The results indicate that decreasing fertility rates had a significant impact on the distribution of household wealth. Again in this table, the cells indicate the percentage of net worth held by households in each segment of the distribution before and after the experiment. The estimates labeled "before" are consistent with the survey estimates included in Table 3–2. The estimates labeled "after" indicate that in each year, starting in 1983, the share of wealth owned by the bottom 40 percent increased markedly. Likewise, the share of net worth owned by households in the middle quintiles increased consistently through the 1980s and 1990s. Correspondingly, the share of wealth owned by the top quintile declined over the 1980s and into the 1990s.

The lesson of the results displayed in this table is not that child rearing should be discouraged among the middle class and poor. Instead, the

Table 5–4. *Simulation Experiment: Family Composition and the Distribution of Wealth*

| | Top 1% | | Top 20% | | 2<sup>nd</sup> 20% | | 3<sup>rd</sup> 20% | | Bottom 40% | |
|---|---|---|---|---|---|---|---|---|---|---|
| | *Before* | *After* | *Before* | *After* | *Before* | *After* | *Before* | *After* | *Before* | *After* |
| 1983 | 35 | 33 | 81 | 75 | 12 | 16 | 5 | 6 | 2 | 3 |
| 1989 | 39 | 35 | 84 | 76 | 12 | 17 | 4 | 5 | −1 | 2 |
| 1992 | 39 | 35 | 85 | 76 | 11 | 16 | 4 | 6 | 0 | 2 |
| 1995 | 39 | 35 | 85 | 75 | 11 | 17 | 4 | 6 | 0 | 2 |

*Note*: Author's simulated estimates. Cells indicate the percentage of net worth held by households in each segment of the distribution before and after manipulation of historical patterns of family composition. Estimates before the experiment correspond to simulated estimates of wealth distribution in Table 3–3 and are consistent with survey estimates in Table 3–2. Values in this table are rounded to the nearest percentage with the exception of absolute values between zero and unity. The experimental conditions involved decreasing the probability that households in the middle and lower classes would have a child in each year between 1962 and 1995. See text for details.

message is that child rearing takes a significant toll on a family's ability to save and invest and thus on the family's relative wealth position. The lesson is that child rearing needs to be more affordable, particularly for households in which saving is already difficult because earnings are insufficient to meet needs.

## Summary and Conclusions

In this chapter, I explored wealth ownership patterns among the non-wealthy, that is, those families in the middle and bottom of the wealth distribution. I began the chapter by examining the wealth that families in the middle and lower segments of the wealth distribution owned between 1962 and 1995. I discussed various aggregate and family-level reasons for trends in these ownership patterns, and then I focused on the role of portfolio behavior in affecting wealth accumulation and distribution. I identified asset- and debt-holding tendencies among the bottom 80 percent of the distribution of wealth, clarified who the families in the middle and lower classes were during the 1960–1995 period, and argued that these patterns affect wealth accumulation and distribution in important ways. For example, an increased propensity for middle-class families to buy stocks and mutual funds during the 1980s and 1990s likely affected the distribution of wealth during that period and will probably continue to affect wealth accumulation and distribution for decades. Finally, I used simulation experiments to explore the distributional impacts of debt holding and family composition of the middle class and poor. The results of the first experiment suggested that decreasing the debt burden of middle class and poor families would redistribute wealth away from the rich toward the poor. Likewise, the results of the second experiment indicated that family composition (specifically, the number of children in a household) impacts the distribution of wealth. The lesson of that experiment was that middle-class and poor families need to be able to raise children *and* save money if inequalities in the distribution of wealth are to be alleviated.

The findings that I have presented in this chapter are largely consistent with the recommendations of policy analysts concerned with fighting poverty. Increasing incentives to save, decreasing obstacles to the equal use of financial services, affecting individual and family behavior are all themes that have long reverberated in the literature on poverty policy (Bane 1986; Danziger and Weinberger 1986; Epstein 1997; Katz 1996; Oliver and Shapiro 1995). The discussion in this chapter is somewhat different because the focus is on poverty of wealth rather than poverty of income. As I do throughout the book, I argued here that the wealth-poor are perhaps more at risk than the income-poor. Often, but not always, these are the same families. In all cases, however, the wealth-poor are at long-term risk of experiencing severe financial crisis. In future chapters, I continue to explore both basic research and policy prescriptions for ending these problems. In subsequent chapters, however, I revisit the issue of poverty and, in particular, inequality through the lens of specific processes that cause poverty, such as economic trends, family processes, and inter-generational processes.

# 6

# ARE AMERICANS GETTING RICHER?

Few matters having to do with economic life have been so much misunderstood as the problem of economic security. And in remarkable degree the problem persists.

(J. K. Galbraith)

In this chapter I ask whether Americans have been getting richer over time. The general question I explore is whether wealth ownership has increased from one generation to the next. The notion of an American dream centers on the idea that children will be better off than their parents were at a similar age, and basic social science research on well-being has long used this notion as a starting point for asking various questions about intergenerational differences in prosperity. Recent literature with more practical policy concerns has begun to ask similar questions, focusing on how baby boomers, in particular, are doing financially relative to their parents. Baby boomers, the large post–World War II generation of people born between 1946 and 1964, have attracted attention at every point of their lives.

As Manchester pointed out in a study for the Congressional Budget Office, one of many government agencies that began to study the finances of boomers in the 1980s and 1990s, the strains that this generation put on resources at every stage of their lives not only attracted attention but also raised concerns that the system might not be able to bear the added pressure of the boomers (Manchester 1993). The baby boomers strained school resources in the 1950s and 1960s as their numbers filled classrooms to capacity. When the baby boomers reached adolescence, crime increased. The baby boomers caused crowding in colleges and universities when they reached their late teens and early twenties, and their entry into the labor force likely contributed to slow wage growth in the 1970s and 1980s.

In the 1990s, the baby boomers again began to attract attention as the first wave of this cohort reached age 50 and began to think about retirement. The thought of this huge generation beginning to draw on the Social Security system raised additional concerns about the nation's retirement system, a system that was already raising questions about whether it could handle the smaller generations that were currently relying on it for income in the postretirement years. Baby boomers will retire between 2010 and 2030, increasing the percentage of the population that is age 65 and over from about 12 percent in 1990 to about 20 percent in 2030. The financial condition of the social security system and other social support programs raises questions about whether public forms of support will be adequate to care for this generation. At the same time, post–World War II decreases in household saving rates suggest that private pensions and other private forms of saving will be inadequate to fill the gap left by public forms of support (Attanasio 1993; Gokhale, Kotlikoff, and Sabelhouse 1996). The questions that naturally arise are whether the baby boom generation has fared as well during their working years as their parents did and, subsequently, whether the boomers will be as well off in retirement as their parents.

I explore these questions in this chapter. While other generations would be equally interesting to examine on the subject of intergenerational differences in well-being, the additional practical concerns associated with the aging of the baby boomers make this a logical generation on which to focus. Baby boomers are the 76 million people born in the birth surge following the Second World War. During the Great Depression, the annual number of births in the United States reached a low point of about 2.3 million, but total annual births increased to more than 4.2 million per year between 1956 and 1961 (Manchester 1993). The first evidence of a baby boom was the 53 percent increase in children under five years old between 1940 and 1950. By 1960, the number of children under five had increased another 26 percent, and births did not fall below 4 million until 1965 (Manchester 1993; Russell 1982). Birth rates remained low during the remainder of the 1960s and 1970s, so the baby boom generation was preceded and followed by relatively small generations (Easterlin, MacDonald, and Macunovich 1990b; Welch 1979).

The baby boom generation has been evident as it has moved through the age distribution, causing a bulge at each point of the life cycle. In 1980, there were almost twice as many people who were 20 to 24 years of age as there were in 1960. In 1990, 22 percent of the population was 35 to 44 years old, an increase of 5 percent in 10 years (Manchester 1993). The baby boom is usually divided into two age groups: the older boomers, born between 1945 and 1954 (also called the leading edge of the cohort), and the younger boomers, born between 1955 and 1964 (also called the trailing edge). In 1995, the older baby boomers were 41 to 50 years old, still active in the labor force, but beginning to contemplate retirement. At the same time, the younger portion of this cohort was between 31 and 40 years of age, far from retirement and thus behaving in quite different ways.

In this chapter, I use two separate methods to explore differences in the well-being of baby boomers and to compare their financial conditions with those of their parents. First, I use survey data to conduct rather traditional cohort comparisons of the boomers' generation and their parents' generation. Unlike past research that has focused on income differentials, however, I focus on differences in the wealth ownership of baby boomers and their parents. When questions of retirement are of interest, the importance of wealth in an analysis of well-being is perhaps greater than at other stages of the life course. The parents of the baby boomers were young adults in or around the early 1960s, while the boomers were young adults in or around the late 1980s. Therefore, it is possible to compare similar age cohorts in the 1962 Survey of Consumer Finances and the 1989 Survey of Consumer Finances to explore differences in the well-being of these cohorts. In the first analyses I present in this chapter, I compare the well-being of those who were 25 to 34 (the younger baby boomers) and 35 to 44 (the older baby boomers) in 1989 to those who were in the same age groups in 1962 (their parents). I estimate the net worth, financial wealth, and ratio of net worth to income for each of these groups. I then use the cohort comparisons to examine demographic differences between the baby boomers and their parents in wealth ownership and portfolio behavior. The results provide answers to many general questions about the relative well-being of these cohorts.

Second, I use the simulation model to compare the well-being of the baby boomers with the well-being of the group of people who are their *actual* parents. The use of the simulation model in this way springs from problems with traditional methods of comparing cohorts. The most obvious problem with these methods is that the cohorts being compared are only roughly the cohorts in which we are interested. The parents of the baby boomers, in particular, might have been born during a whole range of years. Thus, the assumption that they were young adults in 1962 is more than a little unrealistic. Survey data has obvious advantages over simulated data, of course, so it is useful to explore the results of cohort comparisons. At all points in this chapter, when I refer to the wealth of an individual (i.e., an individual member of the baby boom generation or the person's parents), I use the wealth of the individual's family as the wealth indicator.

The added advantage of the simulation model is that it can isolate the group of people who were the *actual* (albeit simulated) parents of the baby boomers and compare their wealth at any age with the wealth of the boomers at the same age. The simulation model allows for the simultaneous examination of trends over the life cycle and across generations. It also allows for investigation of mobility patterns within and across generations, a type of analysis that is impossible with survey data given the types of data currently available on wealth holdings. In the second set of analyses, I take advantage of the simulation model to compare the wealth of baby boomers with the wealth of their actual parents over the entire life span for each group. I also use the model to explore differences in mobility for the two groups and to examine the factors that account for mobility differences both across generations and within the baby boom cohort. While the accuracy of the simulation results presented in previous chapters lends credibility to the model's ability to produce accurate estimates of wealth accumulation, distribution, and mobility patterns, there are assumptions underlying the use of any simulation model. I discuss these prior to discussing the simulation estimates below. Together these two methods allow me to ask: Are Americans getting richer? The answer is yes, but not all of them.

## Research on Baby Boomers

Relatively unfavorable labor market conditions (Berger 1985, 1989; Easterlin 1987; Easterlin, Schaeffer, and Macunovich 1993; Welch 1979) combined with changes in marriage and fertility patterns among baby boomers have raised suspicions that this may be one of the first generations to be less well-off as adults than their parents were at a comparable age (Campbell and O'Rand 1988; Levy and Michel 1986, 1991). Baby boomers faced greater competition in both their educational and occupational pursuits simply because there were more people in their generation to create competition than there were in either the generation immediately preceding theirs or the one following. The baby boom cohort is also, of course, larger than that of their parents' generation, so the competition that the boomers faced was certainly greater than what their parents experienced. Some also argue that economic changes and increased globalization have negatively affected the possibilities that many baby boomers had, as jobs in information industries replaced manufacturing jobs (Braun 1997; Galbraith 1998; Levy and Michel 1991). As a result, career advancement was slower and job security less for baby boomers than for their parents.

Baby boomers also postponed marriage and childbearing, and more boomers than people in their parents' generation remained single, either with or without children (Easterlin, MacDonald, and Macunovich 1990b; Easterlin, Schaeffer, and Macunovich 1993). Postponed marriage and child rearing might imply that the children of baby boomers will reach college age when the boomers are farther along in their careers. It was at this point that the baby boomers' parents did the majority of their saving for retirement. With children entering college late in boomers' careers, soaring college costs, and the increased propensity for children to return home after college, baby boomers will have less time and ability to save for retirement than their parents had. Remaining single and trying to raise children creates additional problems. It is no surprise that two-earner households fare better financially than households with a single earner. Likewise, there is considerable evidence that children are a significant strain on family finances. When a single earner raises children, the effect is more than doubled (Manchester 1993). Because baby boomers are more likely than their parents were to raise children without a partner, they are more likely to be caught in the financial strain this creates. Moreover, while opportunities for women to work outside the home are certainly better for baby boomers, declines in real wage growth have forced many families to have two wage earners simply to get by (Gerson 1985).

The pressures that changing labor market and demographic conditions have created for baby boomers are likely to continue for at least a couple of decades. Levy and Michel (1991) argued that there is no evidence that the conditions faced by baby boomers are going to ease before retirement, suggesting that the likelihood that boomers will have sufficient funds during retirement are low. Media portrayals of the prospects of baby boomers have been equally pessimistic. In an article comparing the early segment of the baby boom to the late segment, the *New York Times* worried that the failure "to save money at the same rate earlier generations did, combined with baby boomers' tendency to delay marriage and children, is likely to cause some financial headaches as the group nears retirement" (Barringer 1992). The article worried, in particular, about the implications of delayed childbearing on the ability of baby boomers to save for retirement. Like their counterparts in policy studies, those in the media who have addressed the financial prospects of the baby boomers share a pressing concern about the ability of the Social Security system to withstand the shock of the baby boomers' retirement (Andrews and Chollet 1988; Lewin-VHI 1994).

Amid all of this pessimism, there have been a few researchers who have begun to recognize that prospects for baby boomers may not be as grim as the simple demographic and economic trends would indicate. A number of studies have documented that baby boomers, on average, have had higher incomes and have accumulated more wealth than other generations, including their parents' generation, at a comparable age. One study compared the earnings of baby boomers with those of the generations immediately preceding and following the baby boom. The results of this study suggested that, despite less favorable labor market conditions, baby boomers were doing considerably better than their immediate predecessors (Easterlin, MacDonald, and Macunovich 1990a). Easterlin and his coauthors suggested that one reason for this success in achieving higher living standards was, indeed, *because* the baby boomers had altered their demographic behavior from that of earlier generations. If remaining single is combined with child rearing, then parents are unlikely to be able to save for retirement. But it was not just single parenthood that increased among baby boomers. Baby boomers were also more likely than earlier generations to have fewer children or to remain childless, both choices that would *increase* rather than *decrease* ability to save for retirement.

A complementary paper found that some of the same demographic differences among baby boomers have resulted in improvements in the boomers' financial well-being compared to their parents' generation as well. Easterlin and his colleagues used data from the Current Population Survey (CPS) and published analyses of data from the Survey of Consumer Finances (SCF) and the Consumer Expenditure Survey (CEX) to conduct generational comparisons. The study focused on comparing the incomes of baby boomers (defined, as I do in this chapter, as those born between 1946 and 1964) and the generation born 25 to 30 years prior (Easterlin, Schaeffer, and Macunovich 1993). Easterlin and his coauthors again found that at the end of the 1980s, members of the baby boom generation were doing considerably better than those in their parents' generation at the same point in the life cycle on income and a limited number of wealth measures.

Manchester, in the study for the Congressional Budget Office (CBO) mentioned in the introduction to this chapter (Manchester 1993), and in a related paper coauthored with Sabelhaus (Sabelhaus and Manchester 1995), found that baby boomers in retirement will probably enjoy higher inflation-adjusted incomes and more wealth than their parents currently do. The studies found that both real income and the ratio of wealth to income will likely be greater for the baby boomers than for those currently in retirement and that older baby boomers will likely fare better than younger baby boomers. The CBO report argued that baby boomers will have higher real retirement incomes in general than older people retiring during the 1980s for several reasons. First, assuming continued real wage growth between 1990 and 2010, the baby boomers will have higher real preretirement incomes than their parents. This increase in wages during working years will increase social security benefits to the baby boomers. The higher wages will increase both pension benefits and the ability of baby boomers to save for retirement. Second, the CBO report argued that increases in women's labor force participation imply that more baby boomers will have acquired labor market experience, and more will have accrued social security benefits prior to retirement (Manchester 1993; Sabelhaus and Manchester 1995).

At the same time these two studies pointed toward pockets of baby boomers who will not do so well in retirement, including many divorced, widowed, and never-married women, poorly educated persons, and non-homeowners. Manchester thus draws two important conclusions. First, single, poorly educated baby boomers may face a bleak future even while other members of their generation fare relatively well. Second, portfolio behavior matters. In particular, homeowners are likely to accumulate more assets than those who do not own homes, allowing them to save even more for retirement (Manchester 1993; Sabelhaus and Manchester 1995). Kingson (1992) found similar results but emphasized that there is a significant amount of difference among those collectively labeled as baby boomers. In particular, he argued that it is important to recognize differences particularly in leading and trailing segments of the baby boomer generation. While these findings are certainly important, gaps in our understanding of intergenerational processes in general and the processes that affect the well-being of baby boomers in particular remain. It is these questions that I address in this chapter.

*Are Americans Getting Richer?*

## The Wealth of Baby Boomers and Their Parents:
## Cohort Comparisons

To conduct the cohort comparisons, I used the 1962 Survey of the Financial Characteristics of Consumers (SFCC) and the 1989 Survey of Consumer Finances (SCF). These are two of the survey data sets I have used throughout this book, and that I describe in Chapter 2. The 1962 SFCC surveyed 2,557 households, and the 1989 SCF surveyed 3,143 households. In both surveys, approximately 25 percent of the sample was a high-income sample designed to oversample those with high wealth holdings. In the cohort analyses, I used the standard weights to account for this oversample (Kennickell and Shack-Marquez 1992; Projector and Weiss 1966). I followed Manchester (1993) in making the two data sets comparable. While the two surveys are generally comparable, there are some differences that required transforming both data sets. The most notable was that the 1989 SCF asked respondents for their total income from all sources for 1988. The 1962 SFCC asked for current-year (1962) income from specific earnings components such as wages and salaries, business income, dividends, and capital gains. In order to make the two comparable, I summed the 1962 numbers and converted both to 1990 dollars. I made similar transformations for the wealth estimates. For each survey, I selected the respondents who were ages 25–34 and 35–44. My rationale is that those in these two age groups in the 1989 SCF would have been born between 1945 and 1964, and would thus be baby boomers. Similarly, those who were in the same age groups in 1962 would have been young adults in that year and would have been the cohort that included the baby boomers' parents. The results of the cohort comparisons are consistent with the results reported by Manchester and the Congressional Budget Office in their analysis of the same data (1993).

The results of the cohort comparisons indicate that most baby boomers had more wealth than the people in their parents' cohort had at a similar age. Table 6–1 reports the median net worth of household heads age 25–34 and 35–44 in 1962 and 1989. The table also includes estimates of the median ratio of net worth to income for these groups and breaks median net worth down by income quintile. The estimates indicate that the

Table 6–1. *The Median Wealth of Baby Boomers and Their Parents*

| | Median Net Worth | | Median Ratio of Net Worth to Income | |
|---|---|---|---|---|
| | *1962* | *1989* | *1962* | *1989* |
| *Household head age 25–34* | | | | |
| All households | 6,411 | 9,450 | 0.24 | 0.42 |
| Top income quintile | 26,782 | 77,280 | 0.62 | 1.07 |
| Fourth income quintile | 18,271 | 17,431 | 0.58 | 0.44 |
| Third income quintile | 7,675 | 11,440 | 0.32 | 0.45 |
| Second income quintile | 2,625 | 3,155 | 0.14 | 0.23 |
| Bottom income quintile | 315 | 210 | 0.02 | 0.02 |
| *Household head age 35–44* | | | | |
| All households | 30,765 | 56,911 | 1.20 | 1.23 |
| Top income quintile | 85,040 | 175,875 | 1.61 | 2.09 |
| Fourth income quintile | 60,480 | 73,394 | 1.64 | 1.32 |
| Third income quintile | 32,660 | 67,620 | 1.19 | 1.73 |
| Second income quintile | 12,180 | 24,140 | 0.73 | 0.85 |
| Bottom income quintile | 1,995 | 1,050 | 0.16 | 0.17 |

*Note*: Author's calculations from the Survey of the Financial Characteristics of Consumers for 1962 and the Survey of Consumer Finances for 1989. All values are adjusted to 1990 dollars, based on a standard CPI-U. Those age 35–44 in 1962 were born between 1918 and 1927. Those age 25–34 in 1962 were born between 1928 and 1937. Those age 35–44 in 1989 are considered the older baby boomers and were born between 1945 and 1954. Those age 25–34 in 1989 are considered the younger baby boomers and were born between 1955 and 1964.

median net worth for all young baby boomers (age 25–34) in 1989 was $9,450, while median net worth for those age 25–34 in 1962 was $6,411. Similarly, the median net worth for the older baby boomers (age 35–44) in 1989 was $56,911, while the median net worth for those age 35–44 in 1962 was only $30,765. The estimates presented in the table indicate that these trends were constant across income categories.

What accounts for these changes in wealth ownership? At least part of the answer lies in aggregate economic trends. Prior research has been quick to point out that the baby boomers faced unfavorable demographic and economic trends, making it unlikely that they would fare better than their parents. As I discussed above, cohort crowding increased the competition the baby boomers felt in their educational and occupational pursuits. Changes in marriage and fertility behavior also likely affected the process by which this group accumulated wealth. Others have noted that baby boomers entered their careers and began to save during the 1970s and 1980s, a period of moderate to slow economic growth. Both aggregate economic growth and real wage growth were strong during the 1950s and 1960s, when the parents of the baby boomers were at the peaks of their careers (Manchester 1993). The baby boomers faced less fortunate economic conditions. During the 1980s, GDP growth (growth in the gross domestic product) was only about 2 percent, and disposable income increased by only 0.7 percent between 1973 and 1988 (Manchester 1993). At the same time, however, stock market and real estate market booms encouraged saving and increased the values of the investments that baby boomers had made. Some of the gains in wealth over their parents' generation, thus, likely reflect increased values of stock holdings and real estate investments, even if overall saving had declined.

The baby boomer advantage appears from the estimates in Table 6–1 to be even greater for older baby boomers. Both median wealth ownership, at all income levels, and the median ratio of net worth to income were greater for the baby boomers than for their parents. The difference between the baby boomers and their parents, however, is generally greater for the leading segment of the baby boom than for the trailing segment. In the top quintile of income owners, for instance, the median net worth for older baby boomers was nearly $176,000 in 1989, while the median for 35–44 year olds in 1962 was only $85,000. Thus the median for the baby boomers was nearly double that of their parents. The difference for the younger baby boomers was not as drastic. Manchester and her colleagues at the CBO interpret similar findings to mean that there was an advantage to being born in the earlier portion of the baby boom (Manchester 1993). While this may be true in part, given the different economic conditions that the two portions of the baby boom cohort faced, it is also likely a life cycle pattern, compounded by aggregate economic trends reflected in these data. When economic growth began to increase in the mid- to late-1980s, the older baby boomers had already accumulated considerable savings. The increased growth likely increased the value of their savings making it appear even more substantial. The younger baby boomers, on the other hand, had only begun to save and invest and were unable to take advantage of the increase in growth. What will be more telling of differences between early and late baby boomers will be a retrospective look at the cohort after both have retired. It is obviously premature for such an analysis.

Although the baby boomers appear to have done better than many predicted, this does not imply that demographic patterns were not important influences on the well-being of the baby boomers. Manchester documented that many of the demographic changes anticipated by those observing the baby boomers indeed appeared (Manchester 1993). According to her comparisons of 1960 census data and data from the 1990 Current Population Survey (CPS), there was a greater percentage of households headed by unmarried individuals in the baby boomers' cohort than in their parents' cohort. In addition, the CBO report indicated that more baby boomers remained childless, more women in the baby boom cohort participated in the labor force, and baby boomers had considerably higher educations than their parents.

While demographic changes appear not to have damaged the wealth accumulation of the baby boomers overall, there were important demographic differences in well-being both within the baby boom cohort and between the baby boomers' cohort and their parents' cohort. Table 6–2 compares the wealth of baby boomers and their parents, separated by demographic characteristics. The estimates in the table indicate that for all cohorts, there was a positive association between median net worth and education. Similarly, median financial wealth increased with education, and the percentage of households whose net worth was less than their income declined with education. The estimates in this table also suggest that, for the most part, baby boomers enjoyed greater returns on education than their parents did. The effects of education were particularly strong for older baby boomers. Median net worth for older baby boomers who had graduated from college, for example, was $107,800, while the median for their college-educated parents was only $71,000. For those age 25–34 in 1989, the younger baby boomers, there was only a $5,000 difference in median net worth when compared with their parents. This difference is likely partially a reflection of the added time the older boomers have had to accumulate wealth, and the younger baby boomers may begin to acquire wealth at an increasing rate. But in 1989, the estimates suggest that there was indeed an advantage to being in the leading segment of the baby boom.

Table 6–2. *The Wealth of Baby Boomers and Their Parents by Education, Marital Status, and Children*

| | Median Net Worth | | Median Financial Wealth | | % with Net Worth Less Than Income | |
|---|---|---|---|---|---|---|
| | *1962* | *1989* | *1962* | *1989* | *1962* | *1989* |
| *Household head age 25–34* | | | | | | |
| All households | 6,411 | 9,450 | 2,520 | 4,410 | // | 70 |
| Some high school | 840 | 1,680 | 300 | 780 | 85 | 80 |
| High school graduate | 9,100 | 8,715 | 3,570 | 3,785 | 72 | 73 |
| College graduate | 24,255 | 29,715 | 11,235 | 13,020 | 75 | 57 |
| Unmarried head | | | | | | |
| All | 420 | 1,890 | 315 | 1,155 | 79 | 82 |
| No children | 945 | 3,255 | 945 | 2,100 | 73 | 79 |
| At least one child | 210 | 735 | 220 | 100 | 87 | 85 |
| Married head | | | | | | |
| All | 8,300 | 18,165 | 3,360 | 8,190 | 77 | 62 |
| No children | 8,190 | 18,070 | 5,670 | 9,450 | 94 | 63 |
| At least one child | 8,400 | 19,745 | 3,150 | 7,670 | 75 | 61 |
| One wage earner | 13,250 | 8,510 | 3,885 | 4,200 | 68 | 65 |
| Two wage earners | 5,880 | 29,715 | 2,520 | 11,866 | 90 | 61 |
| *Household head age 35–44* | | | | | | |
| All households | 30,765 | 56,911 | 12,810 | 18,270 | 47 | 42 |
| Some high school | 14,600 | 6,455 | 4,255 | 1,580 | 58 | 60 |
| High school graduate | 45,380 | 47,885 | 24,780 | 14,385 | 40 | 47 |
| College graduate | 71,820 | 107,840 | 40,100 | 39,060 | 30 | 29 |
| Unmarried head | | | | | | |
| All | 6,615 | 17,535 | 1,995 | 4,200 | 61 | 59 |
| No children | 14,175 | 18,585 | 7,245 | 7,350 | 61 | 60 |
| At least one child | 1,998 | 8,295 | 740 | 2,000 | 60 | 55 |
| Married head | | | | | | |
| All | 38,300 | 73,600 | 16,590 | 24,580 | 45 | 35 |
| No children | 45,255 | 75,495 | 16,590 | 31,605 | 43 | 30 |
| At least one child | 37,280 | 73,600 | 16,590 | 23,835 | 47 | 37 |
| One wage earner | 42,735 | 56,040 | 14,385 | 10,745 | 38 | 43 |
| Two wage earners | 36,355 | 97,025 | 20,895 | 30,555 | 55 | 33 |

*Note*: Author's calculations from the Survey of the Financial Characteristics of Consumers for 1962 and the Survey of Consumer Finances for 1989. All values are adjusted to 1990 dollars, based on a standard CPI-U.

For both baby boomers and their parents, marriage had clear financial advantages. However, it was less detrimental for baby boomers to be unmarried than it was for their parents. Median net worth for married 25–34 year olds in 1962 was $8,300, and median net worth for unmarried 25–34 year olds in that year was a mere 5 percent of that value, or $420. Unmarried 25–34 year olds were doing much better by 1989, and they were also doing better relative to their married counterparts. In 1989, median net worth for unmarried 25–34 year olds was $1,800 and for married couples of the same age, it was $18,000. Thus, in 1989, unmarried net worth was 9 percent of that of married couples. The same patterns held for older baby boomers and for other measures of well-being, including financial wealth and the percentage of the cohort whose net worth was less than their income. Some of the difference in these estimates is likely a result of increases in the numbers of baby boomers who choose to postpone marriage. More of the unmarried group in the baby boomers' cohort are singles who chose to remain single in order to advance in a career. Those who chose careers over family, even if only temporarily, would likely have had more income to save and invest. The growing number of women entering the labor force and increases in the number of women who established permanent careers in higher-income jobs also likely contributed to the relative increase in the well-being of unmarried household heads evidenced in the estimates in Table 6–2.

Having two wage earners in a household would seem to have an obvious positive impact on wealth ownership. Two incomes should allow the family to accumulate wealth faster than one income would. The estimates in Table 6–2 suggest that this pattern is clearly true among the baby boomers (i.e., two-earner households were wealthier than one-earner households). For baby boomers age 25–34 in 1989, median net worth was $8,500 for households with one wage earner and $29,715 for those with two wage earners. Likewise, for those age 35–44 in 1989, median net worth was $56,040 for households with one wage earner and $97,025 for those with two wage earners. The estimates indicate, however, that among those in the parents' cohort, two-earner households actually had less wealth than other households. For those age 25–34 in 1962, median net worth was $13,250 for households with one wage earner and only $5,880 for those with two wage earners. For those age 35–44 in 1962, median net worth was $42,735 for those with one wage earner and $36,355 for those with two wage earners. One likely explanation for this pattern is that wives who worked in the early 1960s did so because the family needed extra money rather than because they were pursuing their own careers. Indeed, using cross tabulations, it is nearly impossible to determine the direction of causation. It might be that the direction changed from one generation to the next. That is, for baby boomers, it is likely that having two earners increased net worth and financial wealth. In contrast, for the parents of this cohort, it is more likely that having low wealth increased the likelihood that the wife would take a job outside the home. In most cases, when the wife (and usually it is the woman who works if a second wage earner is needed) works because her income is necessary, the job she takes is one with a lower income than what a woman who is pursuing an independent career would earn.

For all families, having children considerably decreased both their net worth and financial wealth. There was also a positive association between having children and having less wealth than income. The median financial wealth for younger, unmarried baby boomers in 1989 was $2,100 if they did not have children and only $100 if they had children. Median wealth for the parents of this group was $945 if they did not have children and $220 if they had children. Similar patterns held for older baby boomers. While children had the same general impact on the wealth of both baby boomers and their parents, the effect of children on net worth was considerably stronger for those in the parents' cohorts. The same general tendency held for financial wealth, but the effect was not as strong. Not surprisingly, having children was more detrimental for unmarried individuals than for married couples. The median net worth for unmarried baby boomers age 25–34 in 1989 was $3,255 for those who were childless compared to $735 for those with at least one child. For married couples, the general tendency was also for wealth to decrease if the household had children, but the decrease was less than that for unmarried individuals. Indeed, for one group depicted in Table 6–2, median net worth was actually greater for those with children than for those without. For baby boomers age 25–34 in 1989, median net worth increased slightly from $18,000 to $19,000. The same pattern held for the parents of this group. An explanation may be that this is an age at which most families have little wealth and their children, if they have any, are young. It is not until later in the life course of both the parents and the children that children become expensive and have a noticeable impact on net worth.

In addition to differences in overall wealth ownership, there were also differences in the wealth portfolios of baby boomers in the late 1980s and the portfolios their parents had in the early 1960s. Table 6–3 details the value of the typical wealth portfolio for 25–34 year olds and 35–44 year

Table 6–3. *The Wealth of Baby Boomers and Their Parents: Portfolio Differences*

|  | Age 25–34 | | Age 35–44 | |
|---|---|---|---|---|
|  | *1962* | *1989* | *1962* | *1989* |
| *All households* | | | | |
| Net worth | 6,411 | 9,450 | 30,765 | 56,911 |
| Primary residence | 0 | 0 | 24,470 | 52,550 |
| Other tangible assets | 3,240 | 5,250 | 4,095 | 8,450 |
| Liquid financial assets | 525 | 1,365 | 1,685 | 4,200 |
| Other financial assets | 630 | 210 | 4,935 | 3,150 |
| Mortgages on primary residence | 0 | 0 | 0 | 12,600 |
| Nonmortgage debt | 2,415 | 3,255 | 1,680 | 4,305 |
| *Net worth* | | | | |
| Nonhomeowners | 1,475 | 1,785 | 6,720 | 1,575 |
| Homeowners | 24,255 | 46,340 | 51,135 | 96,665 |

*Note*: Author's calculations from the Survey of the Financial Characteristics of Consumers for 1962 and the Survey of Consumer Finances for 1989. All values are adjusted to 1990 dollars, based on a standard CPI-U.

olds in both 1962 and 1989. Housing assets did not change much as a share of total wealth, but the value of housing assets for older baby boomers was more than double that of their parents. According to the estimates in Table 6–3, median value of housing assets was zero for 25–34 year olds in both 1962 and 1989 because only about 40 percent of these households were homeowners in either year. This is, of course, a problem with survey data. While the estimates are accurate for the sample, small sample sizes for some segments of the population yield unusual estimates for key pieces of information. This being said, it is important to note that the propensity to own a home did not increase greatly from one generation to the next, but for the older cohort, the value of housing assets did increase. For those age 35–44 in 1989, the value of the primary residence was more than $52,000, while home values for those in the same age group in 1962 were just $24,000.

Another sign of well-being is the value of financial assets. Tables 6–1 and 6–2 indicated that financial wealth for the baby boom generation was greater than for that in their parents' generation, and the estimates in Table 6–3 provide additional detail about this increase. The estimates in Table 6–3 indicate that the median value of financial assets was greater for both sets of baby boomers than for their parents. While the median value of liquid financial assets for those who were 25–34 in 1962 was $525, in 1989, the median for 25–34 year olds was 2.6 times that, or $1,365. The increase was comparable for 35–44 year olds. In 1962, the median value of liquid financial assets for 35–44 year olds was $1,685, and the median value for 35–44 year olds in 1989 was 2.5 times greater, or $4,200. This increase in the value of liquid financial assets may reflect increases in the value of stocks, mutual funds, bonds, and other financial assets that investors began to enjoy in the 1980s.

In contrast, the value of other financial assets decreased for both groups. In 1962, the median value of other financial assets was $630 for 25–34 year olds and, in 1989, the median value for this group was $210. Similarly, in 1962, the median value of other financial assets was (a much higher) $4,935 for 35–44 year olds, but the median in 1989 for this group was only $3,150. While it is possible that this result is a consequence of differences in questions on the two surveys, these estimates are comparable to the estimates published by the Congressional Budget Office using the same data (Manchester 1993). A possible explanation would be that changes in the availability of mutual funds, Individual Retirement Accounts, and other financial instruments that would be classified as liquid financial assets have changed the way people invest. More precisely, because these investment instruments were more accessible in 1989, more families may have used them than in the past, creating a difference in the form of saving without actually accounting for much of the magnitude in saving.

While the values of their assets were increasing, the debt holdings of those in the 25–34 year old age bracket also increased between 1962 and 1989. In the previous chapter, I discussed the impact that declining real wages had on debt holdings, particularly those of middle-class and poor families. The estimates in that chapter suggested that the nonwealthy owned a large portion of total outstanding debt by the mid-1990s. The estimates included in Table 6–3 suggest that the value of nonmortgage liabilities held by 25–34 year olds increased from a median of $2,415 in 1962 to a median of $3,255 in 1989. Even more extreme was the increase in debt ownership of those in the 35–44 year old age bracket. The median nonmortgage debt holding for those families was $1,680 in 1962 and 2.6 times that, or $4,305, in 1989. While these increases were indeed large, the percentage of total net worth accounted for by debt did not change by much.

Not only did portfolio behavior differ for those who were young adults in 1962 and 1989, but the owning of particular assets and debts also had different implications for these people. Homeownership, in particular, was a more vital component of a secure wealth portfolio for young adults in 1989 than it had been in 1962. Again the estimates in Table 6–3 provide some evidence that this is the case. The final two estimates in that table are estimates of median net worth for homeowners and nonhomeowners. The estimates indicate that the median net worth of nonhomeowners increased only slightly for 25–34 year olds between 1962 and 1989, and it actually decreased for 35–44 year olds. In 1962, the median net worth for nonhomeowners age 25–34 was $1,475 and, in 1989, these nonhome-owners in the same age group had a median net worth of $1,785. In contrast, homeowners enjoyed huge gains in net worth between 1962 and 1989. The net worth for homeowners age 25–34 in 1962 was $24,255, and the median was $46,340 in 1989. Similarly, for those age 35–44, net worth increased from $51,135 in 1962 to $96,665 in 1989.

During the 1970s and 1980s, there was a dramatic increase in housing prices relative to other prices (Manchester 1993). Yet the share of total net worth accounted for by housing equity did not change appreciably. For those in both age groups, housing equity stayed relatively constant. There were also considerable shocks to real estate values throughout the period in which homeowners in the late 1980s would have been purchasing their homes. Yet, again, housing continued to account for a relatively constant portion of the wealth portfolios of each age group. As the evidence in the previous chapter suggested, Americans see home ownership as a logical primary investment. The propensity for middle-class Americans to invest first in a home and only later in other assets is reflected in the estimates in Table 6–3 as well. The secondary story that these estimates tell is that this may be a very reasonable investment strategy. Certainly homeowner-ship paid off for those who were young adults in the late 1980s.

## Baby Boomers and Their Actual Parents

In the second set of analyses designed to explore wealth differences between baby boomers and their parents, I take advantage of the microsimulation model that I have used throughout this book. In these analyses, I use the model in four distinct ways: (1) as longitudinal data that allow me to simultaneously make intergenerational comparisons and explore trends over the life cycle; (2) to compare the wealth of baby boomers with the wealth of their actual parents, rather than with the wealth of a group of people that might have included their parents (the method I used in the cohort comparisons in the previous section); (3) to examine differences in mobility patterns between baby boomers and their parents; and (4) to project well-being into the future.

The first three of these uses take advantage of one of the unique traits of the simulation model and produce estimates of wealth ownership that are not possible with traditional methods of data analysis because longitudinal data are not available. In the case of simultaneous intergenerational comparisons and life course trends, survey data do not exist that can accommodate such analyses. Similarly, because there is no complete source of longitudinal data on baby boomers and their parents, it is not possible to use survey data to compare the baby boomers with their actual parents. Finally, longitudinal data on wealth ownership from the Panel Study of Income Dynamics have made possible studies of mobility between the mid-1980s and mid-1990s. But wealth mobility typically occurs over much longer periods of time, if it occurs at all. In contrast, the simulation model allows comparisons of mobility over a single life course and can also facilitate intergenerational comparisons of mobility, useful in understanding differences between baby boomers and their parents.

Using the simulation model to estimate future trends is a somewhat different matter. Of course, no survey data can easily answer questions about the future. Survey results can be extrapolated to predict future patterns in much the same way the simulation methods are extrapolated. The advantage of the simulation model, in this case, is that the future projections reflect 35 years (1960–1995) of alignment with much of the most accurate data available on many aspects of individual and family behavior. As I explained in more detail in Chapter 2, wealth ownership and distribution patterns are aligned in the model beginning in 1960 with survey data, estate tax data, and aggregate data. Others elements of the model that interact with wealth ownership are aligned in similar ways. The result is that the simulation model produces future estimates that have learned from past trends that are not reflected in survey-based extrapolations.

The evidence presented here is unique in two respects. First, I concentrate on the *wealth* of the baby boomers and their parents. Most existing treatments of intergenerational changes in well-being focus on income differences. As I argued above, however, wealth differences are perhaps more pertinent to understanding potential well-being during retirement, when income from wealth certainly separates the haves from the have-nots. The baby boomer generation is interesting, in part, because of the strain this huge population bulge puts on resources as they move through their lives. The next major strain that the baby boomers are likely to create will be on the Social Security system. Thus, understanding the potential private saving that this group has done has important implications for understanding their well-being at the end of the work years.

Second, in these analyses, I compare the well-being of baby boomers to their *actual* parents. Like much else, wealth is relative. But in assessing relative wealth situation, it is highly unlikely that individuals literally compare the wealth of their own birth cohort with the wealth of their parents' presumed birth cohort. More likely, individuals assess their relative wealth by comparing their situation to their own particular parents' wealth. They might carry out this comparison in a variety of ways depending upon the particular point at which they make the comparison. For example, they might always remember their family situation when they were growing up, or when they left home. Alternatively, they might compare their situation to their parents at a comparable age. For these reasons, it is probably on balance more meaningful to compare the wealth of a specific person at a given age to the wealth of that person's actual parents at the same age. Moreover, using the same-sex parent controls for the effect of gender on wealth ownership and related processes. In the first section of these analyses, therefore, I compare the wealth of each person with the wealth of the same-sex parent at a comparable age.

While there are definite advantages associated with using the simulated estimates to compare the well-being of baby boomers and their parents, several cautions are also in order before I begin to discuss the results. The simulation model rests on numerous assumptions. Indeed, there are more assumptions built into most simulations than can be articulated in a reasonable amount of space. At the same time, the assumptions are vitally important in understanding the estimates that such a model produces. One important assumption I make in the analyses I present in this chapter is that the family links (i.e., the parent–child links on which the intergenerational comparisons rest) are accurate. There is little way to validate the historical accuracy of these linkages, save for validation of fertility and marriage behaviors. The comparisons of the model output with survey output that I presented in previous chapters indicate that the model produces highly accurate estimates of basic demographic trends in wealth ownership. While this is not sufficient to prove historical consistency in family linkages, it is a vital (perhaps *the* vital) necessary component.

Other important assumptions that I make in this chapter include assuming continued economic growth when I estimate future trends. The U.S. economy might, of course, take many paths. I assume continued growth because the economy has grown steadily in recent decades. In the future analyses, I also assume that there are no significant changes in government tax policies and that no new financial instruments emerge that significantly impact saving behavior. Other assumptions would naturally produce different results. Comparing the results presented here with other possible scenarios is also possible using the simulation model, although I do not take advantage of that feature of the model in this chapter.

In addition, I use the simulation model to estimate trends that cannot be estimated using survey data alone. While this allows me to fill gaps in our knowledge, there is little way to validate the simulated estimates that I provide. In previous chapters, I have provided simulated estimates of basic distributional, longitudinal, portfolio, demographic, and mobility trends, alongside survey estimates where they have been available. The previous analyses have demonstrated that the simulation model is able to produce historically consistent estimates of wealth accumulation distribution patterns both cross-sectionally and over time. My intention in including these simultaneous estimates has largely been as validation of the simulation model where it has been possible. I now venture even farther into territory that cannot be validated against historical estimates. Despite the many assumptions underlying the model, my hope is that these estimates are fairly accurate given the general accuracy that previous analyses have demonstrated.

In the first set of comparisons using the simulation method, I compare the median net worth of baby boomers with their parents at the same age over a 40-year period. Figure 6–1 graphs the median net worth of female baby boomers against the wealth of their mothers. As in other sections of this chapter, when I refer to the wealth of an individual, I am using the wealth of the individual's family as a proxy for the individual measure. In the first graph, the member of the birth cohort is all the females born between 1955 and 1964. The group of women who are the actual mothers in the model of those women born between 1955 and 1964 are labeled

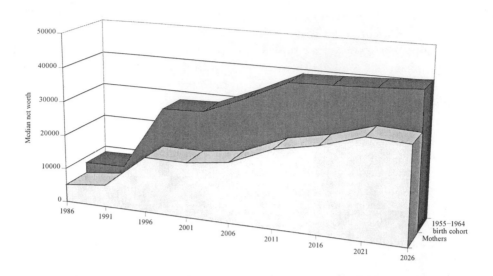

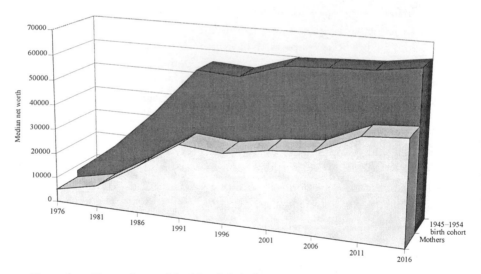

Figure 6–1. The median wealth of female baby boomers and their mothers over the entire life Span.

"mothers." The second graph is set up the same way, although the birth cohort represented in that graph is those women born between 1945 and 1954, and the "mothers" are the actual mothers of those women born between 1945 and 1964. Figure 6–2 includes comparable estimates for

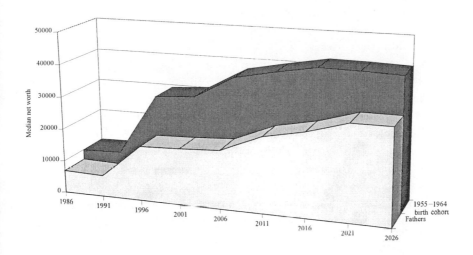

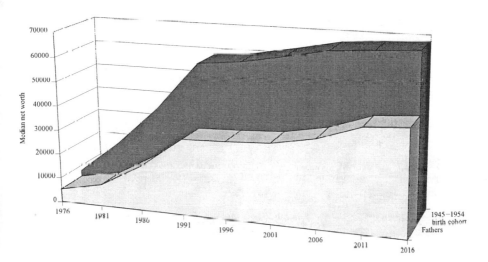

Figure 6–2. The median wealth of male baby boomers and their fathers over the entire life span.

men born during the baby boom and the group of men who were their actual fathers in the model.

In these figures, I compare the wealth of baby boomers and their parents at comparable ages. The age of the baby boomer is the person's age in the year indicated on the horizontal axis. Thus, a hypothetical female baby boomer who was born in 1955 would have been 31 years old in 1986. I sample this woman because her year of birth was between 1955 and 1964, and I include the net worth of the family she lived with in 1986 among the sampled net worth values for that year. I then calculate the median net worth in 1986 over all those born between 1955 and 1964. The process I use for calculating the mothers' net worth is somewhat more complex. I do not use the mothers' net worth in 1986. Rather, for the hypothetical 31-year-old baby boomer, I determine which woman is her mother. I then identify the net worth of the family that the mother lived with when she was 31 years old and include that among the sample of mothers. Thus the median net worth for mothers in the first graph in Figure 6–1 is the median across all mothers in whatever year they were the same age that their actual daughter was in the year shown in the figure. In 1986 in the figure, the younger baby boomers would have been 22–31 years old. Their mothers would likely have been in their twenties in the 1950s and 1960s.

For both the men and the women, net worth comparisons in Figures 6–1 and 6–2 begin when the youngest members of that part of the cohort were 22 years old and continue for 40 years. That is, the comparisons are given for 1986 to 2026 for baby boomers born between 1955 and 1964 (the younger segment of the cohort). For those baby boomers born between 1945 and 1954 (the older segment of the cohort) estimates are given for 1976 to 2016. I extend the estimates for 40 years because, at that point, the youngest of the cohort will have neared retirement. This means that for the younger baby boomers, I extend the estimates through 2026. Extrapolating any further would begin to make little sense, as the model is not aligned to historical data after 1995.

Compared with their actual same-sex parents (in the simulation model), the estimates in Figures 6–1 and 6–2 suggest that baby boomers had (and will have) considerably more wealth at all stages of the life course. In each of the four graphs in the figures, the median net worth is consistently greater than the median net worth for their actual same-sex parents. Each of the graphs has the same basic shape: It begins rather low, when both the baby boomers and their parents were in their early twenties. Across the life cycle, while both young and old baby boomers were consistently better off than their parents in the simulated comparisons, the benefits were somewhat greater for those in the leading segment of the baby boom. While the cohort differences are quite clear in these graphs, there are few noticeable gender differences in wealth ownership. This is likely because most of the respondents are eventually married, as most of the adult population of the United

States has been historically. The wealth of single individuals is consistently less than that of married couples, as the cohort comparisons in the last section demonstrated. In a comparison of single individuals, there would also be noticeable gender differences in wealth ownership. In particular, median net worth for single females would be less than the median for single males. In the figure, because the estimates are based on the family in which the individual lived, the gender differences are not apparent.

As the groups aged, median net worth increased and continued to increase even when a large portion of the groups had reached and passed retirement age. There is some question in the literature on life-cycle processes of wealth accumulation about whether individuals continue to save after retirement. Modigliani (1988a, 1992) was one of the first to posit that after retirement it is likely that household wealth declines as assets are depleted for use as current income. Others have argued, on the contrary, that household wealth continues to increase even after retirement for two reasons: First, people want to leave an inheritance for their children, and second, no one is sure when she or he will die. While further discussion of the life-cycle hypothesis is beyond the scope of this chapter, the continued increase in wealth even after retirement is consistent with the latter argument. The evidence included in these figures also demonstrates a slightly greater increase in median wealth for those in the older segment of the baby boom at the end of the time period depicted. Of course, it would be preferable to extend the estimates farther into the future to examine the life-cycle question in more detail. I do not tackle this question more here, but I do examine this and related questions again in Chapter 8.

### The Mobility of Baby Boomers and Their Parents

Another indicator of financial well-being that is pertinent to a generational comparison is differences in mobility. While survey data on wealth mobility over extended periods of time is not available, it is possible to estimate trends in mobility using the simulation model. In Chapter 3, I used mobility tables to demonstrate trends in wealth mobility. These are useful in illustrating basic trends, but they do not indicate much about the factors that influence mobility. Because I am interested here in demonstrating mobility differences both within the baby boom cohort (i.e., differences between older and younger baby boomers) and differences across cohorts (i.e., differences between baby boomers and their parents), I decided to use a different presentation strategy.

My strategy for comparing mobility has four components. First, I used the simulation model to produce estimates of whether an individual changed deciles in the wealth distribution from year to year in the relevant years between 1960 and 1995. In this case, the relevant years are the years after the person turned 20 years old, continuing until either the person died or 1995 arrived. Second, I created a data set in which the dependent variable was an indicator of upward mobility. The unit of analysis was person-years (one observation for each person for each year). If the individual moved up to a higher wealth decile a given year, I coded the dependent variable 1. Otherwise, I coded the dependent variable 0. I also retained information in the data set about the demographic characteristics of the individual, including an indicator of whether the person was born during the baby boom or had a child born during the baby boom. Third, I estimated logistic regression equations predicting upward mobility, with separate intercepts and independent variable indicators for younger baby boomers, older baby boomers, parents of younger baby boomers, and parents of older baby boomers. The result was a set of coefficients that predict the likelihood of upward wealth mobility.

Using the coefficient estimates from the logistic regression equations, I produced odds ratios that indicate the increase (or decrease) in the odds of upward mobility given that the individual had the specified trait. For example, the odds ratio for being a college graduate in the 1955–1964 birth cohort was 2.132. This suggests that the odds of upward mobility for a member of this birth cohort with a college education were 2.132 times greater than the odds for someone with less than a high school education (the omitted category) in the same birth cohort. Odds ratios less than 1.0 are interpreted as a decrease in the odds of mobility. The odds ratio for members of the 1955–1964 birth cohort who were divorced was 0.995. This implies that the odds of upward mobility for divorced people in this cohort were 1.005 times less than for never married people (the omitted category) in the same birth cohort.

I report the findings of these analyses in Tables 6–4 and 6–5. Table 6–4 reports odds ratios from logistic equations that contained only four variables: four dummy indicators that the individual was in one of the baby boom cohorts or was in one of the groups of parents of baby boomers. The odds ratios in this table indicate the odds of upward mobility broken down simply by cohort. The odds ratios in Table 6–5 separate the individuals by cohort and by demographic characteristics, including education, marital status, family composition, number of wage earners in family, age

Table 6-4. *Lifetime Mobility Differences Between Baby Boomers and Their Actual Parents: Odds Ratios from Logit Model Estimates of Increase in Decile Rank*

|  | Odds Ratio |
|---|---|
| 1955–1964 birth cohort | 1.823 |
| Parents of 1955–1964 cohort | 1.223 |
| | |
| 1945–1954 birth cohort | 2.421 |
| Parents of 1945–1954 cohort | 1.756 |

*Note*: Author's estimates of odds ratios from logistic regression on simulated data. All odds ratios are from the same model. The dependent variable is a dichotomous indicator in family wealth decile, 1960–1995. Cohorts are all people in the specified birth cohort. Parents are all actual mothers and fathers of the sampled cohort members, regardless of the birth year of the parent.

and gender of household head, and whether the household owned a home or stock. Clearly these odds ratios allow for more detailed comparisons of the processes that account for differences in wealth mobility. Using downward mobility as the dependent variable did not change the results substantively. The results were also substantively the same when I estimated multinomial logistic regression with a three-part dependent variable: upward mobility, no mobility, downward mobility. Because it is conceptually easier to interpret the results in terms of upward mobility, I report the odds ratios from those equations.

Older baby boomers, those born between 1945 and 1954, were more likely than the younger baby boomers or either group of parents to move up in the wealth distribution during their lifetime. The odds of upward mobility for the younger baby boomers were also quite high. Indeed, the odds that a member of the 1955–1964 birth cohort was upwardly mobile were 1.823 times greater than for those not in this cohort. Both groups of baby boomers were more likely to be upwardly mobile than either their actual parents or the other parent group. The increase in odds for members of the younger baby boomers and that for the parents of the older baby

Table 6–5. *Baby Boomers and Their Actual Parents: Influences on Mobility*

|  | 1955–64 Birth Cohort | | 1945–54 Birth Cohort | |
|---|---|---|---|---|
|  | *Children* | *Parents* | *Children* | *Parents* |
| Income | 1.017 | 1.000 | 1.000 | 1.100 |
| Some high school | 1.001 | 1.000 | 1.001 | 1.000 |
| High school graduate | 1.879 | 1.430 | 1.654 | 1.000 |
| College graduate | 2.132 | 1.313 | 1.216 | 1.095 |
| Male | 1.089 | 1.206 | 1.166 | 1.613 |
| Married | 1.338 | 2.159 | 1.613 | 2.421 |
| Divorced | 0.995 | 0.721 | 0.794 | 0.329 |
| Has children | 0.804 | 0.590 | 0.728 | 0.790 |
| Single with children | 0.639 | 0.365 | 0.808 | 0.192 |
| Married, two incomes | 1.957 | 1.613 | 1.061 | 1.654 |
| Age 35–54 | 1.061 | 1.095 | 1.099 | 1.089 |
| Age 55–64 | 1.116 | 1.166 | 1.100 | 1.165 |
| Age 65 and above | 1.798 | 1.820 | 1.613 | 1.823 |
| Homeowner | 1.099 | 1.100 | 1.113 | 1.064 |
| Stock owner | 1.216 | 2.159 | 1.418 | 2.262 |

*Note*: Author's estimates of odds ratios from logistic regression on simulated data. All odds ratios are from the same model. The dependent variable is a dichotomous indicator of family wealth decile, 1960–1995. Odds ratios are the ratios between the odds of an increase in decile position for those having the specified trait and those in the omitted category. Children are all people in the specified birth cohort. Parents are all actual mothers and fathers of the sampled cohort members, regardless of the birth year of the parent.

boomers were somewhat comparable. The odds of upward mobility for a member of the younger baby boomer cohort were 1.823 greater than for people not in one of these four groups (anyone who was neither a baby boomer nor the parent of a baby boomer), and the increase in odds for members of the parents of the other group was 1.756.

There were also important demographic differences in the odds of upward mobility both within the baby boom generation and across generations. The estimates displayed in Table 6–5 suggest that education was an important influence on mobility for all four cohorts (for both baby boom cohorts and both groups of their parents). For all four groups, the increase in the odds of upward mobility for having some high school education was about 1.000. Likewise, for the parents of those born between 1945 and 1954, the odds ratio for having graduated from high school was also 1.000. However, for the parents of those born between 1955 and 1964, the increase in the odds of upward mobility for having a high school education was 1.430. Likewise, having a college education was important for both the baby boomers and their parents, but it was more important for the baby boomers. The effects of gender on wealth mobility are evident in these results as well. The increase in odds of upward mobility was greater for males in both the baby boom cohorts and their parents' cohorts. But the increase in odds for being male was greater for the parents. In other words, the handicap of being female appears to have decreased from the parents' to the children's generations.

Marital status and family composition also affected the likelihood of upward mobility among both the baby boomers and their parents. The odds ratios in Table 6–5 suggest that being married was an advantage for each of the groups included in the regression equations, but that being married was more important for the parents than for the baby boomers. The odds ratios also suggest that being married afforded more advantage to older than to younger baby boomers. For those born between 1945 and 1954, the odds of upward wealth mobility increased 1.613 times if the person was married, whereas for those born between 1955 and 1964, the odds of upward mobility increased 1.338 times. The estimates in this table also suggest that being divorced has a negative impact across all four generations but that divorce was more detrimental for the parents of the baby boomers than for the baby boomers themselves. Similarly, having children negatively impacted the odds of upward mobility, but the effect was worse for the parents' cohorts.

Homeownership and stock ownership increased the odds of upward mobility for both baby boomers and their parents. For all four generations included in Table 6–5, the odds of upward mobility increased fairly consistently with homeownership. For those born between 1955 and 1964, the increase in the odds of upward mobility was 1.099 times greater for homeowners than for those who did not own a home. Similarly, for those born between 1945 and 1954, homeowners were 1.113 times more likely

to be upwardly mobile than nonhomeowners. The effect of stock ownership on upward mobility was somewhat greater, particularly for the parents
of the baby boomers. For younger baby boomers, the odds of upward
mobility increased 1.216 times if they owned stock and, for the older baby
boomers, the odds increased 1.418 times with stock ownership. In contrast, the odds of upward mobility increased more than 2 times for each
group of parents if they owned stock. This finding is consistent with evidence that household stock ownership increased in the 1980s and 1990s.
Because it was more common to be a stock owner when the baby boomers
were in their prime working years, the effect appears to have been weaker.
At the same time, it is clear that for each of the generations included
in the table, portfolio behavior, particularly homeownership and stock
ownership, had important effects on upward mobility.

## Summary and Conclusions

Questions about intergenerational differences in well-being have long fas-
cinated those with both basic research and policy interests. Because baby
boomers will continue to dominate demographic trends in this country for
at least three more decades, comparing their well-being to that of their
parents has recently begun to attract attention from various corners.
Research reports and the media alike speculate that these adults may be
the first generation to do worse than their parents financially, yet no solid
empirical evidence documents this trend. In this chapter, I explored some
of these questions by focusing on the well-being of baby boomers and their
parents. I might have picked any generation for the focus of these analyses, but the practical policy issues associated with the aging of baby
boomers made this generation a logical focal point.

I used two distinct methodologies to compare the well-being of baby
boomers and their parents. First I used survey data from the 1962 Survey
of the Financial Characteristics of Consumers (SFCC) and the 1989 Survey
of Consumer Finances (SCF) to compare the wealth of 25–34 year olds in
1989 (the young baby boomers) with those who were 25–34 in 1962,
assuming that 25–34 year olds in 1962 included many of those in the baby
boomers' parents' birth cohort. I also compared wealth ownership patterns
of those who were 35–44 in 1989 with the same age group in 1962. On
balance, the parent–child comparisons suggested that baby boomers accumulated more wealth as young adults than their parents had at a relatively
similar age. Net worth and financial wealth were both uniformly greater

for young adults in the late 1980s than they were for comparable age groups in the early 1960s. Some demographic changes were evident, including changes in the influence of marriage and children on wealth ownership. Remaining single was more common for baby boomers than it had been for their parents, and baby boomers who did eventually get married postponed marriage and family. Some researchers have speculated that these changes could hurt the baby boomers' financial well-being in retirement, but the evidence I found in comparing the 1962 SFCC with the 1989 SCF indicated that these changes had actually improved the situation of some segments of the baby boom cohort.

Consistent with Manchester's findings in her report for the Congressional Budget Office, my results showed that the gains made by baby boomers were not uniform (Manchester 1993). Indeed, there were advantages to being part of the leading segment of the baby boom cohort, although some of these apparent advantages may disappear after younger boomers have had time to acquire more assets during their working years. Consistent with Manchester, my results also indicated that the baby boomers who appeared to still be at a particular disadvantage were those who had no high school degree, married couples with only one earner, single women, and nonhomeowners.

In the second set of analyses I discussed in this chapter, I took advantage of the simulation model to ask questions that were not possible with the survey data. In particular, I used the simulation model to simultaneously explore the wealth ownership patterns of the baby boomers and their parents intergenerationally and over the life cycle. In doing this, I compared the wealth of both the younger and older baby boomers with that of their actual, same-sex parent at a comparable age over a 40-year period. The findings of these analyses indicate that baby boomers had, and will continue to have, considerably more wealth than their parents did at all stages of the life cycle. The analyses revealed strong and consistent patterns of continual increases in net worth over the life cycle and provided no support for the life-cycle hypothesis of postretirement dissaving.

I also used the simulation model to explore differences in mobility between baby boomers and their parents. I found that, on the whole, baby boomers were more likely to be upwardly mobile than their parents, but there were important differences within both the baby boomers' cohorts and their parents' cohorts. Education, particularly a college education, was important for all groups, but more important for baby boomers. Those with little or no education had little chance of mobility. Likewise, marriage and family composition affected mobility in important ways. The results suggested that while being married continued to improve the odds of mobility, its effect decreased in the baby boom generation. Similarly, while divorce was still an impediment to mobility, it was not as strong an impediment as it once was. Finally, the mobility analyses indicated that portfolio behavior affected the odds of mobility. In particular, those who were homeowners and those who owned stocks increased their odds of upward mobility, regardless of their age, but stock ownership, in particular, had a greater effect on mobility for the parents of the baby boomers than it did for the baby boomers themselves.

These findings have implications for both public policy and basic research. From a policy perspective, these results indicate that speculation about baby boomers shocking the Social Security system, for example, may be overstated. Of course, the sheer size of the baby boomer cohort may still worry policy makers, but at least there is reason to believe that the boomers would be able to support themselves in retirement if necessary. These results also have implications for understanding intergenerational processes in general as well as the effects of such things as cohort size on the well-being of members of the cohort. The microsimulation model used here demonstrates an alternative approach to studying intergenerational processes in which linkages between children and their actual parents can be used to understand the effects of family background on a child's outcomes. More substantively, this research suggests that large cohort size is not necessarily a negative factor and that other demographic trends and lifestyle changes may supersede the effects of the size of a birth cohort.

# Part III

## WEALTH ACCUMULATION

# 7

# THE IMPACT OF SOCIAL AND
# ECONOMIC TRENDS ON INEQUALITY

The general movement of wages is exclusively regulated by the expansion and contraction of the industrial reserve army, and these again correspond to the periodic changes of the industrial cycle.

(Karl Marx, *Capital*, Vol. I, Chap. 25)

The past four chapters have focused on the distribution of wealth in various segments of the population. I profiled the entire population in Chapter 3. In Chapters 4 and 5, I concentrated on wealth ownership patterns among the rich, middle class, and poor, and in Chapter 6, I compared patterns of wealth ownership and distribution across generations. I now turn my attention to a more a detailed investigation of the processes that underlie these patterns. I begin, in this chapter, with an examination of the role that social and economic trends play in creating, reproducing, and changing the distribution of wealth. As the quote by Marx above suggests, microlevel changes in well-being correspond in important ways to periodic, and in some cases predictable, changes in aggregate level cycles. In this chapter, I identify some of the aggregate trends that are relevant to understanding wealth inequality, and I specify the nature of the relationships between these trends and microlevel patterns of well-being. I examine the role that demographic patterns, financial and real estate market trends, and government policies play in creating patterns of wealth distribution. As I do in other chapters, I explicitly examine patterns of wealth accumulation and distribution in the United States between 1962 and 1995. I hope, however, that some of the lessons of this period are generalizable to patterns of inequality in the United States and elsewhere both during other historical periods and in future times.

This chapter isolates and examines the macrolevel component of the macro–micro theoretical model that frames this book. Understanding wealth accumulation and distribution processes requires understanding both influences at the level of individuals and families (the microlevel) and influences at the macrolevel. Yet, as I argued in Chapter 1, most research on wealth accumulation and distribution focuses on just one level and attempts to account for most changes in patterns of distribution with an explanation that ignores the other level. In Chapter 1, I introduced some ideas from Coleman's two-level model that guide this analysis (1990). In this model, aggregate structure relations affect microlevel behavior, and these behaviors, in turn, affect the microlevel outcomes such as the amount of wealth owned. Aggregating micro-outcomes, though not a simple matter, can produce aggregate trends such as historical trends in wealth distribution. Modeling a multilevel system of this sort is, of course, challenging, but the simulation methods I use allow me to estimate trends at both levels of aggregation and to explore how these trends interact with and affect each other.

There are four sections in this chapter. In the first section, I explore the effect that demographic trends have on wealth inequality, focusing on the effect of the baby boom. In the second and third sections, I explore the effects of market fluctuations on inequality. I first examine the role of stock market fluctuations, and then I concentrate on the effect of real estate market fluctuations. In the final section, I examine the effect that government policies can have on inequality. In this chapter, I use simulation experiments to isolate specific examples, both historical and theoretical, of aggregate-level changes and to explore their impact on wealth inequality. In each case, there are innumerable patterns I might have simulated. The actual patterns that I have chosen to replicate are simply examples. While I concentrate in this chapter on macrolevel effects as past research has done, the results I present, particularly the simulated results, incorporate both microprocesses and macroprocesses, unlike survey data used in isolation. The experiments I present in this chapter highlight this fact.

## Demographic Trends

Many students of social stratification have hypothesized that the distribution of wealth is largely determined by population size and the total volume of wealth in a society (Homans 1974; Lenski 1966; Mayhew and Schollaert 1980; Millar 1806; Montesquieu 1748; Spencer 1882). Typically, these theorists have argued that increases in either the total volume of wealth (and other status characteristics) or population size will lead to an increase in inequality. Drawing on ideas from early theorists such as Spencer (1882), Lenski, for example, argued that in the simplest societies, goods and services are distributed based on need, but as technology advances, an increasing proportion of goods and services will be distributed based on power (Lenski 1966:46). He concluded that the degree of inequality in distributive systems will vary directly with the size of a society's surplus because a smaller number of powerful people will control a larger amount of goods and services. While Lenski acknowledged that some modifications of the general patterns are possible when persons who lack power are able to organize and thus counterbalance the power of those with greater individual power, he argued that there is generally a direct relationship between size of surplus and inequality (Lenski 1966:85).

Related arguments have addressed the effect of increases in population size on inequality and the distribution of well-being. Lenski's power arguments, for example, have important implications for understanding the effect of demographic shifts on the distribution of wealth. When population size increases, as in a baby boom, there is not necessarily a proportionate increase in the number of those with power. Rather, it is likely that the number of those with little power, and thus little wealth, will increase, while the powerful, wealthy few will remain a relatively small group. The result would be an increase in inequality as a result of a population increase. Others have argued that increases in population size lead to crowding, which in turn leads both directly and indirectly to greater inequality (Easterlin 1980). Greater competition for educational resources, jobs, and other resources spreads limited resources further, making many people worse off (Easterlin 1987). The income-depressant effects of cohort size, in particular, may stay with a cohort throughout their lives (Welch 1979).

Each of these arguments combines mechanisms at both the macrolevel and the microlevels in the spirit of the Coleman model, although the theorists seldom dealt with micro–macro issues explicitly. Lenski argued that macrolevel changes in demographics influenced microlevel control of resources, which, in turn, determined the nature of the distribution of well-being. Thus, increases in population size would increase the wealth of already powerful individuals, leading to greater inequality at the macrolevel. Similarly, while crowding affects inequality directly by spreading limited resources across more people, an increase in cohort size also has important effects on microlevel behaviors that indirectly affect inequality and mobility. Crowding changes the likelihood that a generation will be able to realize the aspirations that developed during childhood. Crowding thus has the potential to change more about the generation than how hard its members have to compete to get ahead.

Drawing on the relative income theory of economic and demographic behavior, Easterlin argued that economic socialization in early life creates the set of material aspirations that one has at adulthood. It is these material aspirations that determine the desired level of living during the adult years (Easterlin, MacDonald, and Macunovich 1990a). The degree to which young adults have to compete with their peers for positions in the labor force determines how difficult it is to achieve the aspirations that were developed during childhood. Competition for educational resources and difficult labor market conditions thus lead to changes in behavior and norms about social and economic behaviors such as how hard one must work to succeed, when to get married, when to have children, and whether women should work.

In this way, generational crowding imprints members of a cohort in ways that affect their behavior throughout the life course. In his work on the effects of the Great Depression on those who grew up during those years, Elder has shown that economic change at the aggregate level affects individual level behaviors in important ways. In one study, Elder and Liker used longitudinal data to examine the consequences of the Great Depression experiences of middle- and working-class women on their well-being in old age (Elder and Liker 1982). The starting point for this study is the notion that adaptations and material loss during the Great Depression varied widely by social class and affected the middle and working classes more than they did the upper classes. They demonstrate that economic depression during the 1930s affected well-being not only during the 1930s but also 30 years later, during the 1960s. Emotional health, intellectual ability, and assertiveness in later life were all negatively related to economic hardship during the Depression. Similarly, economic hardship during the Depression had a direct effect on feelings of helplessness later in life. Elder and Liker posited that Depression hardship affected emotional resources, vitality, and self-efficacy via their effects on resource access, education, and emotional well-being in the early years. Elder's other work on the children of the Great Depression demonstrates similar patterns for various outcomes and provides strong support for the notion that early-life experiences shape the behavior of cohorts in ways that affect not only individual behavior but aggregate social and economic outcomes as well (Elder and Rockwell 1977).

For baby boomers, crowding has the potential to imprint individuals with a sense that it is difficult to get ahead and that it takes more than hard work to succeed. Changes in labor force participation, marriage and divorce, fertility, and related behaviors have been evident among American baby boomers, who faced much greater competition at all points of their adolescent and adult lives than their parents faced. The aspirations that baby boomers developed as children were influenced by their parents' conception that hard work was a likely route to success. When the boomers reached adulthood and discovered that it would take more for them to succeed than it had for their parents, many behavioral patterns changed. The baby boomers postponed marriage, delayed childbirth, and adopted new attitudes toward work behavior and career advancement. Mounting empirical evidence, including the evidence presented in the previous chapter, supports the notion that the indirect effects of cohort size on inequality may indeed allow the baby boomers to fare better than their parents both during their working years and during retirement (Easterlin, MacDonald and Macunovich 1990a, 1990b; Easterlin, Schaeffer, and Macunovich 1993; Manchester 1993; Sabelhaus and Manchester 1995).

Taking this argument a step further, it is likely that demographic changes among baby boomers will impact macrolevel indicators including the distribution of wealth and patterns of mobility among families. However, when we consider the potential effects of cohort crowding on individual-level behavior, it is likely that there is an *indirect* relationship between cohort size and inequality. As people postpone marriage and childbirth, they free up more years to accumulate assets in a way that is not possible in a family with children. Greater female labor participation is also likely to increase family well-being and the prospects for mobility. Because changes in demographic behaviors have been common among those in all classes, there is a potential for those in the middle and lower classes to improve their positions more rapidly than they might have had these changes not occurred. In the previous chapter, I compared patterns of wealth ownership and mobility across generations. The results indicated that baby boomers owned more assets than their same-sex parents had owned at a comparable age. The results also indicated that baby boomers were more likely than their parents to experience upward wealth mobility during their lives. Finally, the results suggested that the processes that accounted for upward mobility were different for baby boomers than they had been for their parents. What the analyses in that chapter did not address was how these differences in wealth accumulation patterns affected the distribution of wealth and wealth mobility across all families.

One way to empirically explore the relationship between demographic trends and distributional outcomes is to compare historically accurate estimates of distribution and mobility patterns with simulated estimates that assume that the demographic changes had not taken place. Survey data allows estimates of actual patterns of distribution and, if the data are adequate, patterns of mobility. Survey data can be used to make intergenerational comparisons of the sort I presented in the previous chapter if they were collected in appropriate years and for appropriate age groups. Standard survey data, however, has little to say about what the world would have looked like if demographic or other patterns had occurred differently. In other words, survey data cannot be used to compare the same subsample under experimental and control conditions. In contrast, a simulation model can be used to conduct the kind of comparisons appropriate to answer questions about whether historical patterns would have been different given a set of changes.

Another advantage of using simulation in this case is that the simulation model can capture much of the complexity that characterizes actual social patterns. Various behaviors and patterns interact in complex ways to produce the distribution of wealth. For example, women's labor force participation is likely an important component, and it is an influence that could be altered in the simulation model to explore its impact on wealth distribution. Yet female labor force participation is certainly not the only determinant of wealth distribution. In a simulation model, patterns of labor force participation interact with the accumulation of income, childbearing, educational attainment, occupational mobility, and other patterns that also affect the outcome of interest. As a result, changing female labor force participation may have some, but not all, of the impact we would expect it to have on wealth distribution, in much the way inputs affect outcomes in reality.

In order to explore the relationship between cohort size and the distribution of wealth, I actually did choose to focus on female labor force participation rates. I selected the labor force participation variable among various demographic changes that I might have examined. By isolating this variable, I do not intend to imply that there is something unique about labor force participation. In fact, similar patterns were evident when I examined fertility, marriage, divorce, and other related patterns that were unique for baby boomers. Rather, my intention is to use labor force participation rates to explore more generally the effect of aggregate demographic changes on outcomes in the aggregate distribution of wealth. In Coleman's terminology, my macrosocial proposition is that an increase in cohort size during the baby boom was indirectly related to a decrease in inequality in the distribution of wealth. Figure 7–1 diagrams this proposition. The mechanism that relates these two constructs, however, requires understanding of microlevel processes as well. In particular, I argued that cohort size led to changes in female labor force participation among baby boomers, and changes in labor force participation increased the likelihood of mobility among baby boomers. Finally, moving back to the macrolevel, changes in wealth accumulation and mobility likely decreased inequality in wealth ownership. Figure 7–2 includes these microlevel propositions as well as the primary, macrolevel proposition.

In order to explore the viability of these propositions, I conducted an experiment designed to explore two of the steps in Figure 7–2. First, I explore the relationship between changes in female labor force participation and wealth accumulation and mobility. Second, I explore the relationship between these outcomes and wealth inequality, or the distribution of wealth. I do not empirically examine the relationship between cohort size and female labor force participation (the first step in the figure). Because there is such strong existing evidence that female labor force participation rates did increase for baby boomers (see the previous chapter in this book as well as Easterlin 1980), there was no need to examine this empirically.

Cohort size                                                 Wealth inequality

Figure 7–1. Macrosocial proposition: Increase in cohort size decreases wealth inequality.

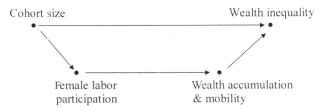

Figure 7–2. Macrolevel and microlevel propositions: cohort size and wealth inequality.

173

The simulation experiment that I conducted had two parts. First, I ran the simulation model using historically accurate labor force participation rates for women and estimated wealth mobility and distribution patterns for baby boomers. This is the control run, the run that reflects historically accurate patterns of work and wealth accumulation. The estimates that I produced from this run are consistent with other base estimates (estimates not part of an experiment) presented throughout this book. Second, I decreased labor force participation rates by 10 percent for all females born between 1945 and 1964 throughout their adult lives. I then ran the model again and estimated the same mobility and distribution patterns for the baby boomers. This is the experimental run. In the results below, I compare mobility and distribution patterns under the two conditions. The probability that a woman works in the model is determined by a stochastic logistic regression equation that includes demographic characteristics of the woman. As it does to determine the ownership of particular assets and debts (see Chapter 2), the model uses the empirically estimated coefficients to predict a probability that a woman works. Using a random number generator, the model produces a random number. If the random number is greater than the predicted probability, the woman works, if not, she does not work. In this experiment, I allowed the stochastic equation to predict a probability of work, and I then decreased that probability by 10 percent and let the random number process proceed as usual. The result was that 10 percent fewer women in the baby boomer cohort, on average, entered the labor force.

My strategy for comparing mobility between the control and experimental runs is similar to the strategy I used in the last chapter to compare mobility patterns across generations. I used the simulation model to estimate (separately for the control and experimental conditions) whether an individual changed deciles in the wealth distribution from year to year in the relevant years between 1960 and 1995. I then created two data sets, one control and one experimental, in which the dependent variable was a dichotomous indicator of upward mobility over the previous year. I then estimated logistic regression equations predicting upward mobility on each data set. The odds ratios that I report in Table 7–1 indicate the increase (or decrease) in the odds of upward mobility given that the individual had the specified trait. The estimates in the table labeled "before" are all from a single model using the historically accurate (control) conditions, and the odds ratios labeled "after" are from a separate model using

Table 7–1. *Simulation Experiment: Women's Labor Force Participation and the Wealth Mobility of Baby Boomers*

|  | 1955–64 Birth Cohort | | 1945–54 Birth Cohort | |
|---|---|---|---|---|
|  | *Before* | *After* | *Before* | *After* |
| Male | 1.089 | 2.241 | 1.166 | 2.611 |
| Married | 1.338 | 2.400 | 1.613 | 1.940 |
| Income | 1.017 | 1.024 | 1.000 | 1.000 |
| Some high school | 1.001 | 1.090 | 1.001 | 1.011 |
| High school graduate | 1.879 | 1.792 | 1.654 | 1.623 |
| College graduate | 2.132 | 2.260 | 1.216 | 1.267 |
| Divorced | 0.995 | 1.010 | 0.794 | 1.000 |
| Has children | 0.804 | 0.824 | 0.728 | 0.800 |
| Single with children | 0.639 | 0.705 | 0.808 | 0.790 |
| Married, two incomes | 1.957 | 2.100 | 1.061 | 1.000 |
| Age 35–54 | 1.061 | 1.095 | 1.099 | 1.100 |
| Age 55–64 | 1.116 | 1.114 | 1.100 | 1.144 |
| Age 65 and above | 1.798 | 1.854 | 1.613 | 1.714 |
| Homeowner | 1.099 | 1.111 | 1.113 | 1.162 |
| Stock owner | 1.216 | 1.334 | 1.418 | 1.390 |

*Note*: Author's estimates of odds ratios from logistic regression on simulated data before and after decrease in women's labor force participation rates for baby boomers. Odds ratios for both cohorts "Before" experiment are all from a single model. Odds ratios "After" experiment are from another model. The dependent variable in each model is a dichotomous indicator of family wealth decile, 1960–1995. Odds ratios are the ratios between the odds of an increase in decile position for those having the specified trait and those in the omitted category. Estimates before the experiment correspond to simulated estimates of wealth mobility in Table 6–5. See text for details.

the experimental conditions in which fewer females participated in the labor market. The estimates derived from the control run correspond to the simulated estimates of wealth mobility in Table 6–5.

The results of the experiment support the proposition that increased female labor force participation among baby boomers increased upward mobility. The odds ratios demonstrate decreased mobility after the experiment particularly for females and those who were not married. In the table, we see that moving from the control scenario (with high female labor force participation) to the experimental scenario (with lower female labor force participation), there is a marked increase in mobility rates for those who were male and for married individuals. For those born between 1955 and 1964, the younger baby boomers, the odds of upward mobility for males were 1.089 greater than for females under the historical conditions, but they increased to 2.241 under the experimental conditions. Because females were not entering the labor force to the extent that they did historically, females accumulated less wealth and experienced less upward mobility. For the older baby boomers, the pattern was similar. In the control scenario, the odds of upward mobility for males were 1.166 times greater than for females, and in the experimental scenario, the odds were 2.611 greater than for females.

Because wealth is a family concept, the models assume that family wealth is an indicator of individual wealth. Thus, the decrease in mobility for females under the experimental conditions reflects a decrease in mobility for single females. The effect of the experiment on the odds of upward mobility for those who were married supports this interpretation of the results. Specifically, the odds of upward mobility for younger baby boomers who were married were 1.338 times greater than for those who were not married under the control conditions and 2.400 times greater under the experimental conditions. The pattern was similar for the older baby boomers. These results reflect the fact that fewer women from the middle and working classes pursued careers under the experimental conditions, decreasing wealth accumulation and thus mobility. There was little change in the odds of upward mobility by the other demographic characteristics included in the model because the experiment did not directly affect individuals with these attributes.

The results of the experiment also support the idea that historical increases in female labor force participation among baby boomers decreased wealth inequality. Because more women from the working and middle classes were pursuing careers, the change in women's labor force participation made the distribution of wealth more equal under the historical conditions than it would have been otherwise. The results presented in Table 7–2 compare the percentage of net worth held by households in each segment of the household wealth distribution before and after the decrease in women's labor force participation for the baby boomers. Again, the "before" estimates refer to the distribution of wealth under the historically accurate, control conditions of high female labor force participation. The

Table 7–2. *Simulation Experiment: Female Labor Force Participation and the Distribution of Wealth*

| | Top 1% | | Top 20% | | 2nd 20% | | 3rd 20% | | Bottom 40% | |
|---|---|---|---|---|---|---|---|---|---|---|
| | *Before* | *After* | *Before* | *After* | *Before* | *After* | *Before* | *After* | *Before* | *After* |
| 1983 | 35 | 37 | 81 | 83 | 12 | 10 | 5 | 5 | 2 | 2 |
| 1989 | 39 | 40 | 84 | 88 | 12 | 10 | 4 | 3 | −1 | −1 |
| 1992 | 39 | 41 | 85 | 89 | 11 | 8 | 4 | 3 | 0 | 0 |
| 1995 | 39 | 43 | 85 | 90 | 11 | 9 | 4 | 2 | 0 | −1 |

*Note*: Author's simulated estimates. Cells indicate the percentage of net worth held by households in each segment of the distribution before and after decrease in women's labor force participation rates for baby boomers. Estimates before the experiment correspond to simulated estimates of wealth distribution in Table 3–3 and are consistent with survey estimates in Table 3–2. Values in this table are rounded to the nearest percentage. See text for details.

"after" estimates refer to the distribution of wealth under the experimental conditions in which the probability of female labor force participation was decreased. The experiment increased the proportion of wealth held by those in the top 20 percent of the distribution, and it decreased the percentage of wealth held by those in the lower percentiles (the bottom 80 percent). This result suggests that the greater female labor force participation by baby boomers decreased the degree of inequality in the distribution of wealth. That is, these results support the hypothesis that there was an inverse relationship between female labor force participation among baby boomers and wealth inequality.

## Financial Markets and Inequality

In addition to aggregate demographic trends, market trends are an important aggregate influence on patterns of wealth distribution. In particular, many academics who study patterns of wealth inequality have noted that financial market fluctuations, particularly stock market fluctuations, are directly related to levels of inequality in wealth ownership (Wolff and

Marley 1989). This is despite the fact that investing in the stock market has long been compared to gambling. In *The General Theory of Employment, Interest, and Money*, John Maynard Keynes observed that:

> The stock market may be likened to those newspaper competitions in which the competitors have to pick out the six prettiest faces from a hundred photographs, the prize being awarded to the competitor whose choice most nearly corresponds to the average preferences of the competitors as a whole; so that each competitor has to pick, not those faces which he himself finds prettiest, but those which he thinks likeliest to catch the fancy of the other competitors, all of whom are looking at the problem from the same point of view. It is not a case of choosing those which, to the best of one's judgment, are really the prettiest, nor even those which average opinion genuinely thinks the prettiest. We have reached the third degree where we devote our intelligence to anticipating what average opinion expects the average opinion to be. And there are some, I believe, who practice the fourth, fifth and higher degrees (Keynes 1936).

As Keynes acknowledged, investing in the stock market can truly be a game, one with its own unique set of rules and that never guarantees a winner. Despite the nature of this game, however, some people invest well enough in the stock market to become quite wealthy, and when the stock market booms, it appears that these people fare the best. My goal in this section is to explore the role that the stock market plays in patterns of wealth inequality. Like demographic patterns such as population size, stock market fluctuations are an aggregate trend. The mechanism by which they affect inequality, however, requires an understanding of how the aggregate trends interact with and change individual-level behaviors and individual-level outcomes. Thus, I begin by exploring patterns in stock ownership. I then examine more closely the effect that aggregate-level stock market trends have on wealth inequality via the changes they have on individual behaviors and the wealth portfolios of individuals.

## Who Owns Stock?

Until the 1980s, typical Americans kept the majority of their wealth in the family home or in checking and savings accounts. Tax incentives combined with the need for shelter encouraged families to first build equity in housing and use only excess savings to make other investments. Furthermore, the risk associated with buying stocks was so great that most people were not willing to chance losing the little excess savings they had playing a game with the sort of rules to which Keynes alluded in the above quote. The result was that only the wealthiest Americans, those who had sufficient excess capital available to invest as well as funds to pay professional investors, owned stocks. With the increasing availability of mutual funds in the 1980s and early 1990s, however, stock ownership became more common, and by the mid-1990s, stocks surpassed housing wealth as the largest component of Americans' portfolios (Norris 1996). This dramatic change in the way Americans invest their savings has important implications for understanding the processes by which wealth is created and destroyed. More than ever, it is important that we understand the roles that stock ownership and the stock market play in determining who has how much wealth and why.

Previous research on stock ownership in America suggests that of all the types of wealth owned by families, the ownership of stocks may be the most concentrated. One study using the U.S. Department of Commerce's 1984 Survey of Income and Program Participation (SIPP) argued that while the average family kept 6.8 percent of its assets in stocks in the mid-1980s, white families (families with a white household head) kept 7.1 percent of their assets in stocks. In contrast, Hispanic families kept only 2.2 percent of assets in stocks and black families kept a mere 0.9 percent in stocks (Winnick 1989). These results suggest not only that there are demographic trends in the investment patterns of American families but also that stock ownership, at least in the mid-1980s, was highly concentrated in the hands of white families.

Evidence from the Surveys of Consumer Finances (SCF) supports this finding and suggests that the families who are more likely to own stock are those whose heads are not only white, but also have a high income, are nearing retirement, and are married with no children. Data from the SCF indicates that in 1983, for example, 22 percent of families with a white head owned stock as opposed to 7 percent of those whose head was nonwhite or Hispanic. Likewise in that year, 51 percent of those earning $50,000 or more in yearly income owned stock while 31 percent of families earning under $50,000 owned stock. Of those whose head was between 55 and 64, 25 percent owned stock. That percentage decreased to 21 percent for families whose head was past retirement age (65 or over) and was no greater than 22 percent for younger family heads. Of families headed by a married couple with no children, 21 percent owned stocks; of all other families, only 17 percent had purchased corporate equities (Avery, Elliehausen, Canner, and Gustafson 1984a; Avery, Elliehausen, Canner, and Gustafson 1984b). Other reports found similar patterns from the 1989 and 1992 Surveys of Consumer Finances (Kennickell and Starr-McCluer 1994).

By 1995, there had been some changes in patterns of stock ownership. Table 7–3 includes estimates of the percentage of families in various demographic categories who owned stocks, mutual funds, bonds, and cash accounts (checking and savings accounts) in 1995. The percentage of families in most categories who were stock owners in 1995 had actually increased over earlier estimates, including the estimates I referred to above. The estimates in Table 7–3, however, are broken down by ownership of stocks (all publicly traded stocks) and mutual funds. I include this distinction because there are important differences in the ownership of each type of equity, and many of these are evident in an examination of simple demographic differences in ownership. The estimates in this table indicate that for most demographic groups, a higher percentage of the families own stocks than mutual funds. Among all families, 15 percent owned stocks and 12 percent owned mutual funds. White families were more likely than nonwhite families to own either stocks or mutual funds, and both white and nonwhite families (by the race of the household head) were more likely to own stocks than mutual funds.

Stock ownership increased with income and with age, although the relationship between age and stock ownership was weaker than one might have anticipated. Eleven percent of those households with a head younger than 35 owned stocks. The percentage of families with stocks increased to the teens for those between the ages of 35 and 74, although there was little variation within subsegments of this large age group. Those in the oldest age category were slightly more likely to own stocks. Indeed, 21 percent of those in the oldest age category were stock owners. These patterns and the similar patterns that existed in the ownership of mutual funds likely reflect increases in the likelihood that younger people bought stocks in the 1980s and 1990s. Finally, the estimates in this table indicate that stock ownership among those who also owned homes was greater than for the general population. While 15 percent of all families owned stocks and 12 percent owned mutual funds in 1995, 20 percent of homeowners owned stocks and 16 percent owned mutual funds. Two possible explanations

Table 7–3. *Ownership of Financial Assets by Demographic Characteristics, 1995*

| | Stocks | Mutual Funds | Bonds | Cash Accounts | All Financial Assets |
|---|---|---|---|---|---|
| All families | 15 | 12 | 3 | 87 | 91 |
| White | 18 | 15 | 4 | 93 | 95 |
| Nonwhite | 6 | 4 | 0 | 70 | 77 |
| *Income (1995 dollars)* | | | | | |
| Less than $10,000 | 3 | 2 | 0 | 61 | 68 |
| $10,000–24,999 | 9 | 5 | 0 | 82 | 88 |
| $25,000–49,999 | 14 | 12 | 3 | 95 | 98 |
| $50,000–99,999 | 26 | 21 | 5 | 99 | 100 |
| $100,000 | 45 | 38 | 15 | 100 | 100 |
| *Age of household head* | | | | | |
| Under 35 | 11 | 9 | 1 | 81 | 87 |
| 35–44 | 15 | 11 | 2 | 87 | 92 |
| 45–54 | 18 | 16 | 5 | 89 | 92 |
| 55–64 | 15 | 15 | 3 | 88 | 91 |
| 65–74 | 18 | 14 | 5 | 91 | 92 |
| 75 and older | 21 | 11 | 7 | 93 | 94 |
| Homeowner | 20 | 16 | 19 | 95 | 96 |

*Note*: Author's calculations from the 1995 Survey of Consumer Finances. Cells indicate the percentage of families in each category who own the asset. Stocks refers to all publicly traded stocks. Bonds are all bonds including both government and corporate bonds. Cash accounts refers to checking and savings accounts.

might account for this pattern. First, despite increases in the overall likelihood of stock ownership in the 1990s, it is likely that most families first invested in the family home and then put savings into stocks. Second, it is possible that a high propensity to save induced the same families to become homeowners and stock owners. In both cases, homeownership should be directly related to stock ownership.

Demographic patterns in the ownership of less-risky investments were rather different than patterns in the ownership of stocks in 1995. Table

7–3 also includes survey-derived estimates of ownership of less-risky investments, including bonds and cash accounts, for comparison. In 1995, few families owned bonds of any sort. I grouped all bonds, including corporate, municipal, state, federal, and international, to calculate the estimates included in this table. Only 3 percent of all families were bond owners in 1995, and fewer than 10 percent of families in any demographic group included in the table owned bonds. Two exceptions to this pattern were those families with high incomes and homeowners. Fifteen percent of those making a total household income of $100,000 (1995 dollars) owned bonds, and 19 percent of homeowners were bond owners. It is not surprising that those with relatively high incomes owned bonds. High income earners tend to have the assets available to diversify their portfolios, and bonds tend to be an investment that most Americans make only after buying a home. The high rate of bond ownership among homeowners supports this idea.

Patterns of ownership of checking and savings accounts were the reverse of patterns of bond ownership. Most families, a full 87 percent, had either a checking or a savings account in 1995. What is more interesting here is the families who do not have cash accounts. There is little variation by age in the ownership of cash assets, and the direct relationship between income and having a cash account is rather predictable. While only 61 percent of those making less than $10,000 in income owned a cash account, at least 95 percent of those making $25,000 or more had a checking or savings account.

Perhaps the most interesting pattern in the ownership of checking and savings accounts is the racial pattern. While 93 percent of white families (those whose household head was identified as white) owned cash accounts, only 70 percent of nonwhite families owned cash accounts. As I mentioned in Chapter 5, not owning a checking account makes families vulnerable to many of the abuses that are associated with using secondary financial markets. As I discussed briefly in the previous chapter, a person who does not have a checking account is often forced to cash paychecks at check-cashing outlets and to pay the often exorbitant fees associated with using these services (Caskey 1994). In both the Caskey study and Kennickell's work on patterns of checking account ownership from the Surveys of Consumer Finances (Kennickell and Starr-McCluer 1994; Kennickell, Starr-McCluer, and Sunden 1997) there is evidence that many families choose not to have checking and savings accounts because they are not convenient. More commonly, however, families do not have cash accounts because they are unable to save enough money for the minimum deposit. Not only do these families pay more for basic banking services, but they lose out during good financial times, if only in relative terms, by not having savings that will accumulate interest. I explore who wins during market upturns in the next section.

Researchers have proposed many explanations for differences in asset ownership among families. The simplest explanation is that families simply have not been willing to risk putting their limited savings in stocks when real estate and checkable deposits (such as checking and savings accounts) offer better guarantees that the money will be secure. Families with less disposable income would tend to own less stock. Other possible explanations for these differences involve differences in people's willingness to postpone consumption. One study used the PSID to demonstrate that college-educated households, white households, and households with high incomes exhibited higher rates of consumption growth between 1975 and 1982 than households headed by someone who was without a college education, non-white, or had a relatively low income (Lawrence 1991). Lawrence argued that households with faster consumption growth have had a greater willingness to defer consumption from early life into later life, whereas households with slower rates of consumption growth were less willing to defer consumption. This implies that some households were willing to save more and thus accumulated wealth more quickly. Other research has also found that wealth accumulation patterns vary among families, suggesting that Lawrence's argument may be correct (Galenson 1972; Parcel 1982). Still others have argued that savings rates do not actually vary among families (Dynan 1993) and have suggested that differences in the wealth of these demographic groups are actually a result of such things as differences in shocks to their wealth (e.g., differences in wage shocks).

Rather than focusing on overall saving, Bertaut asked why there are differences among families in their ownership of risky assets. She argued that households persistently invest in low-risk or riskless assets because they perceive that the information necessary for investing in riskier investments, such as stocks and mutual funds, is too costly relative to the expected benefits of investing (Bertaut 1998). She proposed that risk aversion, income risk, and low resources increase information expense enough that stock investing, in particular, was not feasible for most families. Bertaut then used the 1983–1989 Survey of Consumer Finances to demonstrate that families with lower risk aversion, higher education, and greater wealth were more likely to become stock owners during the 1980s.

Conversely, she showed that those with relatively low resources, more limited education, and high levels of risk aversion were unlikely to become stock owners during that decade.

Because the bulk of previous research on patterns of wealth ownership and inequality has been done by economists, individual-based explanations have been predominant in the literature. More recently, sociologists and others who acknowledge the importance of structural constraints on social behavior have argued that an understanding of wealth ownership must look beyond the individual. Bertaut (1998) acknowledged that limited resources are an important element in an explanation of patterns of stock ownership. What Bertaut and others have not addressed in much detail is why there are differences in resource access. Oliver and Shapiro demonstrated that racial differences in income lead to differences in asset ownership (1995). Similarly, Braun argued that the many structural determinants of poverty of income contribute to wealth inequality as well (Braun 1997). Wage disparities, changes in industrial organization, and productivity declines all force many Americans to live on limited resources. For these families, investing is not a choice. It simply does not happen. Because structural constraints on individual and family behavior and processes are difficult to model, researchers often resort to indicators of constraints that are less than ideal. Racial differences in wealth ownership, for example, suggest structural constraints but do not demonstrate certain differences in access to resources. I address individual and family-level differences in wealth accumulation in more detail in the next chapter. For the remainder of this section, I allow stock ownership to be determined exogenously and ask who wins when the stock market booms.

## Who Wins When the Stock Market Booms?

Past research has suggested that there is a relationship between stock market fluctuations and the concentration of wealth. Researchers have typically relied on survey-based estimates to establish a connection. The most common method is to first demonstrate trends in inequality and then to demonstrate parallel trends in the stock market. Economists, in particular, have argued that when the stock market booms, the distribution of wealth becomes more unequal (Smith 1987; Wolff 1987b, 1992). Smith (1987) demonstrated that between 1972 and 1976, the share of wealth held by the top 0.5 percent of wealth owners dropped from 22 to 14 percent, and the share of the top 1 percent dropped from 28 to 19 percent. He attributed this to a decrease in the value of stocks owned by these top wealth holders. He demonstrated that the total stock owned by the top 1 percent of wealth holders fell from $491 million in 1972 to $297 million in 1976, not because they divested but because share prices declined sharply during that period. Other studies have used the same method to argue that stock market booms in the 1980s and 1990s accounted for much of the growing inequality that was evident during those decades (Wolff 1995b).

Stock market trends did, indeed, parallel trends in wealth inequality in the 1980s and 1990s. I documented trends in inequality throughout Chapters 3 through 6. Figure 7–3 charts the Dow Jones Industrial Average over 1965–1995 and demonstrates that, as inequality was increasing during the 1980s and 1990s, the stock market was growing at unprecedented rates. The figure also depicts the remarkable increases that occurred in the mid-1990s. In 1995, the Dow Jones Industrial Average gained 33.5 percent, exceeding the 2,000-point milestone. During the year, the Dow also reached 69 highs, the largest number of highs ever in a single year (Sloane 1995).

If there is a relationship between the stock market and the concentration of wealth in the United States, certainly it should be evident after this sort of dramatic increase in stock values. In order to further investigate the relationship between fluctuations in the stock market and the concentration of wealth ownership, I take advantage of this particularly dramatic increase and ask: *Who won when the stock market boomed in 1995?* Rather than use traditional methods of comparing survey estimates of inequality with stock market trends, I conducted a simulation experiment in which I allowed household stock values to increase in 1995, but at a constant rate over the previous year rather than at the unusually high rate they actually increased as a result of the stock boom. In this experiment, the control conditions are again the historically accurate conditions. These estimates are highly consistent with survey-based estimates, and they have been aligned to various historical sources of data on wealth.

Consistent with historical reality, the value of family stock holdings increased proportionately to the stock market in 1995. In this simulation experiment, I only allowed family stock values to increase at a constant rate over the previous year. This is the experimental condition, labeled "after" in the tables. My goal was to compare family wealth ownership and the distribution of wealth among families in the two scenarios in order to understand more clearly who won when the stock market boomed. I anticipated, quite simply, that an increase in aggregate-level stock values

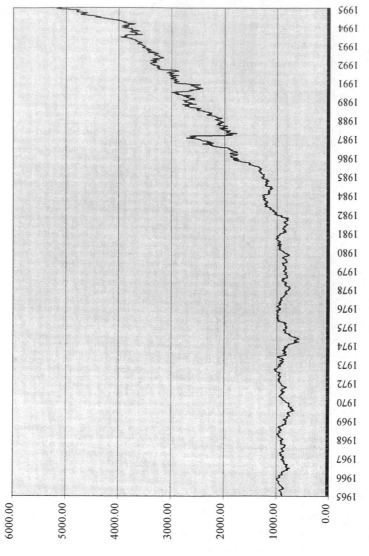

Figure 7–3. The Dow Jones Industrial Average, 1965–1995. *Source:* Dow Jones and Company, Incorporated, 1996.

increased the wealth holdings of those who owned stocks and that these increases did indeed increase inequality. The winners, then, would have been those who owned stocks and mutual funds, and the biggest winners were likely those who had larger investments in stock.

The results of this experiment suggest that the rich did, in fact, get richer after the 1995 stock boom. Table 7–4 includes simulated median stock and mutual fund values by demographic characteristic of the family before and after the experiment. The median net worth values in this table are consistently lower under the experimental ("after") conditions than under the control conditions. That is, the 1995 stock market boom raised median net worth values consistently across demographic groups. Across all families, median net worth was $6,860 in 1995. The experiment decreased that median to $5,119. The estimates in this table demonstrate that those who owned stocks when the boom occurred were, not surprisingly, likely to realize much bigger gains than those who did not own stocks. The estimates in Table 7–3 indicated that whites were much more likely than nonwhites to be stock owners. The complementary finding in Table 7–4 demonstrates that whites gained substantially more wealth in the stock market boom than nonwhites. Historically, the median net worth for white families was $7,370 in 1995. Had the stock market increased at a constant pace, the median would have been closer to $5,400 for whites, according to the estimates in Table 7–4. Thus, the net worth of white families increased by nearly $2,000. By contrast, the median net worth for nonwhite families was $425 in 1995. Had the stock market boom not occurred, the median net worth for nonwhite families would likely have been closer to $300, a decrease of approximately $100. High income families, those with an older head, and homeowners were also likely to win during the 1995 stock market boom.

While net worth increased rather consistently across families, there were some who enjoyed greater percentage increases than others as a result of the stock market boom. Using race as an example again, the median net worth for whites historically was 1.36 times greater than it was under the simulation experiment. For nonwhites, the boom increased median net worth by only 1.34 times. This difference is likely the result of racial differences in education, income, fertility, marriage patterns, work patterns, and other behaviors and processes. In the model, each of these processes interact to produce wealth accumulation processes, and differences in the behaviors and processes affect the rate of wealth accumulation evident under the experimental and control conditions.

Table 7–4. *Simulation Experiment:*
*The 1995 Stock Market Boom and Asset Ownership*
*(median value in 1990 dollars)*

|  | Before | After |
|---|---|---|
| All families | $6,860 | $5,119 |
| White | 7,370 | 5,419 |
| Nonwhite | 425 | 318 |
| *Income (1995 dollars)* | | |
| Less than $10,000 | 1,725 | 1,292 |
| $10,000–24,999 | 4,895 | 1,287 |
| $25,000–49,999 | 5,915 | 3,341 |
| $50,000–99,999 | 4,890 | 3,655 |
| $100,000 | 25,941 | 19,410 |
| *Age of household head* | | |
| Under 35 | 3,175 | 2,374 |
| 35–44 | 3,432 | 2,540 |
| 45–54 | 8,585 | 6,431 |
| 55–64 | 14,585 | 10,882 |
| 65–74 | 12,811 | 9,422 |
| 75 and older | 21,450 | 15,770 |
| Homeowner | 8,582 | 6,310 |

*Note*: Author's simulated estimates. Cells indicate the median value of stocks and mutual funds held by families in each category (including owners only) before and after the simulation experiment. Estimates "Before" the experiment assume that the 1995 stock boom occurred as it did historically. The before estimates are consistent with survey estimates of financial asset ownership from the 1995 Survey of Consumer Finances. The "After" estimates assume a constant rate of stock market growth in 1995 but no stock market boom. All values are adjusted to 1990 dollars, based on a standard CPI-U. See text for details.

The results of the experiment also suggest that the 1995 stock market boom increased inequality in the distribution of household wealth. I anticipated above that there is a direct relationship between stock market increases and inequality. Relatively wealthy families are more likely to be stock owners. When the stock market booms, the value of both total family wealth and the wealth owned by stock owners increases, with stock owners gaining a greater percentage of the total. The estimates in Table 7–5 compare the percentage of net worth held by households in each segment of the wealth distribution before and after the simulation experiment for 1992 and 1995. I included 1992 to demonstrate that because the experiment affected only 1995 (and later years), there was no difference in wealth distribution in 1992. However, in 1995, the estimates demonstrate that the distribution of wealth was considerably more unequal historically (before the experiment) than it was under the experimental conditions. The percentage of total net worth owned by those in the top 1 percent increased from 36 percent assuming a constant historical increase (the "after" estimate) to 39 percent historically (the "before" estimate). The estimates indicate the stock market boom likely increased the percentage of wealth owned by the entire top 20 percent of wealth holders, but it had little effect on the wealth of other families.

### Real Estate Markets and Inequality

The home is certainly more than an investment. It is the central meeting place for the members of a family. For the family who owns and lives in a home, the home is the creator and keeper of memories, and it ideally provides a degree of assurance of safety and stability. For communities, home-ownership assures a degree of aesthetic appeal as homeowners are more likely than tenants to care for the property and physical structure. More-over, homeownership carries with it a degree of social status (Henretta 1984; Henretta and Campbell 1978) and is an important symbol of success (Drelei 1982, Perin 1977). Henretta and Campbell (1978) demonstrated that homeownership is an important component of social prestige, and Perin (1977) argued that homeownership defines "social personhood," giving a person full adult status. Buying a home involves decisions that reach far beyond the financial; neighborhood and school quality, convenience to work and other frequently visited places, and aesthetic appeal all affect the decision. Families are aware of status differentials in neighborhood quality, and they invest considerable energies in making decisions about the neighborhoods in which they want to live (Logan and Collver 1983). Similarly, selling a home and moving to another is often an emotional, highly disruptive affair.

Yet the home is also a physical possession. It is a real asset, rather than

Table 7–5. *Simulation Experiment: The 1995 Stock Market Boom and Wealth Distribution*

|  | Top 1% | | Top 20% | | 2nd 20% | | 3rd 20% | | Bottom 40% | |
|---|---|---|---|---|---|---|---|---|---|---|
|  | *Before* | *After* | *Before* | *After* | *Before* | *After* | *Before* | *After* | *Before* | *After* |
| 1992 | 39 | 39 | 85 | 85 | 11 | 11 | 4 | 4 | 0 | 0 |
| 1995 | 39 | 36 | 85 | 83 | 11 | 11 | 4 | 5 | 0 | 1 |

*Note*: Author's simulated estimates. Cells indicate the percentage of net worth held by households in each segment of the distribution before and after the simulation experiment. Estimates "Before" the experiment assume that the 1995 stock boom occurred as it did historically. The before estimates correspond to simulated estimates of wealth distribution in Table 3–3 and are consistent with survey estimates in Table 3–2. The "After" estimates assume a constant rate of stock market growth in 1995 but no stock market boom. Values in this table are rounded to the nearest percentage. See text for details.

a financial asset like stocks and bonds, because it has use-value as well as financial value. But the use-value of a home in no way diminishes its central position in the typical family wealth portfolio in America. Indeed, the home is often a family's single most valuable possession and the single largest component of the family's investment portfolio. As I have mentioned before, many Americans invest in the home first and in all other assets only after they have bought a home. There are certainly those who cannot buy a home because they lack the financial resources, but given the size of the investment involved in buying a home, homeownership is surprisingly accessible to a wide range of families. Indeed, the 1995 Survey of Consumer Finances indicated that 65 percent of families owned their primary residence in that year (see Table 7–6). Kennickell and his coauthors produced a similar estimate for 1995 (Kennickell, Starr-McCluer, and Sunden 1997) and demonstrated that the 1995 figure represented a slight increase over homeownership rates in the late 1980s and early 1990s (Kennickell and Starr-McCluer 1994). In both the 1989 and 1992 Surveys of Consumer Finances, 63 percent of families were homeowners (Kennickell, Starr-McCluer, and Sunden 1997). The SCF data also provide

Table 7–6. *Ownership of Home Assets and Real Estate by Demographic Characteristic, 1995*

|  | Primary Residence | Investment Real Estate |
|---|---|---|
| All families | 65 | 18 |
| White | 70 | 20 |
| Nonwhite | 48 | 10 |
| *Income (1995 dollars)* | | |
| Less than $10,000 | 38 | 7 |
| $10,000–24,999 | 55 | 12 |
| $25,000–49,999 | 68 | 17 |
| $50,000–99,999 | 84 | 25 |
| $100,000 | 91 | 52 |
| *Age of household head* | | |
| Under 35 | 38 | 7 |
| 35–44 | 65 | 14 |
| 45–54 | 75 | 24 |
| 55–64 | 82 | 27 |
| 65–74 | 79 | 27 |
| 75 and older | 73 | 17 |
| Homeowner | 100 | 22 |

*Note:* Author's calculations from the 1995 Survey of Consumer Finances. Cells indicate the percentage of families in each category who own the asset. Primary residence refers to the family's home. Investment real estate is all other land, vacation homes, and real estate owned by the family.

evidence that the bulk of household sector debt, as much as 60 percent of total liabilities, was mortgage debt in the 1980s and 1990s (Kennickell, Starr-McCluer, and Sunden 1997). As such, homeownership played a central role in determining who owned how much wealth and why. That is, because the majority of families owned the primary residence, real estate market trends were closely related to trends in family net worth and in the distribution of wealth among households.

A related component of family wealth, that is, investments in real estate other than the family home, also have an important impact on the distribution of household wealth. Investment real estate refers to all real estate other than the primary residence that the family owns. Vacation homes, other apartments and homes, rental property, vacant land, buildings, and any other real estate in which the family does not reside permanently are included as investment real estate. In 1995, only 18 percent of families owned investment real estate, so the impact of these investments affected a smaller number of families. However, because those who do own investment real estate tend to own large amounts, and because values of investment real estate are closely linked to values of real estate that are used as the primary residence, investment real estate is related to trends in household wealth distribution.

My intention in this section of the chapter is to explore how aggregate trends in real estate values affect aggregate trends in the distribution of household wealth. My premise here, as it has been throughout this chapter and the book, is that aggregate trends such as real estate market fluctuations affect wealth distribution via their impact on the behavior and wealth ownership of microlevel actors. Thus in order to understand how trends in real estate values affect trends in wealth distribution, I first examine patterns of homeownership and ownership of other real estate at the microlevel. The experiment that I discussed in the previous section involving trends in the stock market indicated that when the stock market boomed, stock owners gained net worth and the distribution of wealth became more unequal.

Similar to the relationship between stock market trends and ownership, aggregate changes in real estate values affect both the value of the homes families own and the propensity of families to sell existing homes and buy new ones. Unlike stock ownership, the ownership of homes tends to be dispersed across a wider range of families. When home values increase, the increase in net worth is spread across a wide range of families and has little effect on wealth distribution. Of course, the value of investment real estate rises and falls with the value of homes. When real estate markets boom, those who own investment real estate also win. Because the median value of primary residence assets is considerably greater than the median value of investment real estate, gains to owners of investment real estate do not have a measurable independent effect on the distribution of wealth. In 1995, the median value of the primary residence was $77,000, while the median value of household-owned investment real estate was closer to $40,000.[1]

Thus, because real estate ownership is more equitable than stock ownership, I would expect that a boom or a bust in real estate values would have only a minor overall effect on the distribution of household wealth. Indeed, when I conducted simulation experiments in which I allowed real estate market booms and busts to affect wealth accumulation and distribution, the effect on wealth distribution was neither statistically significant nor in a consistent direction. That is, there were differences in the distribution after introducing the boom or bust, but the differences did not tell a consistent story about whether a real estate market boom, for example, increased or decreased inequality. Moreover, the differences in the distribution were so minor, they likely reflected chance variation in the estimates rather than any real difference in outcomes. I do not include the results of these experiments here because the distribution of wealth before and after the real estate market experiments is much like the distribution of wealth historically, and the estimates of wealth ownership would look much like the results in Table 3–3.

Even though real estate market booms and busts do not have a noticeable impact on the distribution of wealth, real estate market fluctuations do change the value of the portfolios of those who are real estate owners. I briefly explore patterns of real estate ownership in the remainder of this section in order to understand who benefits from aggregate-level real estate market booms and who suffers from real estate busts. However, I reserve the bulk of my discussion of microlevel patterns of wealth ownership for the next chapter.

There are differences in the demographic characteristics of homeowners and owners of investment real estate. Table 7–6 presents estimates of the percentage of families in various demographic categories who owned the home and investment real estate in 1995. The estimates are from the 1995 Survey of Consumer Finances. The estimates indicate that whites were 1.5 times more likely than nonwhites to own the primary residence and 2 times more likely to own investment real estate. Naturally, there is

---

[1] Both estimates are author's calculations from the 1995 Survey of Consumer Finances, and both are in 1990 dollars. These estimates are consistent with the estimates that Kennickell, Starr-McCluer, and Sunden (1997) have produced using the Surveys of Consumer Finances.

a direct relationship between income and ownership of both assets. Of those who made less than $10,000 a year, 38 percent owned their homes and, surprisingly, 7 percent owned investment real estate. Homeownership rates increased considerably with income. Real estate ownership, on the other hand, increased gradually across income brackets until the highest income bracket. Of those making between $10,000 and $24,999, 55 percent owned the primary residence and 12 percent owned investment real estate. In the highest income bracket (those making more than $100,000 in total income), 91 percent of families owned the primary residence and 52 percent owned investment real estate. These estimates support the idea that most families, at all income levels, make investments in the primary residence but few invest in other real estate. Only those with particularly high incomes have vacation homes, income-generating real estate, and other real estate investments in their portfolios.

There is a similar relationship between the age of the household head and the ownership of real estate. In particular, those who had entered the middle years were likely to own investment real estate. Of those under 35, 38 percent owned the primary residence and 7 percent owned investment real estate. In the older age brackets, however, the majority of households were homeowners, but fewer than 30 percent of households in this older age bracket owned investment real estate. Of those age 35–44, 65 percent were homeowners, and homeownership increased through age 64, when 82 percent owned the home. Of those in the retirement years, ages 65 and older, a majority continued to own the home, but the percentage owning the home declined. Ownership of investment real estate followed similar, although less pronounced, patterns. Of those in the middle years (age 35–64), 14–27 percent owned investment real estate, and 27 percent of those aged 65–74 continued to be real estate owners. After age 75, however, only 17 percent of families continued to own real estate.

Various factors influence the propensity of a family to own real estate. Naturally, there are different factors underlying the ownership of most real assets, particularly the family home, and the ownership of financial assets such as stocks and bonds. Different processes also influence ownership of the primary residence and investment real estate. Structural constraints certainly account for much of the variation that is evident in real estate ownership by income level and race. Wage inequality, declining national productivity, declining real wages, decreased occupational mobility, and related problems prevent many families from accumulating the income that would allow them to buy a home (Braun 1997). Persistent discrimination in lending and other inequities in home and real estate ownership also certainly account for some of the racial differences in homeownership that are evident in the estimates in Table 7–6 and in other studies of racial differences in wealth accumulation.

In *Black Wealth/White Wealth*, Oliver and Shapiro demonstrated that blacks are denied mortgages more often than whites, pay higher mortgage rates than whites, and own homes that appreciate more slowly than homes owned by whites (Oliver and Shapiro 1995). Others have found similar patterns over longer periods of time. Long and Caudill, for example, found that between 1970 and 1986, black couples were less likely than white couples to be homeowners and that blacks owned a disproportionately lower share of housing wealth than white couples (Long and Caudill 1992). There is some evidence that whites overestimate the values of their homes more than blacks in surveys (Ihlanfeldt and Marinez-Vazquez 1986), but even controlling for this difference bias, Long and Caudill found considerable racial differences in market values that indicated systemic barriers to wealth accumulation and mobility.

Economists also point to age differences and use the life-cycle hypothesis to account for many of the differences that are evident in real estate ownership. Practical concerns, such as the need to assure that the elderly have homes, have motivated research about change in homeownership across the life cycle. Several studies have found patterns similar to that in Table 7–6. That is, researchers tend to find that levels of homeownership decline significantly with age, even when cohort effects are taken into account. Similarly, researchers typically find that the amount of housing assets owned declines after retirement (Greenwood and Wolff 1990; McDermed, Clark, and Allen 1989; Mirer 1979; Sheiner and Weil 1992).

One study found that the amount of housing held by people near death is quite low compared to what is seen in cross sections (Sheiner and Weil 1992). Sheiner and Weil estimated that 42 percent of households had a home when the last member of the family died. They also found that the degree to which families decrease homeownership between age 65 and death did not vary greatly between those in upper- and lower-income deciles or between those who had children and those who were childless. Sheiner and Weil did find that increases in real estate values made it more likely that the elderly would reduce their homeownership, but that the value of houses sold by the elderly did not stay in their portfolios after the sale of the house. In a related study, Vanderhart found that predictable demographic factors, such as retirement, marital status, income, and housing costs, affected the

likelihood of real estate ownership, particularly among the elderly (Vanderhart 1993). Vanderhart also demonstrated that health concerns were
important, as were factors related to attachment to the home. Related to his
finding that emotional attachment was a key determinant of ownership
decisions, his results also showed that government strategies to make homeownership more affordable to the elderly likely have little effect on the
propensity to own a home, but that efforts to deal with nonfinancial aspects
of homeownership were quite effective.

Studies of the relationship between age and homeownership often rely
on ideas from the life-cycle hypothesis to explain their findings. The life-
cycle hypothesis is the proposition that individuals accumulate assets
through their working years and deplete their savings during retirement
(Modigliani 1992). While it is a simple idea, the life-cycle hypothesis
explains much about the wealth accumulation behavior of households and
is particularly useful because it is a process-oriented theory. Studies of
housing ownership tend to support the life-cycle hypothesis, as do the findings that I report in Table 7–6 and the studies I described above. Overall,
however, empirical support for the hypothesis has been mixed because
there is some evidence that accumulation of assets differs from the accumulation of housing assets. Uncertainty about the timing of death and a
desire to leave an inheritance for children are two factors that affect patterns of dissaving after retirement and make studying wealth accumulation over the life course more complex than it might appear initially.
I address issues related to individual and family-level wealth accumulation
processes (including racial differences, life-course variations, and other
patterns) in more detail in the next chapter.

## The Impact of Government Policies

Government policies of many sorts, of course, have the potential to affect
changes in the distribution of household wealth. Welfare policies, other
social programs, and tax policies are only some of the many tools the government can use, whether deliberately or not, to influence levels of inequality. Tax policies are particularly effective methods of changing inequality.
Income taxes, estate taxes, and wealth taxes can all be used to redistribute income and wealth in important ways. Some have argued that the real
influence on inequality is declining real wages and that policies designed
to improve occupational mobility opportunities and to assure that low-
income families retain a greater proportion of their earnings are needed

(see Braun 1997, Chapter 5, for a discussion of declining real wages and its effect on inequality). Perhaps the most direct way to affect wealth inequality is to tax assets.

Capital gains taxes already do this to some extent, and many argue that these are important because changes in capital gains account for a large percentage of changes in wealth ownership. Greenwood and Wolff found that capital gains were the major factor explaining changes in wealth holdings between 1962 and 1983. They argued that more than 70 percent of increases in wealth ownership could be accounted for by changes in capital gains (Greenwood and Wolff 1992). In another study, Wolff argued that the United States needs a personal tax on wealth holdings (Wolff 1995a). Drawing on evidence from the Survey of Consumer Finances, Wolff contended that a combination of income and wealth provides a better indicator of a household's ability to pay taxes, and that a tax on wealth would improve wealth inequality considerably. Wolff provided evidence from other advanced economies such as Sweden's to support his argument that introducing a modest wealth tax would have a deleterious effect on household incentives to save or the probability of capital flight (i.e., investing wealth outside of the country to avoid paying the wealth tax).

Another relatively direct way to redistribute wealth is via estate taxes. Currently, when the wealthy die, they pay a tax on the value of their net worth. I discussed this tax in Chapter 2 and presented the federal estate tax filing requirements in Table 2–1. In the 1980s, the rate at which a deceased individual had to pay estate taxes increased several times. In real dollar values, the estate tax cut-off increased from $170,000 in 1980 to $600,000 in 1987. In 1990 dollars, the cut-off increased from $268,000 to $680,000. The implication of this increase was that an individual had to be increasingly wealthy to be affected by estate taxes. If the estate tax cut-off had been lower, more of the population would have paid estate taxes, and wealth inequality would likely have been decreased.

In order to explore the validity of this proposal, I conducted a simulation experiment in which I forced the estate tax cut-off (the level at which the deceased were required to pay estate taxes) to remain lower than it did historically during the 1980s. Specifically, I forced the estate tax cut-off to remain at $250,000 (in 1990 dollars), roughly the level it was in 1979, each year between 1980 and 1995. In real terms, that meant that the cut-off increased, but it only increased enough to keep pace with inflation. In current terms, the cut-off remained low relative to where it was historically in the late 1980s and 1990s. The estimates of household wealth

Table 7–7. *Simulation Experiment: Estate Tax Rates and the Distribution of Wealth*

| | Top 1% | | Top 20% | | 2nd 20% | | 3rd 20% | | Bottom 40% | |
| | *Before* | *After* | *Before* | *After* | *Before* | *After* | *Before* | *After* | *Before* | *After* |
|---|---|---|---|---|---|---|---|---|---|---|
| 1983 | 35 | 30 | 81 | 74 | 12 | 16 | 5 | 6 | 2 | 4 |
| 1989 | 39 | 34 | 84 | 75 | 12 | 17 | 4 | 7 | −1 | 1 |
| 1992 | 39 | 33 | 85 | 74 | 11 | 17 | 4 | 8 | 0 | 1 |
| 1995 | 39 | 32 | 85 | 74 | 11 | 18 | 4 | 7 | 0 | 1 |

*Note*: Author's simulated estimates. Cells indicate the percentage of net worth held by households in each segment of the distribution before and after manipulation of estate tax filing requirements. Estimates before the experiment correspond to simulated estimates of wealth distribution in Table 3–3 and are consistent with survey estimates in Table 3–2. Values in this table are rounded to the nearest percentage. The experimental conditions involved decreasing the net worth level at which filing estate taxes was required. See text for details.

distribution included in Table 7–7 demonstrate the result of this change on household wealth distribution between 1983 and 1995. This table compares the percentage of net worth owned by families in the top 1 percent and each quintile of the wealth distribution assuming the estate tax cut-off was at the historical levels (the "before" estimates) and assuming the cut-off was at the lower, experimental levels (the "after" estimates). The before values in the table are consistent with survey-based estimates discussed in Chapter 3.

Decreasing the estate tax cut-off decreased wealth inequality dramatically. The percentage of total wealth owned by those in the top 1 percent decreased by 5 to 7 percent in each year depicted in the table. In 1983, for instance, the top 1 percent historically owned 35 percent of total household net worth. Only three years into the experiment, the percentage of total wealth owned by this group was only 30 percent of the total. The results are even more dramatic in later years and are equally dramatic for the entire top quintile of wealth owners. The gains from this experiment was clearly felt by those in the middle class. The share of wealth owned by families in the second and third quintiles increased markedly, as early as 1983, and continued to increase through 1995. Clearly, there was still considerable inequality in wealth ownership. In fact, families in the bottom quintile still owned almost no wealth after the experiment. Yet, the redistribution of wealth that resulted from this experiment were more dramatic than any of the other redistributions that I have presented throughout this book.

## Summary and Conclusions

In this chapter, I examined the impact of social and economic trends on wealth inequality, focusing on demographic trends and trends in financial markets and real estate markets. I found that, while theorists have argued that increases in population size will lead to an increase in inequality, cohort size affects microbehavior in ways that actually reverse this relationship. Following Easterlin and others (Easterlin 1987; Easterlin, Schaeffer, and Macunovich 1993; Elder 1974; Manchester 1993), I argued that competition for educational resources and difficult labor market conditions can effect changes in behavior and norms about work, marriage, and childbearing. Some of these microlevel behavioral changes, such as postponing childbearing and increasing female labor participation rates, are likely to increase wealth accumulation and mobility and to decrease inequalities in the distribution of wealth. An experiment in which I simulated a decrease in historical rates of female labor force participation for baby boomers provided support for these arguments.

I then explored the effect of market trends on wealth inequality. I first focused on the effect that financial markets have on wealth inequality. This relationship has permeated much of the literature on wealth because there is clear evidence of empirical correlations between stock market booms and inequalities in the distribution of wealth. I conducted a simulation experiment that provided support for the idea that stock market booms make the rich richer and the distribution of wealth more unequal. Wealthy families are more likely to own stocks, and when the stock market booms, these families benefit. Not only does the value of their assets increase, but the share of total wealth that they own also increases. In the experiment I discussed in this section, I altered the 1995 stock market boom. That is, I allowed household stock values to increase at a constant rate over the previous year. I then compared wealth accumulation and distribution under the constant increase to accumulation and distribution under the historically accurate stock market boom conditions. I found that those who owned stock, not surprisingly, did get considerably richer during the 1995 boom. I also found that the boom increased inequality as I anticipated.

Because real estate ownership is more equally distributed, real estate market booms and busts have a much less dramatic effect on levels of inequality. However, there have been considerable demographic variations in homeownership and the ownership of investment real estate (e.g., second homes, vacation homes, vacant land, rental properties). Demographic and structural influences have made some families much more likely than others to own real estate, and it is these families who win when real estate markets boom. In the final section of this chapter, I explored the impact of estate tax levels on the distribution of household wealth. The wealthy pay taxes on the value of their net worth at the time of death, and some have argued that not enough of the wealthy are affected by these taxes. I simulated a decrease in the net worth level at which filing an estate tax return is required and found that making such a change decreased inequalities in the distribution of household wealth considerably.

In each section of this chapter, I focused on a particular example of an aggregate influence to examine the relationship between aggregate-level social and economic trends and the distribution of wealth among households. I might have chosen any of a number of other experiments to examine, for example, the relationship between stock market trends and the distribution of wealth. Likewise I might have focused on an entirely different aspect of the financial market, such as reliance on fringe banking institutions, to examine how financial market processes interact with and shape wealth distribution. I chose the examples included here because they demonstrate clearly that, while the relationships in which we might be interested are often purely aggregate-level relationships (e.g., the relationship between stock market trends and wealth distribution), an explanation of the process by which this influence occurs must include an analysis of microlevel processes as well. In the next chapter, I focus more closely on the microlevel influences at which I only hinted in this chapter. Together these chapters provide some insight into the processes that account for wealth accumulation and distribution.

# 8

## FAMILIES AND WEALTH INEQUALITY

Money doesn't make you different. It makes your circumstances different. Money enables you either to do more with your life or to insulate yourself more from life.

(Malcolm Forbes)

Discussing aggregate and microlevel processes in separate chapters implies a separation that is highly artificial. In reality, the processes that underlie wealth accumulation and distribution are interconnected in complex ways. I separate them to parse out the relative strength and direction of influences and to make the discussion more manageable. In this chapter, I explore several individual and family-level behaviors and processes that influence wealth accumulation, processes to which I alluded in previous chapters. My focus is primarily empirical, but the findings I present in this chapter are an integral part of the theoretical model that has guided my discussion throughout the book. My basic assumption is that changes in aggregate processes, such as the distribution of wealth, reflect changes in numerous, interacting aggregate processes and microprocesses. Aggregate processes are the structure within which individual and family-level behaviors occur. While there are aggregate processes that affect wealth accumulation, there are also individual and family processes that directly affect accumulation. These microlevel behaviors and processes determine which families accumulate wealth and thus determine a great deal about how wealth is distributed. They are my focus here.

Specifically, I explore the effects of age and life-cycle patterns, race, family structure, income, and education on wealth accumulation. The role that these behaviors and processes play in the accumulation and distribution of wealth has received a considerable amount of research attention, at least in part because of their policy implications. For example, economists have debated for decades how wealth changes as a person ages. Some argue that asset ownership increases until retirement and then decreases markedly as households draw on savings to replace earned income. Others have cited uncertainty about the length of life and the desire to leave an inheritance for one's children as possible reasons that wealth would continue to increase (or at least not decrease much) after retirement. Answers to questions about the way wealth changes over the life cycle would allow policy makers to deal more effectively with issues regarding taxes and transfer payments before and after retirement.

In this chapter, I also examine in more detail variations in wealth ownership by race. Race is clearly an important influence on wealth ownership at the microlevel and on wealth distribution across families. In Chapter 4, I presented the results of a simulation experiment that explored how distribution would be affected if race, as an independent influence on wealth ownership, did not affect wealth accumulation. The impact on wealth distribution was quite stark, though it did not completely eradicate race-based wealth inequality. In this chapter, I explore the role that race plays in more depth. I examine existing literature on race and explore how racial differences in portfolio behavior affect wealth accumulation. I also examine the influences of other microlevel processes on wealth ownership. There are similar implications for understanding how education, marriage, divorce, children, income, and other microlevel influences affect wealth accumulation and distribution. In each section of this chapter, I introduce the research that has been conducted in these areas, and I present survey estimates of wealth ownership. I focus on demographic differences in wealth ownership to highlight microlevel patterns that affect wealth distribution. I draw on the simulation model to explore how these processes have changed over time and how they affect wealth mobility. I also draw on the model to explore how changes and variations in these processes might affect changes in wealth ownership and distribution. In this chapter, I concentrate on microlevel effects, but as I argued in the last chapter, the results I present, particularly the simulated results, incorporate both microprocesses and macroprocesses. Again, the simulations, which allow me to alter processes at either level and explore the effects at both levels, highlight this.

## *Wealth Ownership Over the Life Course*

One of the fundamental concerns of social scientists has long been accounting for changes in well-being over the life course. A growing body of literature has demonstrated that both age and birth cohort affect the well-being of individuals as they move through their lives. As I discussed in the previous chapter, aggregate factors such as cohort size and the distribution of demographic traits within an age group have been shown to affect the fertility and marriage behavior, work and earnings, and wealth accumulation of members of an age group. These effects have played a prominent role in scholarly literature as well (Berger 1984, 1985; Connelly 1986; Freeman 1979; Quinn 1985). Extreme examples are age groups born during baby booms such as the one that occurred in the United States following World War II. Members of such generations face increased competition for resources that affect opportunities throughout their lives that, in turn, affect well-being both directly and via their indirect effects on behaviors, attitudes, and motivation.

In addition to cohort effects, there are, of course, independent effects of age on well-being and on the behaviors and processes that affect well-being. Studies of the distribution of resources among generations have demonstrated considerable age-related inequalities in well-being even within age groups. Among the elderly, for example, one study showed that while mean income among elderly households increased substantially between 1949 and 1979, the income of younger elderly households was always greater and always increased more rapidly than that of older elderly households during that period (Ross, Danziger, and Smolensky 1987). Another study showed that well-being is unequally distributed even among the elderly. In the 1980s poverty rates among individuals age 65 and older were 6.9% for white men, 13.3% for white women, 24.2% for black men, 35.5% for black women, 18.8% for Hispanic men, and 25.2% for Hispanic women (Quinn 1985). Similar patterns hold for wealth ownership, although research on age effects on wealth ownership has been more focused on life-cycle patterns than on differences within segments of the population. The motivation for this focus is the notion that households often need to rely on their assets to provide income during retirement. Because behaviors and processes that occur during the working years produce retirement wealth, they tend to be the focus of research on age-related wealth processes.

Researchers have developed and tested theories about the nature of the effect of age on wealth accumulation, but both theorizing and empirical investigation of these theories are complex for at least two reasons. The first reason is conceptual, the second is empirical. Separating age from cohort effects is difficult. Indeed, understanding age effects without the interaction of cohort effects is highly complex. I explore both age and cohort effects in this book. I also examine various explanations of age effects and approaches to studying age effects below. Nearly all of the empirical studies I will discuss deal either directly or indirectly with the second problem that arises in studies of wealth accumulation over the life cycle: data difficulties. As I have mentioned before, data on wealth accumulation and distribution in the United States have long been scarce, and longitudinal data is particularly difficult to come by. Researchers are often forced to use cross-sectional data when they would prefer longitudinal measures. In this chapter, I use the same methods that others have used, but I also draw on the simulation model as a proxy for actual longitudinal data.

The life-cycle hypothesis is an explanation of changes in wealth over the life course that is widely used in economics. This hypothesis, which suggests that people accumulate assets throughout their lives and spend them during retirement, was initially a response to Keynesian economics (Modigliani 1992; Modigliani and Brumberg 1954). Keynesian economics, the predominant approach to economic behavior in the 1930s and 1940s, emphasized the role that individual saving played in the larger economy. Keynesians argued that oversaving was a potential economic threat because it caused inadequate demand that would lead to decreased output and employment, lowering the capacity of the economy. Inadequate saving was seen as a source of cyclical fluctuations and long-run stagnation and was considered to be a primary cause of the Great Depression (Modigliani 1992). Because saving was assigned such a central role in determining economic outcomes, extensive research on the determinants of saving was conducted by Keynesian economists. This research generally held that current income is the sole determinant of saving and that saving is a superior commodity, one on which expenditure increases with income (Keynes 1936; Modigliani 1992).

In response to Keynesian theory, Modigliani and Brumberg posited the Life Cycle Hypothesis of Saving and Wealth Accumulation (Modigliani and Brumberg 1952, 1954). Modigliani and Brumberg argued that the Keynesians could not adequately justify why individuals would choose to save. The Keynesians had argued that the saving rate increased as a function not of the absolute income of a family but instead by the family's income relative to mean income across families (Friedman 1957). In response, Modigliani and Brumberg proposed that saving is not a function of *current* income but rather of *permanent* income (the present value of the expected lifetime labor earnings and bequests). While Modigliani and Brumberg (1952, 1954) are generally credited with conceiving of the life-cycle hypothesis, Milton Friedman also contributed to the development of the concept of permanent income (Friedman 1957). The rate of saving over long periods is relatively constant, not increasing as suggested by Keynesian economics. The saving rate over short periods, then, varies to the extent to which current income diverges from average lifetime income (Modigliani 1992). In terms of wealth accumulation, this hypothesis implies that households accumulate assets throughout the working years and use these assets to support consumption in old age. Net worth, therefore, should increase until retirement and then fall sharply (Ando and Modigliani 1963).

Results of empirical tests of the life-cycle hypothesis, however, have been mixed. Some empirical evidence has supported the life-cycle hypothesis prediction that wealth increases until about age 60 or 65 and then declines at a relatively constant rate (Ando and Kennickell 1985; King and Dicks-Mireaux 1982). Based on analyses of the 1953 Oxford Savings Survey, for example, Straw concluded that the hump pattern proposed by Modigliani holds empirically. He found that asset ownership increased with income and age but declined in the highest age groups (Straw 1956). Likewise, much of Modigliani's own research has confirmed the life-cycle hypothesis. In a coauthored study, Modigliani also analyzed the Oxford Savings Studies and found results that supported his hypothesis. Janet Fisher's analyses of a similar survey in the United States produced similar results (Fisher 1952).

Yet other analyses suggest that while the elderly do dissave, they do so at a rate much slower than that predicted by the life-cycle hypothesis (Darby 1979; Hurd 1987, 1990; Mirer 1979, 1980; Sheiner and Weil 1992; Shorrocks 1975; White 1978). For instance, Shorrocks (1975) used data from the Inland Revenue Reports for seven years between 1912 and 1971 to demonstrate that wealth ownership varies considerably with age and that lifetime ownership of assets does follow the hump pattern. Shorrock's research demonstrated, however, that the hump pattern over the life cycle was not evident unless corrections were made for mortality within the population. He also showed that the rate of dissaving among the elderly was lower than predicted by the life-cycle hypothesis. Similarly, Mirer (1980) used the 1963 and 1964 Surveys of Consumer Finances to study changes in net worth across age groups and demonstrated, once again, that retired households did not dissave as rapidly as the life-cycle hypothesis predicts. Using the SIPP, Land and Russell (1996) found the quadratic age-wealth relationship predicted by the life-cycle hypothesis. However, they demonstrated that when status attainment variables were controlled, the age at which net worth begins to decline is far beyond the normal retirement age.

Another approach to testing the life-cycle hypothesis empirically is to examine the effects of age on the ownership of particular assets. One study used the 1988 Survey of Income and Program Participation (SIPP) and the 1983 Survey of Consumer Finances (SCF) to examine the degree to which the elderly reduce homeownership with age (Sheiner and Weil 1992). Sheiner and Weil found that reductions in homeownership in later years did not vary between upper- and lower-income households and that households without children did not reduce homeownership more slowly than those with children. They also found that these declines in homeownership happen at a relatively slow rate and that increases in state housing prices were directly related to reductions in home equity. Further, their research demonstrated that the value of housing assets does not typically remain in the household's portfolio once the house is sold. In contrast, a study that used data from the Survey of Income and Program Participation to examine the effect of personal retirement accounts on the assets of recent retirees and persons who are approaching retirement found that personal retirement saving may actually increase the savings of older households (Venti and Wise 1993).

Other empirical studies have observed that wealth accumulation behavior directly contradicts the life-cycle hypothesis (Bernheim 1987; Danziger, VanDerGaag, Smolensky, and Taussig 1982; David and Menchik 1988; Menchick and David 1983; Torrey 1988; Torrey and Taeuber 1986). Bernheim (1987) used the Longitudinal Retirement History Survey, which followed 11,000 retirees over a 10-year period, to produce evidence that the life-cycle hypothesis fails almost entirely to account for savings behavior after retirement. His analyses showed, instead, that retirees continued to save throughout retirement. Similarly, David and Menchik (1988) found that wealth continues to increase through retirement. Their analyses of longitudinal data from the Social Security Administration estimated the effects of age on saving; their results implied that dissaving does not occur after age retirement.

One response to this empirical dissensus has been the development of a theory of inheritance that suggests that the elderly do not dissave because they are motivated to leave an inheritance to their offspring. While there are several different approaches to the theory of inheritance, and empirical results have again been inconsistent (Cheal 1983; Davies 1982; Hurd and Mundaca 1989; Osberg 1984), Modigliani has argued that the life-cycle model implies that "the bulk of wealth might be acquired not by intergenerational transfers but instead be accumulated from scratch by each generation to be consumed eventually by the end of life" (Modigliani 1988b:16). Modigliani found that transfers, both inter vivos (made between living persons) and bequests (made after the death of the giver), account for only 20 percent of the net worth of U.S. families (Modigliani 1988a, 1988b). Data on inheritance are even more rare than data on wealth, making it difficult to ascertain the true relationship between inheritance and wealth ownership (see Miller and McNamee 1998, for a relatively comprehensive overview of work from several disciplines on inheritance).

Others have argued persuasively that a bequest motive prevents elderly households from depleting their assets during retirement. The desire to leave an inheritance to children, grandchildren, and other relatives would motivate those with the financial means to continue to save during retirement, or to limit dissaving so that assets either continued to accumulate or were depleted at a relatively low rate. Research in this tradition has provided convincing empirical support for the notion that a bequest motive affects wealth accumulation. Gale and Scholz found that inter-vivos transfers (transfers between generations while both are still alive) and bequests accounted for more than 50 percent of net worth (Gale and Scholz 1994). Similarly, Kotlikoff and Summers estimated that such transfers account for perhaps more than 80 percent of the net worth of U.S. families (Kotlikoff and Summers 1981:706). While this literature has not produced decisive evidence of the weight that transfers carry in determining wealth, it has clearly indicated that transfers are important. Moreover, this evidence suggests that transfers significantly impact the distribution of wealth among families and that inequalities in the distribution of wealth will tend to have an inertial quality. In other words, the wealthy tend to remain wealthy not only because a percentage gain in assets benefits them more than it would a middle-class family, but also because the wealthy family starts at a higher level in the beginning of life.

Still other research has suggested that elderly households do not deplete their assets, but that they behave this way for reasons other than a bequest motive. Many have pointed out that because the length of life is uncertain and because people are generally risk averse, they do not dissave in order to avoid spending their last years in poverty (Davies 1981; Hurd 1990). A very practical, very simple explanation, risk aversion, certainly explains much about the behavior of those households who do not deplete their assets during retirement. The combination of medical advances that have extended life expectancies with increasing costs of medical care, health insurance, and retirement and nursing homes force the elderly to use discretion in depleting their assets in the early stage of retirement.

Others have demonstrated that emotional factors may influence wealth accumulation behaviors in retirement. Many elderly households have most of their assets in owner-occupied housing. Many have spent a large portion of their lives paying for the home, raising children in it, and becoming emotionally and psychologically attached to it. Many elderly households sell their homes when they no longer need as much space or when the physical demands of homeownership become overly burdensome. For many, however, emotional attachment to the home prevents them from liquidating this asset (Kendig 1984; Lawton 1980; Vanderhart 1993). Because the primary residence has long been the largest component of most households' portfolios, not selling the home implies that wealth ownership will be relatively constant during the retirement years.

Cross-sectional estimates from recent Surveys of Consumer Finances support the idea that between 1983 and 1995, wealth ownership increased through retirement and then decreased. However, the survey estimates are also consistent with arguments that suggest the elderly will deplete their assets minimally during retirement. Table 8–1 includes estimates of median household net worth from the 1983, 1989, 1992, and 1995 surveys by the age of the household head. In 1983, median net worth for those younger than 35 was $11,300 (in 1990 dollars). Wealth ownership increased to more than $51,000 for those age 35–44, and even further for those in the next two age groups. For those households at retirement age, median wealth was $81,900. In the years immediately following retirement, the median continued to rise, presumably as households began to draw on their savings. As the life-cycle hypothesis predicts, median wealth was substantially lower for those age 75 and older. Similar patterns existed in the late 1980s and the 1990s, although in those years, the decline in wealth in the retirement years was evident beginning with the 65–74 age group. In 1989, for example, median wealth for those age 55–64 was $94,800, and it was $75,800 for those age 65–74. While median wealth holdings did decline in retirement, the decline was not as significant as the life-cycle hypothesis

Table 8–1. *Wealth Ownership by Age, 1983–1995*

|  | 1983 | 1989 | 1992 | 1995 |
|---|---|---|---|---|
| All families | 45.0 | 48.5 | 45.3 | 48.4 |
| *Age of household head* |  |  |  |  |
| Under 35 | 11.3 | 7.9 | 8.7 | 9.8 |
| 35–44 | 51.3 | 59.4 | 39.5 | 41.6 |
| 45–54 | 74.7 | 97.8 | 71.6 | 77.6 |
| 55–64 | 73.4 | 94.8 | 105.1 | 95.0 |
| 65–74 | 81.9 | 75.8 | 90.8 | 89.3 |
| 75 and older | 66.2 | 71.4 | 79.6 | 81.6 |

*Note*: Author's calculations from the 1983, 1989, 1992, and 1995 Surveys of Consumer Finances. Cells are median net worth in thousands of 1990 dollars. Age refers to the age of the household head. Net worth is family net worth.

would have predicted. Median wealth was greater than $65,000 for those older than 75 in each year included in the table, and the decline in wealth between ages 55–64 and 65–74 was not greater than 20 percent of wealth in the preretirement years.

Similar patterns were evident when I explored life-course patterns of wealth accumulation using the simulation model. When studying life-course patterns of wealth ownership, longitudinal data are preferable to cross-sectional data because the same individuals can be followed over their entire lives. As I have reiterated, longitudinal data on wealth holdings are not available. In their place, I drew on the simulation model to produce estimates of net worth for the 35 years between 1960 and 1995. I then produced a variable indicating whether household net worth was greater than total household income for each person-year. I estimated logistic regression equations in which the dependent variable was the dichotomous indicator that wealth was greater than income. I report the odds ratios for the coefficients in Table 8–2. These results suggest that the odds of having wealth greater than income increased substantially with age. Controlling for other microlevel influences, the odds were 1.518 times greater that

Table 8–2. *Wealth by Demographic Group: Odds of*
*Having Wealth Greater Than Income, 1960–1995*

|  | Odds Ratio |
| --- | --- |
| *Age of household head* | |
| 35–44 | 1.518 |
| 45–54 | 2.877 |
| 55–64 | 7.566 |
| 65–74 | 7.678 |
| 75 and older | 7.619 |
| | |
| White | 1.531 |
| | |
| *Marital status* | |
| Married | 1.456 |
| Divorced | 0.671 |
| Widowed | 3.360 |
| | |
| No children | 2.128 |
| | |
| *Education* | |
| Some high school | 1.053 |
| High school graduate | 1.913 |
| College graduate | 2.961 |

*Note*: Author's estimates of odds ratios from logistic regression on simulated data. All odds ratios are from the same model. The dependent variable is a dichotomous variable indicating that household net worth was greater than total household income before taxes. Demographic characteristics refer to the household head.

household heads age 35–44 would have more net worth than income than they were for those younger than 35 (the omitted category). The odds ratio increased to 2.877 for those age 45–54 and increased dramatically for those age 55–64 (to 7.566). The odds continued to increase, although only slightly, for those in the older age categories. In short, the relationship between age and the net worth–income ratio was increasing through retirement and then decreasing slightly after that.

While the net worth and income estimates in this simulated output are consistent with survey estimates given in other tables both in this chapter and throughout the book, the pattern that is evident in Table 8–2 reflects more than just the survey data findings. The wealth estimates produced by the simulation model are indeed consistent with known, historical patterns of wealth holding, as the tables in Chapters 3 through 5 demonstrated. However, various other processes interact with wealth accumulation processes in the simulation model to produce the model estimates. Moreover, rather than comparing cross sections of people as is done in survey estimates of the relationship between age and wealth, the simulated estimates examine patterns over the life cycle. Thus, while the estimates in Table 8–2 support the survey findings substantively, they are based on a wholly different methodology, with some advantages over the traditional survey methodology employed in Table 8–1. In particular, these estimates are longitudinal. That is, they track changes in wealth ownership over an individual's entire life rather than looking simply at cross sections of data.

In contrast, there was almost no relationship between age and patterns of upward wealth mobility. To explore age patterns of mobility, I again drew on the simulation model. I used the model to produce estimates of whether an individual changed deciles in the wealth distribution yearly between 1960 and 1995, after the person turned 20 years old. The model continues until either the person died or 1995 arrived. I then created a data set in which the dependent variable was an indicator of upward mobility. The unit of analysis was person-years (one observation for each person for each year), and the dependent variable was coded 1 if the person experienced upward mobility over the previous year. I then estimated logistic regression equations predicting upward mobility. I report the findings of these analyses in Table 8–3. While there was a clear effect of age on mobility, the effect did not change much as age increased. The odds ratio of upward mobility was approximately 1.000 for all age groups included in the model with a slight increase in the middle years. An odds ratio of 1 indicates that there is no difference in the odds between the specified group and the omitted group.

## Race and Wealth Ownership

Racial inequality in socioeconomic well-being has been documented extensively in the social sciences. Evidence that blacks, in particular, have

Table 8–3. *Mobility by Demographic Group: Odds of Increase in Decile Position, 1960–1995*

|  | Odds Ratio |
|---|---|
| *Age of household head* | |
| 35–44 | 1.000 |
| 45–54 | 1.000 |
| 55–64 | 1.038 |
| 65–74 | 1.198 |
| 75 and older | 1.036 |
| | |
| White | 2.961 |
| | |
| *Income* | |
| $10,000–24,999 | 1.402 |
| $25,000–49,999 | 2.448 |
| $50,000–99,999 | 5.751 |
| $100,000 | 7.535 |
| | |
| *Marital status* | |
| Married | 1.985 |
| Divorced | 0.684 |
| Widowed | 1.036 |
| | |
| No children | 1.300 |
| | |
| *Education* | |
| Some high school | 1.005 |
| High school graduate | 1.036 |
| College graduate | 3.330 |

*Note*: Author's estimates of odds ratios from logistic regression on simulated data. All odds ratios are from the same model. The dependent variable is a dichotomous indicator in family wealth decile, 1960–1995. Demographic characteristics refer to the household head.

not kept pace with whites is clear in research that highlights differences
in such indicators as earnings (Cancio, Evans, and Maume 1996), labor
force participation and labor force outcomes (Browne 1997; Petterson
1997), and quality of living conditions (Henretta 1979; Massey, Condron,
and Denton 1987). Researchers have shown that when net worth is
included as an indicator of well-being, racial inequality is even more severe
than other indicators suggest. Oliver and Shapiro observed that while representation of blacks among the nation's top income holders has increased,
there are still very few blacks among the highest wealth owners. They drew
on both quantitative and qualitative data to demonstrate that in the late
1980s, the median income for black families was only about 60 percent
of that of white families. Median income for blacks was about $15,000 per
year according to survey estimates from the Survey of Income and Program
Participation. For whites, the median was approximately $25,000 at that
time. It was even more shocking that the median net worth of black
families was a mere 8 percent of that of white families ($43,800 for white
families versus $3,700 for black families). Similarly, while 25 percent of
white families had zero or negative assets in 1992, more than 60 percent
of black families were in such bleak financial straits in the late 1980s
(Oliver and Shapiro 1989, 1990, 1995).

Status attainment theorists acknowledged long ago the relationship
between race and wealth. In a series of papers that examined wealth ownership processes from a sociologist's perspective, well before most sociologists expressed much interest in studying wealth accumulation and
distribution formally, John Henretta and Richard Campbell explored the
individual and family processes that create differences in wealth ownership. Their work demonstrated substantial race differences in net worth
and the ownership of the components of wealth, particularly home ownership. For example, Henretta and Campbell (1978) used the National
Longitudinal Studies of Labor Force Participation to estimate status attainment models of net worth ownership. They found positive relationships
between total wealth in 1971 and family background, education, marriage,
and income. They also found strong evidence of racial differences in wealth
ownership. In this paper, Henretta and Campbell took a somewhat typical
status attainment approach and argued that status, and thus wealth, is
transmitted from parents to children via education. Because racial minorities have more limited educational opportunities, they are likely to accumulate less wealth in each generation and to transmit less wealth across
generations.

In a related piece, Henretta (1979) used the National Longitudinal Survey (NLS) to demonstrate that levels of home assets were greater for whites than nonwhites. Again Henretta suggested that education was the crucial link between parental status and the status of offspring. Henretta (1984) continued this line of research by using data from the Panel Study of Income Dynamics (PSID) to demonstrate that those with parents who had high social status are more likely to own homes than those whose parents had lower status. Race and status were again correlated. In yet another examination of related processes, Campbell and Henretta (1980) demonstrated a relationship between demographic characteristics of families, including race, and the ownership of home equity, savings, real estate, business assets, and pensions in 1971. To talk about status attainment is somewhat awkward because it is a static concept, implying that people attain certain positions that can be understood to represent their well-being. In reality the processes that generate well-being are dynamic. Education can increase throughout life, income changes, and families get larger and then smaller as children grow. As these events unfold, wealth changes as well. At the same time, some of the basic processes that status attainment theorists identified are worth understanding.

Outside of the status attainment literature, one of the most lucid and comprehensive treatments of race and wealth ownership was Oliver and Shapiro's *Black Wealth/White Wealth* (1995). Oliver and Shapiro used the 1987–1989 panel of the Survey of Income and Program Participation (SIPP) to conduct the bulk of their quantitative analyses of the way race interacts with wealth. They argued that when assets rather than income are examined, it is difficult to make a case for the existence of a black middle class. According to Oliver and Shapiro, black families may have gained in income attainment in recent years, but their wealth portfolios indicate that they have not achieved the level of financial well-being enjoyed by white families with the same characteristics other than race. Oliver and Shapiro demonstrated that, as a result of historical inequalities and institutionalized racism, extreme inequality existed between white and black families in the early 1990s. They demonstrated that while 16 percent of white families owned less than $1,000 in net worth, 40 percent of black families were this asset-poor. Similarly, Oliver and Shapiro illustrated that while 30 percent of white families had net worth in excess of $100,000, only 6 percent of blacks were so fortunate.

Evidence from the Surveys of Consumer Finances supports Oliver and Shapiro's findings of extreme racial differences in wealth ownership

Table 8–4. *Simulation Experiment: Education, Race, and Wealth Ownership, 1989–1995*

|  | 1989 | | 1992 | | 1995 | |
|---|---|---|---|---|---|---|
|  | *Before* | *After* | *Before* | *After* | *Before* | *After* |
| All families | 48.5 | 54.32 | 45.3 | 51.6 | 48.4 | 58.6 |
| White | 72.6 | 72.6 | 61.5 | 61.5 | 63.4 | 63.4 |
| Nonwhite | 5.8 | 6.5 | 14.5 | 16.5 | 14.1 | 17.0 |

*Note:* Survey estimates are author's calculations from the 1989, 1992, and 1995 Surveys of Consumer Finances. Simulated estimates are from the simulation model. Cells are median net worth in thousands of 1990 dollars. Race refers to the race of the household head. The nonwhite category includes Hispanics. Estimates before the experiment are consistent with other estimates from the SCF data sets (Kennickell, Starr-McCluer, and Sunden 1997). "Before" and "After" labels refer to estimates before and after the simulation experiment that increased education for nonwhites. See text for details.

(Keister forthcoming). Indeed, the SCF estimates suggest that racial differences in wealth ownership may be more even severe than evidence from the SIPP indicates. The estimates in Table 8–4 support this finding. This table includes median net worth values (labeled "before") for 1989, 1992, and 1995 that correspond to estimates from the Surveys of Consumer Finances for those years. In each year, the estimates demonstrate that median net worth for whites (that is, those households with a head who was identified as white) was dramatically higher than for nonwhites. In 1989, the median net worth for whites was more than 12 times that for nonwhites. Median net worth for whites was $72,600 (in 1990 dollars), while the median net worth for nonwhites was less than $6,000. The racial difference was less extreme in the 1990s, but the differences were still dramatic. In 1992, median net worth was $61,500 for whites and $14,500 for nonwhites. Three years later, in 1995, the medians had not changed appreciably. These estimates confirm Oliver and Shapiro's findings and suggest that wealth ownership was, perhaps, more unequal than they suggested. While the SCF data included a high-income sample, the data that Oliver and Shapiro used, the SIPP, was a nationally representative sample of adults. Because wealth ownership is highly concentrated, it is not surprising that the data set that includes more of those families in the upper tail indicates higher levels of inequality. What is surprising is that inequality could possibly be worse than suggested by Oliver and Shapiro's already extremely bleak estimates.

As the status attainment theorists argued, at least some of the racial differences in wealth ownership that are evident in estimates like those in Table 8–4 reflect differences in educational attainment. To explore the relationship between education, race, and wealth ownership, I conducted a simulation experiment in which I increased the educational attainment of all nonwhites in the model. In the model, educational attainment is determined with a series of stochastic equations that predict continuing in school for the current year as a function of past education and multiple other demographic and behavioral characteristics of the individual. In the experiment, I began in 1980 to increase the likelihood that nonwhites would continue in school by 10 percent. The "after" estimates in Table 8–4 are the estimates of wealth ownership given this change. In each of the years depicted, wealth ownership for nonwhites increased at least 10 percent over the preexperiment levels. In 1989, the experiment increased the median net worth for nonwhite families 12 percent. That is, median net worth increased from \$5,800 before the experiment to \$6,500 after the experiment. In 1992, the experiment resulted in a 14 percent increase, and in 1995, the increase was more than 20 percent.

In each year, the increase in wealth ownership that resulted from the change in education was greater, in percentage terms, than the change in education because education affects wealth ownership both directly and through the race effect. Indeed, the effect appears to be almost exponential. In reality, increases in education for nonwhites would likely produce substantial increases in wealth ownership, and the effect might well be more dramatic than a linear relationship. But the effect would probably diminish after some threshold level. Whatever the actual relationship, the point is that education and race interact in important ways to impede racial inequality in wealth ownership.

In the experiment that I discussed in Chapter 4, in which I removed the direct effect of race on wealth accumulation, the distribution of wealth changed in favor of nonwhites. In that experiment, however, the improvement in inequality was less pronounced than we might have expected. At that point, I argued that persistent racial differences, including differences in educational attainment, allowed the differences to remain. The combination of the two experiments provides additional support for the importance of race as a determinant of wealth accumulation and suggests that one method of changing these differences would be to lessen educational disparities.

Race also affects the odds that a family's wealth is greater than its total income. The estimates included in Table 8–2, discussed above, include an indicator of the race of the household head. Again, these are estimates of the wealth-to-income ratio for households included in the simulation model. I calculated the odds ratios from a logistic regression model estimated on simulated 1960–1995 wealth values. The estimates indicate that the odds that a white household had wealth that was greater than income were 1.531 times greater than the odds of a nonwhite family being in that position. Likewise, the estimates in Table 8–3 indicate that the odds of upward wealth mobility for whites over that same period were nearly 3 times greater than the odds of upward mobility for nonwhites.

Oliver and Shapiro, and others who have explored racial differences in wealth ownership in the past, have concentrated on the role structural barriers play in creating these differences (Baer 1992; Blau and Graham 1990; Galenson 1972; Henretta 1979; Oliver and Shapiro 1995; Parcel 1982; Terrel 1971). Indeed, pure structural barriers are a vital part of the explanation of racial inequalities in wealth ownership. That discrimination, redlining in housing, dampened educational and occupational opportunities for minorities, and other structural constraints contribute to inequality has become orthodoxy in the social sciences (Baer 1992; Barth, Cordes, and Yezer 1980; Ong and Grisby 1988), particularly in sociology (Henretta 1979; Horton 1992; Jackman and Jackman 1980; Oliver and Shapiro 1989; Williams 1975). Indeed, the media have even begun to take these constraints for granted to a large degree (Brenner and Spayd 1993). That these structural barriers constrain wealth ownership has also become well accepted. The experimental results that I presented in Table 8–4 demonstrated the dramatic differences that education has on wealth ownership. If structural barriers to educational opportunity were lessened, wealth inequality would no doubt decline. Another manifestation of structural constraints, which leads directly to racial differences in wealth accumulation, is differences in portfolio behavior. That is, structural barriers and other influences lead to important racial differences in the ownership of assets and the holding of debts. These portfolio differences, in turn, can affect inequality.

Differences in portfolio behavior result from both aggregate and microlevel influences. The accessibility of assets (housing assets versus stocks versus bonds), market values, cohort patterns, and other aggregate processes affect portfolio behavior. When market values are favorable, for example, investors are more likely to buy stocks. At the microlevel, demographic characteristics also affect portfolio behavior directly. Older investors, for example, might be less risk averse with their retirement savings than younger investors. In turn, portfolio behavior affects wealth accumulation and thus the distribution of wealth among families. Savings that are kept in relatively risky investments such as stocks and mutual funds naturally accumulate faster, particularly during times of prosperity.

Until the 1980s in the United States, the single largest component of total wealth for most families was the primary residence (Holloway 1991; Levy and Michel 1991). In the 1990s, however, an increasing number of Americans began putting their savings into stocks and stock-based mutual funds (including Individual Retirement Accounts and pension plans), hoping to reap some of the benefits of a stock market that experienced record increases in the eight years between 1988 and 1995 (Norris 1996). Moreover, the increasing availability of mutual funds in the 1980s and early 1990s made stock ownership more feasible for more people, and by the mid-1990s, stocks surpassed housing wealth as the largest component of Americans' portfolios (Sloane 1995). While the stock market spiraled upward, the housing market topped out, making real estate investments less appealing and stock investments more appealing. Because increased numbers of households were investing in stocks, stock market booms in the 1990s had a less dramatic effect on inequality than they had had in the past. Thus, as a result of aggregate changes, microlevel portfolio behavior changed. When stock values increased, the wealth of those who owned stocks increased without further change of investing behavior.

The relationship between stock ownership and wealth inequality indicates that the combination of assets owned affects wealth distribution, but how might asset ownership be linked to racial differences in wealth ownership? There is nothing unique about stock ownership. In fact, any wealth component whose value increases relative to other components would have the same effect. Researchers have speculated that white and black families save differently and that these differences have important implications for wealth inequality (Brimmer 1988; Keister forthcoming; Parcel 1982). Certain wealth components, such as stocks, because they involve higher relative risks tend to have a more noticeable effect on wealth distribution. If families of different races tend to make different decisions about which assets to own or, more importantly, if structural constraints restrict ownership in systematic ways, the link would be unambiguous. Prior research suggests that there is reason to suspect that there are indeed systematic variations between blacks and whites in asset ownership for various reasons (Oliver and Shapiro 1995). Economists explain differences in asset ownership by resorting to discussion of differences in preferences to save, that is, differences in willingness to postpone consumption (Brimmer 1988; Lawrence 1991).

While there may indeed be black-white differences in willingness to postpone consumption, structural factors lead to even greater racial differences in portfolio decisions than would be expected from a pure postponed-consumption argument. Opportunities to make investments vary systematically because income varies systematically by race and affects ability to save. A discussion of reasons that income varies systematically with race is beyond the scope of this book. Whether such differences result from discrimination in hiring and promotion or differences in labor force participation and career preferences, the implications for wealth ownership are the same. In addition, the socioeconomic well-being of family of origin varies systematically by race. Blacks tend to start out in families that are less well-off and experience lower rates of upward mobility than whites as well (Oliver and Shapiro 1995). This directly affects portfolio behavior. If a family does not have savings available initially, they will be unable to invest in risky assets. As a result, the family will not enjoy high returns on savings, and they will not be able to make high-risk investments in subsequent time periods. My point is not to deny structural influences on inequality, yet one can also not deny that increases in wealth inequality do correspond empirically with increases in prosperity and macroeconomic booms (Oliver and Shapiro 1995).

In addition to demographics and family background, other direct structural influences are also likely to influence the portfolio behavior of black and white families differently. In particular, discrimination in lending and interest rate differences experienced by families of different races also make some assets less attractive or even unreachable to some groups of people or in some regions or neighborhoods in the United States. Opportunities to invest (determined by such factors as the location of banks) are structurally constrained, and they, therefore, also systematically influence the types of assets families own (Oliver and Shapiro 1995). Not only do investment opportunities vary systematically by race, but the ability to save money that might be invested varies systematically because families without savings must often pay more than other families for basic financial services (Caskey 1994). As Caskey observed in his work on fringe banking, a household that does not have savings is much less likely to begin saving simply because the cost is too high. In addition, families with little or no savings are often forced to assume additional credit and are unable to improve their debt to income ratios sufficiently to gain access to mainstream financial instruments, including both assets and liabilities. Caskey demonstrated that these conditions became much worse during the 1980s and 1990s, exacerbating increases in inequality that originated with stock market booms and the stagnation of the housing market.

Simulation experiments in which portfolio behavior is altered produce results that resemble those presented in Table 8–4. Specifically, increasing the propensity for nonwhites to own high-risk assets, particularly stocks, during the 1980s and 1990s increases their wealth holdings by 15 to 20 percent. Moreover, as with education, the extent of the improvement in the wealth holdings of nonwhites increases over time. Of course, the 1980s and 1990s were a period of stock market growth, and changing the propensity to own stock in earlier decades had less of an effect on the wealth of nonwhites. However, experiments such as these demonstrate the importance of portfolio behavior in the wealth accumulation processes. Whether it is a relatively pure structural effect constraining wealth ownership or the indirect effect of structure on portfolio behavior, mounting evidence suggests that race may be the single dimension along which wealth is most unequally distributed. Efforts to affect change in wealth inequality might well begin by targeting racial differences in wealth ownership.

## Other Individual and Family Processes

### Family Structure: Marriage, Divorce, and Children

According to popular perceptions, family structure and composition are extremely important in explaining well-being. The amount of media attention alone that is devoted to the role of family structure in creating and maintaining poverty suggests that family structure creates poverty. Popular perceptions also suggest that if changes in family structure had not occurred in the second half of the twentieth century, levels of poverty would have been much less than they actually were. The "feminization of poverty" refers to the disproportionate representation of females, particularly single mothers, among the poor. In the 1970s and 1980s, in particular, the concentration of poverty in single, particularly single female, households increased substantially. At the same time, divorce rates were increasing, more children were spending time between primary homes and homes with a remarried parent, more women who had never been married were having children and choosing to raise them alone, and the number of elderly living alone grew dramatically (Bane 1986). Given the correlation between the trends, it is not surprising that both popular opinion and academic speculation suggested that the correlation might be causal.

Actually, researchers had begun to demonstrate as early as the mid-1980s that a relatively small percentage of the change in poverty in the 1970s, 1980s, and 1990s was accounted for by changes in family structure. One study estimated that the 1982 poverty rate was only 1.8 percent higher than it would have been if demographic composition had not changed since 1967 (Gottschalk and Danziger 1984). Similarly, Bane demonstrated that the "feminization of poverty" between 1960 and the mid-1980s was a result of changes in relative poverty rates for various household compositions rather than changes in family structure, particularly for blacks (Bane 1986). Using data from the Census, Bane provided evidence that less than half of the poverty of single-person households and female-headed households resulted from changes in household composition such as divorce. She also demonstrated that about 20 to 25 percent of all poverty was, therefore, attributable to such changes. Danziger and his coauthors arrived at similar conclusion using different methods (Danziger, Haveman, and Plotnick 1986). Analyzing trends in poverty over the 1965–1983 period, they concluded that economic growth, job creation, and increases in earnings have more impact on lessening poverty than changes in family composition.

While changes in family structure have not impacted changes in poverty as much as we might expect, there are still very important relationships between family structure, family composition, and well-being. An extensive literature in sociology documents the importance of family circumstances on the well-being of children, and much of this literature starts with principles from the life-course paradigm. The notion that lives are interdependent, that the timing of life events is important, and that there are vital links between the lives of those in different generations permeates much thinking in sociology (Elder 1985, 1995). Research in this tradition has shown that family structure and composition affect children's emotional well-being, cognitive development (Baydar 1988; Clausen 1991; Cooksey 1997; Cooksey and Fondell 1996; Cooksey, Menaghan, and Jekielek 1996; Demo and Acock 1988), and educational progress (Downey

1995). There is also evidence that family structure is related to levels and quality of parental involvement and nurturance and related outcomes (Blake 1989; Cooksey and Fondell 1996; Menaghan 1991; Menaghan and Parcel 1991). Financial well-being also varies with family structure. Income in a single-parent household is often less than that in a two-earner household, married couples combine their assets to increase their net worth, widowed individuals may have benefited from insurance payments at the death of a partner, women's labor force participation affects resources and the amount of time both parents spend with their children, and so forth (Treas 1987). Indeed, most measures of socioeconomic well-being vary considerably by family structures. Thus, it would not be surprising to find that wealth varies with family structure as well.

The results of the simulation analysis presented in Table 8–2 included multiple indicators of family structure that indicate the strength of the relationship between structure and well-being. The outcome variable in this analysis was the likelihood that the family's wealth was greater than its income. This outcome is an indicator of both the current and potential future well-being of the family. For instance, if the family were to experience a financial crisis, having substantial wealth reserves would provide a cushion. Any of a number of crises might necessitate additional funds, including job loss, the death of a primary income earner, major medical expenses, and other major expenses. The table presents the increase in the odds of having wealth greater than income, given the characteristics of the household.

Controlling for other influences on well-being, the results in Table 8–2 indicate that being married or widowed and not having children increase the odds that the family's net worth was greater than their income over the entire 1960–1995 period. The odds that a married couple had greater net worth than income were 1.456 times greater than the odds for households headed by a single person. An important reason that married couples fair so well on this measure, as well as the many other measures that I have examined in this book, is simply economies of scale. Households headed by a single individual can have, at most, one income earner to contribute to savings. Similarly, as the old adage "two can live as cheaply as one" suggests, expenses for two people living together are not simply the sum of the expenses of the individuals. Thus, saving rates can be greater for those who have pooled their resources. When singles marry and combine their assets, of course, their wealth is greater. Likewise when couples separate or divorce, splitting assets eliminates the benefit of economies of scale.

The odds ratios from the simulated mobility analysis presented in Table 8–3 indicate that married couples were also more likely to experience upward mobility between 1960 and 1995 than households headed by single people. The odds ratios in this table are from logistic regression equations estimated on the simulated output that I have used throughout this book. The outcome of interest in this segment of the analyses was movement upward into a higher net worth decile. The odds that a married couple was upwardly mobile were 1.985 times greater than for a household headed by a single individual. Again, economies of scale were probably part of the reason that married couples had such an advantage over their single peers. Married couples were also the most likely to be engaged in an active program of saving, often in preparation to start a family or to pay for major expenses, such as college expenses, for the children they already had. Divorce had predictably adverse effects on both the likelihood that wealth was greater than income and upward mobility. In the analyses displayed in Tables 8-2 and 8–3, divorce had a deleterious effect on the probability that net worth was greater than income and on the probability of upward mobility. Similarly, having children had an adverse effect on both measures of wealth ownership and mobility.

Widowed people (both widows and widowers) were also more likely to have more wealth than income, but the reasons for their relative well-being were likely different than for their married counterparts. The results in Table 8–2 suggest that the odds that a household headed by a widowed individual had more wealth than income were 3.360 times greater than the odds that a household headed by a single (never-married) individual was this well-off. The results in Table 8–3 indicate that the widowed were also more likely than those who had never been married to have experienced upward mobility as well, but the effect was not as great as it was for the more general measure of well-being included in Table 8–2. The increase in odds enjoyed by the widowed was 1.036 times greater than for the never married. Widows and widowers tend to be older and thus have had time to accumulate wealth. But the effects that are evident in the table were net of the effects of age, suggesting that some other influence produced this result. One likely explanation is the fact that many elderly individuals are both widowed and no longer working, creating a strong association between having high net worth relative to income and being in the widowed category. Another possible explanation of these effects is rooted in gains from life insurance received at the death of a spouse. Often life insurance benefits received at the death of a spouse increase the wealth of the remaining partner, and occasionally the benefits move the remaining partner into a higher wealth bracket. In either case, the widow or widower is likely to be financially secure.

   Life insurance is an asset to which I have given little attention in this book, but it is one that deserves at least a mention, particularly in the context of family processes related to wealth ownership. Widows and widowers do, of course, sometimes benefit from life insurance assets and experience an improvement in relative wealth standing. Life insurance can also be an integral part of the wealth portfolio of the living, and, in fact, some families make life insurance a central element of their wealth holdings, whether deliberately or not. The wealthy often use life insurance to ensure the financial well-being of their families in the case of the death of a major breadwinner. Middle-class and poor families often buy life insurance with the same intention, although the investment is not nearly as substantial. The middle class and poor are also more likely to use whole life insurance accounts as savings plans (estimates from the Surveys of Consumer Finances for 1962–1995 support this claim).

   Family structure clearly affects decisions about the ownership of life insurance, particularly the presence of dependent children or a nonworking spouse. Much of the research done on the demand for life insurance has been conducted by economists working from a life-cycle perspective, and much of the work in this subfield takes a classic work by Menahem Yaari as a starting point (Yaari 1965). The principle underlying this work is that individuals increase expected utility by purchasing life insurance (referred to as fair life insurance in the literature) or a comparable annuity (Fischer 1973; Pissarides 1980; Yaari 1965). Lewis (1989) extended this line of thinking to include consideration of dependents in the calculation of demand for life insurance. He showed that life insurance purchases are made to maximize the expected lifetime utilities of beneficiaries rather than simply the insured.

   While rational, financial utility–maximizing calculations explain some of the propensity for families to purchase life insurance, it is also likely that social elements contribute to behavior in this area. Many families use life insurance as savings plans. Whole life insurance (as opposed to term life insurance) accumulates a cash value that can be drawn on as any other investment. Life insurance is a relatively low-risk investment, but its returns are often less favorable than other investments that have comparable levels of risk, including many bonds, certificates of deposit, and money market accounts. My estimates from the 1962–1995 Surveys of Consumer Finances suggest that minority and poor families are more likely than others to invest in life insurance. The same estimates suggest that households headed by a single female (whether never married, separated, divorced, or widowed) have tended to invest more in life insurance than comparable households with a male head. Descriptive statistics using the same data and conducted by others demonstrate this pattern as well (Kennickell and Shack-Marquez 1992; Kennickell and Starr-McCluer 1994; Kennickell, Starr-McCluer, and Sunden 1997). Controlling for income, education, family structure, and other demographic characteristics, the pattern holds.

Many families save money in whole life insurance, and life insurance is the one asset that nonwhites have been consistently more likely than whites to own. Minorities and women tend to invest in low-risk assets in general (Bajtelsmit and VanDerhei 1997). This preference combined with social influence (i.e., the encouragement of friends and family who have also used life insurance as an investment), unscrupulous life insurance salesmen who take advantage of poor and minority families, and other social processes might create the empirical difference. Of course, it is possible that because the poor or minority breadwinner has a lower life expectancy, calculations of beneficiaries' expected lifetime utility are maximized at higher levels of life insurance ownership. In any case, existing research has not explored this question, though the subject certainly deserves greater attention.

## Income and Wealth Ownership

Income had a predictably positive effect on wealth ownership. Table 8–5 includes estimates of wealth ownership by income level from the 1983, 1989, 1992, and 1995 Surveys of Consumer Finances. The cells in the table are median household net worth in thousands of 1990 dollars. Income is total household income before taxes in the year specified. The results suggest that net worth declined over the 1983–1995 period for most of the groups, but that there was a clear positive association between income and net worth. For the lowest income group included in the table, net worth was $5,000 in 1983 and declined to $1,400 by the end of the 1980s. This group's wealth holdings increased through the mid-1990s, but by 1995 their median wealth was still less than it had been in 1983. Those making between $10,000 and $24,999 were the only group whose net worth consistently increased over the period depicted in the table. The net worth for this group was also considerably greater than that of the

Table 8–5. *Wealth Ownership by Income, 1983–1995*

|  | 1983 | 1989 | 1992 | 1995 |
|---|---|---|---|---|
| All families | 45.0 | 48.5 | 45.3 | 48.4 |
| *Income* |  |  |  |  |
| Less than $10,000 | 5.0 | 1.4 | 2.9 | 4.1 |
| $10,000–24,999 | 23.3 | 22.0 | 24.2 | 25.7 |
| $25,000–49,999 | 62.6 | 48.0 | 47.0 | 47.1 |
| $50,000–99,999 | 120.8 | 109.9 | 104.0 | 103.9 |
| $100,000 and greater | 751.2 | 407.3 | 434.2 | 416.9 |

*Note*: Author's calculations from the 1983, 1989, 1992, and 1995 Surveys of Consumer Finances. Cells are median net worth in thousands of 1990 dollars. Income is total household income in 1990 dollars before taxes.

bottom income group. The other middle-income groups lost net worth value during the 1980s and early 1990s as well, as did the highest-income group. Despite these relative declines in wealth over time, the pattern of increasing wealth across income groups is evident in each year. The reasons for this pattern need little explanation. Those with higher incomes have more to save and invest.

Income also increased the likelihood of mobility in predictable ways. The estimates in Table 8–3, odds ratios calculated from a logistic regression estimated on output from the simulation model, indicate that there was a strong positive association between income and upward wealth mobility. The odds of experiencing an increase in decile wealth position for those in the $10,000 to $24,999 income group were 1.402 times greater than for those who had income totaling less than $10,000 (the omitted category). For the next two income categories, the increase in odds was even greater: 2.448 for those making between $25,000 and $49,999 and 5.751 for those making between $50,000 and $99,999. For those making more than $100,000, the increase in the odds of upward mobility was a remarkable 7.535 times greater than for those in the omitted income category. These increases in odds are even more incredible given that they are estimated with many other demographic influences on wealth ownership and mobility controlled.

For comparison, I also include a demographic breakdown of income earners. Table 8–6 includes estimates of median total household income before taxes. The estimates are for 1989, 1992, and 1995 and are in thousands of 1990 dollars. According to the estimates in this table, in each year depicted, income increased with age through retirement age. At retirement age, income declined sharply. Median income in 1989 for those under 35, for example, was about $22,000. Income increased to nearly $40,000 for those age 45–54, but it declined again to under $30,000 after age 55. The decline in income by age is greater than the decline in net worth by age (that was evident in the estimates included in Table 8–1). The decline in income also began at an earlier age than the decline in net worth. The greater decline likely reflects the fact that most people certainly do retire. At retirement, income ceases, even while net worth may continue to grow. The earlier age for the start of the decline is most likely a reflection of early retirement that has become common in some occupations. Racial and educational differences in income were quite pronounced according to these estimates, but the differences were not nearly as dramatic as the differences in wealth ownership. Consistent with Oliver and Shapiro's findings in the Survey of Income and Program Participation, median income for whites was more than twice the median income for nonwhites (Oliver and Shapiro focused on blacks, not all nonwhite families, but still the findings are substantively similar). In contrast, median net worth for whites was more than 14 times greater than the median net worth for nonwhites. Educational differences in net worth were also more extreme than educational differences in income (see below for more discussion of the role education plays in wealth accumulation).

While there is a clear positive association between wealth ownership and income, wealth and income are not perfectly correlated. As I mentioned in Chapter 1, the Pearson's correlation between income and wealth was actually only 0.49 in 1983, and it dropped to 0.26 when asset income (income generated by wealth) was removed from total income. The estimates in Tables 8–5 and 8–6 refer to total income, including asset income. When asset income is removed, the association between income and wealth in these tables decreases as well. There are many reasons for this low correlation, including the work behavior of the extremely wealthy. As the Malcolm Forbes quote that opened this chapter said, "Money doesn't make you different. It makes your circumstances different. Money

Table 8–6. *Family Income, 1989–1995*

|  | 1989 | 1992 | 1995 |
|---|---|---|---|
| All families | 27.3 | 25.0 | 26.4 |
| *Age of household head* | | | |
| Under 35 | 22.1 | 23.0 | 22.9 |
| 35–44 | 39.7 | 33.6 | 33.6 |
| 45–54 | 39.2 | 39.1 | 35.3 |
| 55–64 | 27.5 | 27.1 | 30.9 |
| 65–74 | 16.6 | 16.6 | 16.8 |
| 75 and older | 14.3 | 12.7 | 14.9 |
| White | 32.0 | 28.7 | 28.6 |
| Nonwhite | 15.4 | 17.2 | 18.1 |
| *Net worth* | | | |
| Less than $10,000 | 11.9 | 12.7 | 13.2 |
| $10,000–24,999 | 23.3 | 22.5 | 22.1 |
| $25,000–49,999 | 25.4 | 22.1 | 27.5 |
| $50,000–99,999 | 30.9 | 28.1 | 30.2 |
| $100,000–249,000 | 36.8 | 35.1 | 33.8 |
| $250,000 and greater | 61.8 | 60.1 | 58.7 |
| *Education* | | | |
| Some high school | 14.3 | 11.5 | 13.5 |
| High school graduate | 23.5 | 22.1 | 22.9 |
| College graduate | 44.1 | 41.7 | 39.7 |

*Note*: Author's calculations from the 1989, 1992, and 1995 Surveys of Consumer Finances. Cells are median household income before taxes in thousands of 1990 dollars.

enables you either to do more with your life or to insulate yourself more from life." Money, or wealth, also allows you to chose whether to work or not to work. Some of the wealthy do, in fact, chose to work, but it is a choice, not a necessity. Schervish and his coauthors in *Gospels of Wealth: How the Rich Portray Their Lives* recounted conversations with Camille Gray, a 25-year-old woman who was born into an extremely rich family.

Camille told them about the job she had in college: "I was working full-time the last two years of college, or year and a half. I was in charge of Kids Stuff [part of her family's large business]. We had 10, we had 12 at the time, we were franchising and I was responsible for all the marketing" (Schervish, Coutsoukis, and Lewis 1994:227). While Camille was certainly working, her job was much different from the job that a work study student might have held. Moreover, Camille *chose* to work, while the less wealthy certainly do not. After college, many of the wealthy work and earn income only sporadically. Thus while their net worth might be substantial, in any year, they may have earned little or no income.

## Education

In most research on wealth ownership, education has a positive effect on net worth, even net of other demographic influences. That is, people with more education tend to be wealthier at all levels of income and even within the same occupation. The results included in Table 8–7 provide support for this argument. Median net worth for those without a high school degree was never greater than $26,000 between 1983 and 1995. In contrast, median net worth for college graduates ranged from $88,000 to more than $113,000 in the years included in the table. Results from the simulation model indicated that education also increased the probability of having net worth greater than income, and these results were robust when income and other demographic influences were controlled. Likewise, education increased the likelihood of mobility. The results in Tables 8–2 and 8–3 demonstrate that the increase in odds for those with a college education, in particular, was considerably greater than for those in the omitted category, those who did not attend high school.

The positive association between education and income is particularly interesting given that, in Tables 8–2 and 8–3, the relationship persists even when other demographic influences are controlled. While I do not report them here, I have also estimated cross-sectional logistic regression equations on each of the survey data sets I use. The results, including the coefficient estimates for the education coefficients, were substantively consistent with the results in Tables 8–2 and 8–3. This implies that there is something about those with more education that, net of income, occupation, and other likely influences, leads them to acquire greater wealth. One possible explanation for this relationship is that people who are highly

Table 8–7. *Education and Wealth Ownership,*
*1983–1995*

|                      | 1983 | 1989  | 1992 | 1995 |
|----------------------|------|-------|------|------|
| All families         | 45.0 | 48.5  | 45.3 | 48.4 |
| Some high school     | 25.7 | 24.4  | 18.5 | 22.6 |
| High school graduate | 39.9 | 37.3  | 35.5 | 42.9 |
| College graduate     | 95.6 | 113.3 | 88.5 | 89.3 |

*Note*: Author's calculations from the 1983, 1989, 1992, and 1995 Surveys of Consumer Finances. Cells are median net worth in thousands of 1990 dollars. Educational attainment refers to household head in the given year. Net worth is family net worth.

educated are more willing to postpone consumption and consequently enjoy higher net worth than their less-educated peers (Dynan 1993).

Of course, it is difficult to decipher time-ordering in most analyses of wealth ownership because most are conducted on cross-sectional data sets. It is possible that the education effect is really a reflection of the fact that wealthy people are more likely to be more highly educated because this is the expectation for them as adolescents, they are more likely to have the resources to attend college, and they are more likely to be encouraged and have the resources to continue education beyond college. The simulated estimates in Tables 8–2 and 8–3 use lagged education to predict net worth and thus address this problem as much as possible, and the results remain. Of course, we would ideally have longitudinal survey data on which to test these ideas further.

## Debt

Before concluding my discussion of individual and family influences on wealth ownership, a word about differences in debt holding is in order. Table 8–8 describes family debt holdings in 1995 by demographic characteristic of the family. The results included in this table demonstrate that patterns of debt holding are similar to trends in net worth that I examined throughout this chapter. The table includes survey estimates of the

Table 8–8. *Family Debt Holdings, 1995*

|  | Any Debt | Mortgages, Home | Mortgages, Other | Credit Card |
|---|---|---|---|---|
| All families | 23.6 | 53.6 | 29.4 | 1.6 |
| *Age of household head* | | | | |
| Under 35 | 16.0 | 66.2 | 23.9 | 1.5 |
| 35–44 | 39.5 | 63.0 | 31.5 | 1.9 |
| 45–54 | 43.1 | 50.4 | 29.5 | 2.1 |
| 55–64 | 27.1 | 37.8 | 27.3 | 1.3 |
| 65–74 | 8.1 | 20.0 | 37.8 | 0.7 |
| 75 and older | 2.1 | 16.8 | 8.4 | 0.4 |
| White | 28.6 | 56.7 | 31.0 | 1.6 |
| Nonwhite | 12.8 | 38.3 | 25.2 | 1.3 |
| *Income* | | | | |
| Less than $10,000 | 2.7 | 14.7 | 15.8 | 0.6 |
| $10,000–24,999 | 9.7 | 27.3 | 19.2 | 1.3 |
| $25,000–49,999 | 24.6 | 48.3 | 26.3 | 1.5 |
| $50,000–99,999 | 68.3 | 71.4 | 35.7 | 2.3 |
| $100,000 and greater | 117.8 | 109.4 | 38.3 | 3.4 |

*Note:* Author's calculations from the 1995 Survey of Consumer Finances. Cells are medians and are in thousands of 1990 dollars. Demographic characteristics refer to the household head. Debt values are total family liabilities.

median value of debt holdings in 1995 in four categories. I include total debt, home mortgages (that is, all mortgages on the primary residence), other mortgages (that is, mortgages on investment real estate, vacation homes, other homes, rental properties, and all other real estate), and credit card debt. In 1995, debt holdings increased with age, but declined rather sharply after age 55–64. Whites had considerably more debt than non-whites, especially mortgage debt. What is perhaps most interesting in this table is the fact that those with extremely high incomes also had considerable debt, although this is less surprising when the type of debt held by these families is included. Those making more than $100,000 had more than $100,000 in mortgage debt on the primary residence alone, though these families also held other debt as well.

## Summary and Conclusions

In this chapter, I explored the processes at the levels of individuals and families that affect patterns of wealth accumulation. I examined the effects of age, race, family structure, income, education, and other individual and family processes. The results that I presented provided support for the life-cycle hypothesis: Wealth accumulation continued through the working years and began to trail off during retirement. The results suggested, however, that dissaving during retirement was less extreme than the life-cycle hypothesis predicts. Influences such as a bequest motive, uncertainty about the length of life, and attachment to the family home likely influenced the wealth behavior of the elderly and prevented them from depleting their assets as significantly as they might otherwise have done. Both the survey data and the simulation model that I drew on demonstrated dramatic racial differences in wealth ownership. Using the simulation model, I conducted an experiment that increased the educational attainment of nonwhites. The results suggested that returns to education for nonwhites were considerable when net worth was the outcome of interest. Within a decade of making the change, median wealth ownership for nonwhites had increased between 14 and 20 percent over historical values.

Family structure, income, and education also had important effects on wealth. Married people, especially those without children, and the widowed had a greater chance than their never married peers to have more net worth than income and to experience upward mobility. The opposite was true for the divorced and those with children. Income had a predictably positive effect on all aspects of wealth ownership and mobility. Yet, as I mentioned, the correlation between wealth and income (particularly when asset income is not considered part of total income) is rather low. I discussed possible explanations for this pattern. I also explored the positive association that I found between education and net worth. It was a pattern that remained even when other demographic influences were controlled, suggesting perhaps that those who pursue higher education are people who are also willing to postpone consumption in order to save. I concluded the chapter with a brief description of demographic patterns of debt holding.

# 9

## WEALTH MOBILITY

I've been rich and I've been poor. Believe me, rich is better.

(Sophie Tucker, Entertainer, 1884–1966)

Throughout this book, I have occasionally discussed the processes that account for wealth mobility, that is, movement among segments of the wealth distribution over the life course. In Chapter 3, I presented survey estimates of wealth mobility and pointed out that such estimates are rare because longitudinal data on wealth ownership is rare. I also included estimates from the simulation model to demonstrate that the model produces mobility estimates that are comparable to estimates available from survey data. In subsequent analyses and subsequent chapters, I used the simulation model to estimate patterns of mobility where survey data have not been available. I compared the mobility patterns of baby boomers and their parents, examined the effects of aggregate processes such as demographics on patterns of upward mobility, and explored how individual and family-level processes affect mobility. In previous chapters, I combined discussion of mobility patterns with other discussions. In this chapter, I focus exclusively on patterns of mobility and the processes that underlie those patterns. I explore movement into the top segments of the wealth distribution, movement out of poverty, and movement into the bottom segments of the distribution. I use the simulation model to estimate mobility patterns and to examine the effects of aggregate processes and microprocesses on this movement. I end the chapter with a discussion of a related process: inheritance.

Although the study of wealth distribution dates back to the writings of Smith, Mill, and Ricardo, discussions of wealth mobility are relatively rare. Cross-sectional analyses that sketch differences and trends became increasingly common in the 1980s, particularly in light of growing evidence that wealth inequality was worsening. Debates regarding the degree to which wealth was unequally distributed, the causes of inequality, and the relative merit of solutions to growing inequality increasingly filled academic and popular writing. While these discussions were certainly informative, they gave little insight into the intertemporal processes that lead to these patterns. Similarly, while the preceding chapters provide valuable insight into trends in wealth distribution between 1960 and 1995, they would be lacking without at least a brief discussion of the mobility processes that underlie patterns of distribution. Not only does the degree of mobility affect distributional outcomes, but mobility patterns also affect interpretation of cross-sectional distributional measures, particularly when inequality is worsening (Steckel and Krishman 1992). As with other approaches to studying wealth inequality, studying mobility is limited by the lack of longitudinal data. For that reason, I draw almost exclusively on simulated estimates in this chapter.

One of the first studies of mobility using multivariate methods of data analysis was Blau and Duncan's *The American Occupational Structure* (Blau and Duncan 1967). When Blau and Duncan's volume appeared, Lyndon Johnson had recently declared a war on poverty and mobility had become a topic of interest among scholars and academics alike. Much like other status attainment works that I referred to in the previous chapter, Blau and Duncan concluded that poverty and thus wealth as well were transmitted from parents to their children, typically via education. Using mobility tables of the sort used earlier in this book (i.e., Tables 3–6 and 3–7), Blau and Duncan focused on occupational mobility among white men and found that education was a better predictor of occupational status than family background. Based on these findings, they rejected the "vicious cycle of poverty" hypothesis. Other researchers extended Blau and Duncan's work and found similar patterns around that time (Corcoran 1995; Duncan, Featherman, and Duncan 1972; Featherman and Hauser 1978; Jencks, Smith, Acland et al. 1972; Sewell and Hauser 1975). Studies consistently found relatively weak, although statistically significant, correlations between parents' and children's income and concluded that mobility was, indeed, possible in the United States.

Many of these studies, however, relied on nonrandom, relatively homogenous samples of white working men. Those who were nonwhite, jobless, or female were neglected. There was also reason to question the methodology used in these studies. Most used earnings or income estimates from a single year to generalize about lifetime earnings. They relied heavily on cross-sectional data and retrospective reports of background to draw conclusions about longitudinal processes. Moreover, these early research projects typically did not examine the effects of family structure, welfare receipt, neighborhood characteristics, or changing labor market conditions (Corcoran and Datcher 1981). As Corcoran also pointed out, these early studies were consistent with a scenario in which there was overall mobility amidst pockets of permanent poverty.

By the late 1980s, new longitudinal data sets became available and researchers began to uncover more evidence of status inheritance. In particular, the Panel Study of Income Dynamics (PSID), a longitudinal study of 5,000 families that started in 1968 and followed both original respondents and their children, allowed researchers to explore longitudinal trends about which they had previously been able to offer only speculation. Studies of intergenerational poverty and welfare receipt, longitudinal patterns of sibling correlation, and longitudinal patterns of correlation between parents' and children's income began to clarify understanding of various longitudinal patterns, including mobility. Later panels of the PSID specifically asked about wealth ownership, but those questions were only included starting in the 1980s. Using PSID data, researchers estimated correlations of 0.4 and greater between the income of parents and that of their children (Behrman and Taubman 1990; Zimmerman 1992). Solon (1992) took a somewhat different approach. He defined the amount of income a family needed for basic survival and calculated an income-to-needs ratio for both fathers and sons. He found a correlation of 0.5 between the income-to-needs ratio of fathers and sons, and he concluded that a finding of this magnitude indicated a severely less mobile society than reported in previous research. Peters (1992) computed transition matrices using the PSID data and found what she called a "positive but moderate" overall relationship between both parents' and children's earned income and total income. The least mobility appeared to be in the highest and lowest quartiles. For example, children born into the lowest quartile had an approximately 40 percent chance of remaining in the lowest quartile in adulthood.

Several researchers have taken advantage of the longitudinal PSID data to specifically examine the intergenerational transmission of poverty and wealth. For instance, Levy (1980) compared the income-to-needs ratio of parents and their children and found that approximately 28 percent of children from poor families and more than 11 percent of children from nonpoor families were poor as adults. Levy concluded that there was intergenerational transmission of poverty but that it was less severe than some have suggested. Others have found that parental income positively affects other indicators of well-being in adult children. The earnings and educational attainment of adult children, for example, increase with the income of their parents (Corcoran and Datcher 1981; Kiker and Condon 1981).

Moving beyond simple economic outcomes, Hill and Duncan explored the impact that the source of income has on children's attainment. They argued that economic models of intergenerational attainment overemphasize income amount and neglect the source of that income. They drew on sociological theory that has suggested that labor income from a mother or father may indicate that positive role models were present in the household, while welfare receipt would imply that the household had adopted "counterproductive norms and values of a welfare culture" (Hill and Duncan 1987). Hill and Duncan used the PSID to explore these questions and found that working mothers were not necessarily positive role models for children. In fact, they found that the additional dollars of a mother's labor income had a less positive effect on children's attainment than did income from other sources. They also found no support for the hypothesis that welfare receipt had a negative effect on children. Overall they reported that parental income did have a significant effect on children's later earnings, even controlling for parental education and occupation.

Rodgers (1995) used more recent panels of the PSID to examine the extent to which poverty is inherited in the United States, allowing her to examine longer-term patterns than her predecessors. Rodgers estimated that, in part, because of declining real wages in the 1970s and 1980s, children of poor parents had a 16 to 28 percent chance of being poor as adults. Of those who escaped poverty, half remained near-poor with family incomes less than twice the poverty line. Only 13 percent of poor children had moved to the most affluent category as adults. Approximately 6 percent of poor adults had been raised in affluent families. Of those nonpoor children who fell into poverty as adults, 75 percent were raised in near-poor families. Rodgers emphasized differences in mobility by race, demonstrating that nonwhites were less likely to escape poverty and more likely to fall into poverty as adults. She estimated that 91 percent of whites escaped from poverty, while only 68 percent of nonwhites escaped. Overall, the rate at which individuals moved out of poverty was 78 percent. Rodgers concluded that economic claims of mobility and equality of economic opportunity are exaggerated and that in reality there is considerable persistence in income across generations.

In presenting the findings of this research, I do not intend to provide a comprehensive review of the mobility literature. Indeed, others have compiled much more comprehensive collections of work done on the subject (Corcoran 1995). Rather, I intend to demonstrate that a considerable amount of research has been conducted on economic mobility, but this research has focused almost exclusively on income mobility. Moreover, while I have not attempted to mention every piece of sociological research that has been conducted on mobility, I have attempted to demonstrate that economists have conducted the bulk of the research on economic mobility. Because wealth is more unequally distributed than income, understanding persistence in poverty and movement into high-wealth categories is at least as important as understanding income mobility. Data availability has made examination of wealth mobility largely impossible in the past. The researchers who have dominated the field of wealth distribution have occasionally used the 1983–1989 panel of the Survey of Consumer Finances to estimate short-term trends in wealth ownership (see, e.g., Wolff 1998). Short-term trends in mobility, however, tell us little about the intergenerational or life-course processes that lead to the persistence of either wealth or poverty. Of course, what is needed is longitudinal data on wealth ownership that would facilitate studies comparable to those conducted using the PSID's information on income.

In the absence of such data, estimates of wealth mobility and its causes (or impediments) will have to come from artificial data sources. In the remainder of this chapter, I draw on the simulation model to estimate the patterns that we would be likely to find if survey data were available. I refer the reader to the simulated mobility estimates I included in Chapter 3 (Table 3–6) for evidence that the simulated estimates correspond extremely well to survey estimates. The simulated estimates included in that table are also consistent with other published estimates of short-term mobility patterns derived from the Survey of Consumer Finances (Wolff 1998). I have also produced evidence throughout the book that the simulated estimates are highly consistent with patterns of wealth accumulation and distribution available from survey data. While this does not provide conclusive evidence that the mobility estimates I present in the pages that follow are historically accurate, it does suggest that the simulated estimates are reliable estimates. They, of course, should not be taken as anything more than estimates of mobility patterns.

## *From Income to Wealth Mobility*

In the next three sections, I present simulated estimates of the log odds of three types of mobility. In the first section, I examine who gets rich. That is, I explore the factors that are related to movement into the top 10 percent of the wealth distribution. In the second section, I explore movement out of poverty, that is, escaping poverty. Finally, I examine movement into poverty, or becoming poor. I used the simulation model to estimate the net worth of all families every three years between 1960 and 1995. In each year, I then ranked the families by net worth, estimated decile and quintile cut-offs, and determined each individual's position in the distribution. I compared each individual's quintile position in the current year (excluding the first year) with that individual's quintile position in the prior year. While the unit of analysis in these mobility estimates was the individual, I used family wealth as a characteristic of the individual.

In estimating the models, I included only adults age 20 or older in the analysis, and I created three dummy variables to be used as dependent variables. The first was a dummy variable indicating movement into the top 10 percent, the second was a dummy variable indicating movement out of the bottom quintile, and the third was a dummy variable indicating movement into the bottom quintile. I estimated standard logistic regression equations, using person-years as the unit of analysis, to produce coefficient estimates for various potential influences. I report the log odds of movement from these equations in Tables 9–1, 9–2, and 9–3.

### Getting Rich: Who Becomes Rich and How?

America likes to view itself as a place where equality of opportunity means that everyone has a chance to experience upward mobility. As we saw above, most research on social and economic mobility has focused on income mobility even though wealth mobility perhaps captures more of our sense of what upward mobility is all about. Table 9–1 includes the results of the first set of analyses in which the dependent variable was movement into the top 10 percent of the wealth distribution. The odds ratios reported in this table are from a single equation, although the equation included separate coefficient estimates for each of three time periods. Specifically, I included separate intercepts and separate coefficients for each variable for 1960–1969, 1970–1979, and 1980–1995. Changing aggre-

Table 9–1. *Getting Rich: Odds of Movement into Top 10%, 1960–1995*

|  | 1960–1969 | 1970–1979 | 1980–1995 |
|---|---|---|---|
| *Age* |  |  |  |
| 35–44 | 1.000 | 1.030 | 1.000 |
| 45–54 | 1.011 | 0.999 | 1.073 |
| 55–64 | 1.010 | 1.000 | 1.000 |
| 65–74 | 2.448 | 2.939 | 2.448 |
| 75 and older | 1.297 | 1.432 | 1.237 |
|  |  |  |  |
| White | 3.498 | 3.109 | 2.448 |
|  |  |  |  |
| *Income* |  |  |  |
| $10,000–24,999 | 1.518 | 1.531 | 1.589 |
| $25,000–49,999 | 2.877 | 2.128 | 2.448 |
| $50,000–99,999 | 3.360 | 3.330 | 3.400 |
| $100,000 | 5.474 | 5.907 | 5.916 |
|  |  |  |  |
| *Marital status* |  |  |  |
| Married | 2.343 | 1.998 | 1.508 |
| Divorced | 0.547 | 0.551 | 0.754 |
| Widowed | 1.082 | 1.000 | 1.000 |
|  |  |  |  |
| No children | 1.297 | 1.297 | 1.301 |
|  |  |  |  |
| *Education* |  |  |  |
| Some high school | 1.036 | 1.049 | 1.053 |
| High school graduate | 1.189 | 1.212 | 1.273 |
| College graduate | 2.345 | 2.516 | 3.400 |
|  |  |  |  |
| *Birth cohort* |  |  |  |
| 1945–1954 | 1.273 | 2.128 | 2.961 |
| 1955–1964 | – | – | 1.402 |
|  |  |  |  |
| Upwardly mobile parents | 5.751 | 6.099 | 6.182 |

*Note*: Author's estimates of odds ratios from logistic regression on simulated data. All odds ratios are from the same model. The dependent variable is a dichotomous indicator of movement into the top 10 percent of family wealth owners, 1960–1995. Demographic characteristics refer to the household head.

Table 9–2. *Escaping Poverty: Odds of Movement Out of Bottom 20%, 1960–1995*

|  | 1960–1995 |
| --- | --- |
| *Age* |  |
| 35–44 | 2.877 |
| 45–54 | 1.531 |
| 55–64 | 1.331 |
| 65–74 | 1.003 |
| 75 and older | 1.000 |
| White | 3.360 |
| *Income* |  |
| $10,000–24,999 | 1.985 |
| $25,000–49,999 | 1.913 |
| $50,000–99,999 | 2.711 |
| $100,000 | 7.678 |
| *Marital status* |  |
| Married | 1.000 |
| Divorced | 0.713 |
| Widowed | 1.068 |
| No children | 1.895 |
| *Education* |  |
| Some high school | 1.033 |
| High school graduate | 1.127 |
| College graduate | 2.345 |
| *Birth cohort* |  |
| 1945–1954 | 1.187 |
| 1955–1964 | 1.058 |

*Note*: Author's estimates of odds ratios from logistic regression on simulated data. All odds ratios are from the same model. The dependent variable is a dichotomous indicator of movement into the top 10 percent of family wealth owners, 1960–1995. Demographic characteristics refer to the household head.

gate trends during those time periods suggested that different processes might underlie upward mobility at different points, and initial investigations confirmed that there were significant differences between coefficients in the different time periods.

Table 9–3. *Becoming Poor: Odds of Movement into Bottom
20%, 1960–1995*

|  | 1960–1995 |
| --- | --- |
| *Age* | |
| 35–44 | 2.343 |
| 45–54 | 1.187 |
| 55–64 | 1.000 |
| 65–74 | 1.000 |
| 75 and older | 1.570 |
| White | 0.746 |
| *Income* | |
| $10,000–24,999 | 2.343 |
| $25,000–49,999 | 0.717 |
| $50,000–99,999 | 0.260 |
| $100,000 | 0.240 |
| *Marital status* | |
| Married | 1.000 |
| Divorced | 2.370 |
| Widowed | 1.013 |
| No children | 0.387 |
| *Education* | |
| Some high school | 1.069 |
| High school graduate | 0.453 |
| College graduate | 0.748 |
| *Birth cohort* | |
| 1945–1954 | 1.000 |
| 1955–1964 | 1.058 |

*Note*: Author's estimates of odds ratios from logistic regression on
simulated data. All odds ratios are from the same model. The
dependent variable is a dichotomous indicator of movement into
the top 10 percent of family wealth owners, 1960–1995. Demographic characteristics refer to the household head.

The final results, presented in the table, indeed demonstrate that there
were changes in the importance of certain influences over the three decades
included in the table. Not all influences changed, but decreasing real
wages, changes in social patterns and norms, recessions and economic

booms, and other aggregate influences appear to have combined to produce different effects at different points during history. I included 15 years in the third time period because differences in the 1990s were not distinct enough from the 1980s to justify the loss in degrees of freedom from including separate estimates for a fourth time period (1990–1995). Statistical tests, including Wald tests for differences in coefficient estimates, confirmed this choice of time periods. I discuss the details of these changes below in my presentation of the actual results.

Both microinfluences and macroinfluences appear to have influenced individual propensities for upward mobility between 1960 and 1995. One of the key influences on wealth accumulation, age was certainly related to the odds of upward mobility. However, the effects of age appeared only after retirement in all three time periods. The reference group for the age categories is the under 35 group. For those in the 35–44, 45–54, and 55–64 age groups, the odds of upward mobility were virtually indistinguishable from the odds for those in the reference group. In other words, there was no discernible mobility advantage to being in any of the age groups under 65. In contrast, the odds of movement into the top decile for those age 65 and older were considerably greater than for those under 35 in each of the three time periods. Between 1960 and 1969, for example, the odds of becoming rich for those age 65–74 were 2.448 times greater than for those under 35. Similarly, for those 75 and older, the odds of upward mobility were 1.297 times greater than for the youngest age group. These patterns were consistent across the three time periods, that is, there was no noticeable period effect on the relationship between age and upward wealth mobility.

Life-cycle arguments of wealth accumulation would suggest the opposite, that is, that the propensity for upward mobility would decline after retirement as savings are depleted for current consumption (Modigliani 1992). Yet these results are consistent with counterarguments, examined in more depth in Chapter 8, that bequest motives, uncertainty about the length of the future, risk aversion, and emotional attachment to the home discourage dissaving and result in continued wealth accumulation even after retirement (Ando and Modigliani 1963; Bernheim 1991; King and Dicks-Mireaux 1982; Menchick and David 1983; Modigliani 1992; White 1978; Wolff 1988). Indeed, the results presented in that chapter provided evidence that the elderly did continue to save between 1960 and 1995. Those results showed some decline in wealth holdings, but the decline was less dramatic than the life-cycle hypothesis would predict. The age effects evident in Table 9–1 provide additional evidence that wealth accumulation does not strictly follow the pattern proposed by the life-cycle hypothesis. In contrast, these results demonstrate that upward wealth mobility was likely for those who had reached retirement.

There was a very clear and relatively strong association between being white and the odds of upward mobility. Between 1960 and 1969, the odds that whites would move into the top decile of the wealth distribution were 3.498 times greater than for nonwhites. Likewise the odds ratio for whites was 3.109 in the 1970s and 2.448 between 1980 and 1995. This result provides support for the conjectures that Oliver and Shapiro made in *Black Wealth/White Wealth* (1995). They suggested that racial differences in mobility were likely quite pronounced, but their data was not able to support tests of such claims. Of course, it would be preferable to have longitudinal survey data to test the effects I am discussing here. Given that it is unavailable, the simulated estimates provide a useful approximation. The strength of this result, in particular, suggests that the relationship between race and mobility was quite strong.

The reasons that race, net of income, family structure, education, and other potential effects on mobility continued to be associated with mobility are less clear. Wilson's social isolation arguments likely explain much of the effect. Wilson (1987) argued that the movement of manufacturing jobs out of urban centers along with the outmigration of middle-class blacks, left uneducated, low-skilled blacks in areas where unemployment was high and chances of escaping poverty were correspondingly low. The movement of middle class blacks out of these urban centers weakened social institutions such as churches and community organizations that had exposed middle-class residents to mainstream alternatives (Corcoran 1995). While these arguments are specifically about movement out of poverty, high rates of joblessness, declining wages, and "ghettoization" among blacks certainly affected the propensity of nonwhites to be upwardly mobile. These arguments also ignore other racial and ethnic minorities, including Asians, who may have had very different mobility patterns but who were included in the nonwhite category in my analyses. Ideally I would have included these other groups, but I omitted them because the sample numbers are too small for these other nonwhite groups in the survey data that underlie the simulation estimates to calculate accurate wealth accumulation measures. The effect of patterns of mobility among blacks, however, was so strong during this period, and these patterns were consistent with patterns among Hispanics and other poor minority groups, that the opposite effects of many Asian groups were likely invisible.

Income had a predictably positive relationship with the odds of movement into the top 10 percent of the distribution, and the effect was relatively constant across time periods. Income refers to total household income from all sources: Earned income, transfer payments, asset income (such as interest and dividends), alimony, and any other income source are included in the total. All values are in 1990 dollars. The estimates indicate that greater income is associated with higher odds of becoming rich. The omitted category is total household income less than $10,000. Thus the results suggest that the odds of moving into the top decile of the wealth distribution for someone in a household with total income between $10,000 and $24,999 were 1.518 times greater than for someone with an income less than $10,000. The odds ratio for that income category was approximately 1.5 times greater than for the omitted category for each of the three time periods. For those making more income, the odds ratios were even greater. For example, in the 1960s, the odds of "getting rich" or moving into the top decile were 2.877 times greater for those in the $25,000 to $49,999 income bracket than for those in the omitted category.

For those in the top income category, the odds of upward mobility were, not surprisingly, quite high. In fact, the odds that someone in the top income category would be upwardly mobile were more than 5 times greater than the odds ratio for those in the lowest income group. The explanation of the income effect is relatively straightforward as well. Higher income means that a household has more funds available to save and invest. The odds of upward mobility for those in the higher-income categories were even greater when I isolated those who were not already in the top decile. In the reported results, I include both those who were not in the richest category and those who were, making the results slightly more conservative than they might otherwise have been.

Family structure had important effects on upward mobility, and the relationship between family structure and mobility changed over the three decades included in Table 9–1. In all three decades, the odds of upward mobility were greater for married couples than for those who had never been married (the omitted category). However, the strength of the relationship between being married and mobility into the top decile decreased over time. Because these odds ratios are based on coefficients from a single equation with three separate intercepts, it is possible to compare the odds ratios over the three time periods. The results indicate that during the 1960s, the odds of getting rich for married couples were 2.343 times greater than for those who were never married. During the 1970s, the odds ratio was only about 2 (1.998), and for the years between 1980 and 1995, the odds ratio was 1.508.

The decline in the significance of marriage likely reflects the demographic changes that I explored in my discussion of baby boomers and their parents in Chapter 6. Norms regarding female labor force participation, education for women, childbearing, and related behaviors and processes changed during the 1960s and 1970s. As a result, women's work behavior changed, people postponed marriage and childbearing, and other work and family patterns changed as well. As a result, it became less critical for women to be married to experience upward mobility. The results in the table likely reflect some of these changes. Similarly, both divorce and childbirth generally have negative effects on family finances, particularly for women. In all three periods, both divorce and having children decreased the odds of upward mobility. However, consistent with the finding that the importance of marriage decreased over the three decades, the liability of divorce decreased. Being widowed had almost no effect on upward mobility.

Consistent with arguments that attribute a great deal of the impetus for mobility to education, the odds of upward mobility increased markedly with education, even with other influences controlled. Because returns to education appear to be different at different levels of education, I used four educational categories. Some high school refers to those who started but did not finish high school. High school graduates are those who graduated from high school, including both those who started college and did not finish and those who never started college. College graduates are those who completed a college degree, including a two-year degree. The omitted category was those who never started high school.

The results indicate that the odds of movement into the top decile were only slightly, and then not consistently, greater for those with some high school education and high school graduates, when compared to those who never started high school. The odds that a high school graduate in the 1970s and 1980s would move into the top decile were approximately 1.2 times greater than for someone who had never started high school, and the importance of a high school education became greater over the three decades. Over the three time periods included in Table 9–1, college graduates had considerably higher odds of moving into the top wealth decile. Moreover, the strength of the relationship between education and upward mobility appears to have increased between 1960 and 1995. In the 1960s, the odds of upward mobility for college graduates were 2.345 times greater than for those without even a high school education. By the 1970s, the odds ratio for college graduates had increased to 2.516, and in the 1980s and 1990s, the odds for college graduates were 3.4 times greater than for those with less than a high school education.

We saw in previous chapters that education has a relatively strong and highly consistent effect on wealth accumulation. The results included in Table 9–1 suggest that upward mobility is also positively related to educational attainment, particularly college education. As they were in other analyses in this book, the education results in Table 9–1 are net of the effects of income, age, race, family structure, and other influences on mobility. The benefits of human capital obtained through higher education are certainly likely to affect saving and wealth accumulation. Yet the income control probably captures some of the human capital effect. The strong education effect, net of the other influences included in the model, implies that there is something unique about education, particularly advanced degrees, that increases the likelihood of economic mobility. It is possible that college graduates are more willing than non–college graduates to postpone consumption. The same character or personality trait might result in both educational advancement and a relatively high propensity to save (Dynan 1993). Parental expectation, exposure to others who have achieved high levels of education, knowledge about investing, and networks of contacts who invest might also produce an independent education effect on saving and wealth accumulation.

The positive association between education and upward mobility may also reflect patterns of social reproduction. In addition to the human capital acquired during college, students acquire social and cultural capital that might impact wealth accumulation and mobility. Research on social reproduction, the continuation of power and privilege across generations, has debated whether there is equality of opportunity for upward mobility or whether power and privilege are re-created from generation to generation, with the same group of families retaining elite positions for decades or longer. Education has played a central role in these debates. Status attainment researchers have argued that education imparts skills and knowledge that facilitate mobility (Alexander 1976; Alexander, Cook, and McDill 1978; Alexander and Eckland 1975; Blau and Duncan 1967;

Kerckhoff 1976). The emphasis in this literature has been largely on the meritocratic aspects of educational attainment.

Others have argued that nonmeritocratic features of the educational process might also affect later well-being (Bowles and Gintis 1976; Collins 1979). Bowles and Gintis suggested that education produces and reinforces many noncognitive personality traits that produce and reproduce social relations and lead to class persistence for those in the upward classes and upward mobility for those who are similarly indoctrinated (Bowles and Gintis 1976). Collins suggested that schools create status groups that protect desired market positions for those with similar backgrounds (Collins 1979). Meyers argued that charters, "the social definition of the products of [an] organization," reserve certain social rights for those with access to the charters and create structural limitations for others by denying them these same rights. Admission to graduate schools, access to key jobs, and admission to elite social circles are all privileges that may be reserved for those who have passed through the appropriate segments of the educational system.

Indeed, a rather substantial collection of literature has documented that graduation from certain schools carries advantages that lead to social reproduction. For those who are not born in the upper class, access to these schools dramatically increases the likelihood of mobility. In particular, there is evidence that elite secondary boarding schools and universities are central to the reproduction of an upper class (Domhoff 1970; Persell and Cookson 1986; Useem 1984). Only a small fraction of American adults ever attended these schools, yet that small group has been increasingly recognized as a very central and powerful segment of the population (Persell and Cookson 1986). These elite schools provide excellent college preparation for their graduates, but they also cultivate human and social capital in their students and work to acquire sought-after positions for their graduates in elite universities and companies (Persell and Cookson 1986).

The schools also actively cultivate social networks that span geographic barriers and lead to tightly connected adult business and social networks. Researchers have shown that graduation from an elite secondary school is positively associated with attending a four-year college (Falsey and Heyns 1984), attending a highly selective or Ivy League college or university (Hammack and Cookson 1980; Persell and Cookson 1986), and earning higher income after graduation from college (Lewis and Wanner 1979). Useem also showed that graduates of 14 elite secondary boarding schools were much more likely than those who did not graduate from these schools to become leaders (part of the "inner circle" of leaders) of Fortune 500 companies (Useem 1984). These advantages might well underlie the wealth mobility effects of education that are evident in the results presented in Table 9–1. Using the simulation model alone, I cannot identify the mechanism by which education and mobility are related, but it is possible that the processes described in the social reproduction literature are operative here as well. Future survey data or qualitative data on upward mobility may be able to better identify this mechanism.

Being a baby boomer also had clear advantages for mobility prospects. Table 9–1 includes odds ratios for baby boomers, both young and old boomers, that indicate the increase in odds that those born between 1945 and 1964 enjoyed. We saw in Chapter 6 that baby boomers, particularly older boomers, were more likely than their parents to be upwardly mobile. The results in Table 9–1 build on this finding in two ways. First, in this set of analyses, baby boomers are compared to all people in the model, not just their parents. Second, the analyses in Table 9–1 explore movement into the top decile rather than any upward mobility. The mobility advantages of being a boomer were relatively strong and increasing, particularly for those born between 1945 and 1954. For example, the odds of mobility into the top decile for those born between 1945 and 1954 were 1.273 times greater than for all other people during the 1960s. As the baby boomers aged, their relative odds of upward mobility increased. During the 1970s, the odds of upward mobility for older baby boomers were more than 2 times greater than for non–baby boomers, and between 1980 and 1995, the odds ratio was nearly 3 times greater than for non–baby boomers. The increase in the odds over the three periods likely reflected the aging of this group. In the 1960s, the older baby boomers were just entering adulthood, but by 1980, even the youngest of those born between 1945 and 1954 were adults and many had established careers and were at the peak of their working years.

There were also apparent advantages to being a member of the younger portion of the baby boom. Again, we saw in Chapter 6 that younger boomers were also likely to be more upwardly mobile than their parents. The results in Table 9–1 suggest that perhaps this mobility advantage was even more general. In addition to the dummy variable indicating that the individual was an older baby boomer, I also included a dummy for being a young boomer in the third time period. I did not include this variable in the first two time periods because the younger baby boomers, those born between 1955 and 1964, were either children or just reaching adulthood. In both the 1960s and 1970s, there would not have been enough members of this group to estimate the equations. The odds of moving into the top decile of the wealth distribution in the 1980s and early 1990s were 1.402 times greater for younger boomers than for non–baby boomers. Both cohort effects reflect the propensity for baby boomers to accumulate wealth quickly as a result of postponed childbearing, increased female labor force participation, and related behaviors.

Early status attainment literature emphasized the importance of parental influence on children's status in adulthood, and as I discussed above, the debate about the role that parental influence plays in mobility continues today. The estimates in Table 9–1 suggest that the effect of parents' mobility on the wealth mobility of the child was extremely strong. Indeed, the strongest overall influence on mobility into the top decile of the wealth distribution in the simulation model was having parents who had been upwardly mobile during their own adult lives. The variable is a dummy indicating that one or both of the individual's parents experienced upward mobility of any kind during his or her lifetime. The effect increased slightly over the three periods, but the real story is the relative magnitude of the effect. Again, it is important to emphasize that the mobility patterns estimated from the simulation model are only estimates of historical patterns. The strength of the parental effect, however, suggests that there was indeed a strong intergenerational effect on mobility, beyond the effect of parents' behavior on income, education, and family structure.

One possible explanation for this effect is that parents who are upwardly mobile influence human and social capital in ways that are not fully captured by education and income measures. Perhaps children from upwardly mobile homes are exposed to attitudes about saving and work ethics that others do not experience. In much the same way that long-term parental poverty affects adulthood poverty in children (Corcoran 1995), it is possible that long-term exposure to upward mobility impacts children cognitively in ways that enhance their prospects for mobility in their own adult lives. It is also possible that children benefit from the improved social connections, or social capital, that their parents acquire with upward mobility. Of course, the modeling method I used to estimate the relationships presented in Table 9–1 could not answer such detailed questions. Perhaps future surveys will be more effective in identifying the mechanism by which well-being is transferred across generations.

### Escaping Poverty and Becoming Poor

Much of the research on social and economic mobility has been motivated by a desire to end poverty. Determining how it is that some people are able to escape poverty while others are persistently poor is also at the heart of both the study and practice of social policy. The notion that poverty may be passed along from parents to children violates the notion of equality of opportunity that is revered in the United States, yet researchers have produced considerable evidence that poverty is highly intergenerational (see Corcoran 1995 for an excellent review). In this literature, however, the emphasis is almost exclusively on income rather than wealth. In Table 9–2, I present a second set of estimates derived from the simulation model. These are estimated odds ratios for movement out of the bottom quintile of the wealth distribution between 1960 to 1995. Again, I included only adults in the analyses. The odds ratios are from a single logistic regression equation with a single intercept. I did not separate the equation by time period in this case because preliminary analyses suggested that the differences across time period were not sufficient to warrant the more complex specification.

The results indicate that age had the reverse effect on escaping poverty from what it had on mobility into the top of the wealth distribution. The odds ratio for the youngest age group included in the equation was considerably greater than those for the older groups. The implication of this finding is that most movement out of poverty occurred in early adulthood, but after age 35. After 45, movement out of poverty slowed drastically, and there was little effect of age after 65. Whites, again, were much more likely to escape poverty than nonwhites, and income had a predictably positive association with upward mobility. Likewise, baby boomers were more likely than those born in other generations to escape poverty. Education, particularly higher education, was again one of the strongest predictors of upward mobility. The odds of escaping poverty for those with less than a high school education and those with only some high school education were virtually the same. However, the odds of escaping poverty for those who graduated from high school were 1.127 times greater than the odds for those with less than a high school education. Again, the strongest educational effect was the effect of higher education. The odds of movement out of poverty for college graduates were 2.345 times greater than for those who never attended high school.

The processes that allowed some to escape poverty were the same processes that, in reverse, caused others to enter the ranks of the poor. Demographics, decisions about family formation and dissolution, and education all contributed to movement into poverty between 1960 and 1995. In Table 9–3, I present the results of a third set of analyses. As with escaping poverty, it appears that movement into poverty occurred most often in early adulthood. It was more rare for whites than nonwhites to become poor, and those with children were less likely to move into the bottom quintile of the household wealth distribution. Education and income were relatively strongly associated with becoming poor. The odds of becoming poor for those who graduated from high school, for example, were nearly 0.453 times less than for those who did not attend high school. Likewise, the odds of downward mobility decreased markedly with income.

A particularly strong relationship was that between being divorced and downward mobility. Literature on the social and economic impact of divorce suggests that women bear more of the negative effect of marital dissolution (Cherlin 1981; Huber and Spitze 1980; Stirling 1989; Weitzman 1985). Although there has been some controversy over empirical findings in this literature (Peterson 1996), there is reason to believe that women's economic well-being decreases more than men's well-being after divorce. This literature includes homeownership among its outcome variables, but overall wealth seldom enters the debate explicitly because it is a family-level concept. Moreover, in the already sparse wealth data that are available, there is little information that would facilitate analysis of gender differences in wealth changes following divorce. For these reasons, I do not include a gender indicator in the analyses presented in the tables in this chapter. This does not imply that the issue of gender differences in well-being following divorce is not important. Rather, the strong relationship between divorce and downward mobility evident in the results in Table 9–3 suggests that data are needed that would allow examination of the issue.

## Inheritance

J. K. Vanderbilt once said, "Inherited wealth is a big handicap to happiness. It is as certain death to ambition as cocaine is to morality." Yet Vanderbilt might have agreed with the sentiment that Sophie Tucker expressed in the quote at the beginning of this chapter, that is (to paraphrase), those who have been both rich and poor generally find that being rich is better. Those who enjoy wealth know this, and they typically want to ensure that their children are also able to enjoy the benefits of financial security. Transferring their wealth to their children is one of the most certain ways to ensure the financial security of future generations. We know a considerable amount about individual attainment and life-course changes in social and economic well-being, and the bulk of literature on wealth accumulation and distribution focuses on these processes. Yet, by some accounts, the transfer of wealth from one generation to the next may be the single most important determinant of who owns what, how they got it, and what effects it has on both individual- and system-level outcomes. In the 1960s, there is evidence that less than 5 percent of the population had inherited any wealth, and newer estimates suggest that baby boomers are going to inherit nearly $7 trillion dollars in the late 1990s and into the next century. More striking is evidence that suggests that approximately 80 percent of the richest Americans were born to wealthy families (Oliver and Shapiro 1995:152).

Inheritance comes in at least three forms. Those who are born into wealth are likely to acquire large lump-sum inheritances at the death of one or both parents. In addition, the wealthy enjoy significant inter-vivos transfers (transfers of resources from living parents to their children) and transfers of cultural capital from their parents, and each of these transfers has the potential to facilitate social reproduction, the intergeneration re-creation of class. Lump-sum inheritance, the transfer of the bulk of an estate at the time of death of the estate's owner, is what we usually think of as inheritance. These transfers certainly have the potential to secure the economic and social positions of the receiver, adding to the persistence of wealth in the same families.

In contrast, inter-vivos transfers are gifts given while the parent is still alive. These are usually monetary gifts or gifts that have some monetary value attached to them. Monetary transfers, vehicles, the down payment for a home, the home itself, furniture, money for educational expenses, assistance getting a job, and similar gifts to children and grandchildren are all inter-vivos transfers. These transfers are not inheritance in the traditional sense of the word, but they do have a critical impact on the well-being of the receiver, both short- and long-term. Moreover, there is evidence that inter-vivos transfers account for a greater proportion of inter-generational transfers than lump-sum transfers at death (Gale and Scholz 1994; Kurz 1984). Indeed, Kurz (1984) estimated that inter-vivos transfers account for nearly 90 percent of intergenerational wealth transfers.

Cultural capital also contributes to the total effect of inheritance on inequality. The notion of social reproduction rests on the idea that there are nonmonetary benefits that wealthy parents can give their children that allow them to get ahead. While financial wealth is not a prerequisite to having cultural capital, cultural capital typically occurs where financial wealth is high. Cultural capital is an understanding of norms, behaviors, tastes, styles of interaction, and other intangible preferences that are associated with the upper class (Bourdieu 1973). As Miller and McNamee pointed out, cultural capital is an important part of the inheritance of an heir to great wealth. It is transferred through formal education, other more informal educational experiences, social connections, and proficiency with cultural codes and nuances. Cultural capital is "an important resource, and individuals inherit differential opportunities for its acquisition. Since cultural capital is required for entry and acceptance into higher status social circles, lack of cultural capital for individuals from modest backgrounds poses a significant impediment to their prospects for upward social mobility. In this way, barriers of entry are created and existing forms of inequality are reinforced" (Miller and McNamee 1998:3).

Americans are ambivalent about inheritance (Miller and McNamee 1998:1). They like to think of their society as granting equal opportunity and rewarding individual merit (Huber and Form 1973; Kluegel and Smith 1986). Yet they also embrace the idea that individuals ought to be able to leave the things they accumulate during their lives to their heirs. These two beliefs are at direct odds with each other: If resources are inherited, they cannot be gained through merit. Trying to preserve both rights has created friction between individual-level choice and system-level equality for decades, yet both beliefs have survived. Researchers have long debated the relative impact of individual attainment and inheritance on financial well-being. Some have argued that great wealth is primarily acquired through risk-taking, entrepreneurship, and other behaviors that reflect individual motivation, hard work, and, to some extent, luck. Others, however, have argued that the bulk of wealth is transferred intergenerationally, preventing most individuals from entering the wealthy class because they were born in more modest circumstances.

Unfortunately, however, we know almost nothing about the process of inheritance. There is little reliable data on inheritance, and the research that has been done on inheritance processes has emerged in disparate literatures from various disciplines. Because there is almost no available data on inheritance, I do not produce survey estimates of inheritance processes in this section. For the same reason, I did not model inheritance processes explicitly in the simulation model. Of course, in the simulation model, the process of inheritance is captured by the change coefficients that age people and their wealth holdings.[1] Because distributional, accumulation, and mobility estimates produced by the model are highly consistent with known survey data, there is reason to believe that the inheritance processes that are included are somewhat accurate. However, in an ideal model, inheritance would be an influence that could be manipulated for experimental purposes. Perhaps when more complete data on wealth accumulation processes are available, it will be possible to model inheritance. For now, however, I will rely on secondary sources to discuss inheritance and its effect on wealth accumulation and distribution.

In the remainder of this section, I draw on these secondary accounts to explore the role that inheritance plays in creating and maintaining inequalities in the distribution of household wealth. A small but growing group of researchers from various academic disciplines has acknowledged the importance of inheritance and has begun to document what is known about the process. I do not attempt to provide a comprehensive review of the inheritance literature as others have already compiled such collections (see, e.g., Miller and McNamee's 1998 collection of essays on inheritance and related processes *Inheritance and Wealth in America*). Rather, my goal is to speculate from these secondary sources about the role that inheritance plays in creating wealth inequality and to argue for the importance of collecting data that would allow empirical exploration of these processes.

Bequeathing wealth to future generations has been common practice throughout history in nearly all industrialized societies, including the United States. However, as Chester (1998:23) pointed out, since the American Revolution, the right to transfer wealth at the death of its owner has been considered a civil, not a natural, right. That is, inheritance was a custom that conscious decision making over the course of decades turned into law. As such, inheritance has long been subject to legislative control, regulation, and taxation. Some have argued that a 1980s court case (*Hodel*

---

[1] That is, in each equation in the model that determines the likelihood of ownership and the value owned for each asset and debt, there is a lagged dependent variable. This variable indicates that change in the family's ownership or value over the prior period (three years prior). Because this variable indicates change in the total amount owned, it indirectly captures the effects of inheriting. However, there is no way to distinguish between inheriting and other means by which families increase their wealth.

*v. Irving*), regarding the fragmentation of Indian lands as a result of property ownership regulations, brought into question the very nature of inheritance (Chester 1998; Kornstein 1984). As a result of this case, some have argued that it is possible that inheritance will be redefined as a natural right for the first time in American history. Johnson and Eller's (1998) description of debates over whether inheritance should be considered a right or a privilege parallel Chester's legal history. Johnson and Eller provided a detailed overview of the origins and character of modern estate taxation practices, and they concluded that much debate over the effects of these taxes had its origins in disagreements about whether inheritance is a natural or a civic right.

Johnson and Eller were less optimistic than Chester, however, when they argued that such issues are unlikely to be resolved in the near future. Until they are, and very probably for much longer, federal inheritance taxation will continue. After all, the federal government has long relied on estate and inheritance taxes as well as taxes on inter-vivos transfers for revenue and to enforce policy prescriptions. Attempts to determine how much wealth is actually transferred across generations and, thus, how much revenue the government should be receiving from taxes on these transfers, has long been debated. Menchik and Jiankoplos (1998) discussed problems with such calculations and showed that, according to estimates from a wide range of years from the 1970s through the 1990s, as little as 20 and as much as 80 percent of total wealth could be inherited. The reasons that people leave an inheritance, whether motivated by altruism, exchange, or strategic desires, are equally uncertain. Yet, as I have mentioned throughout this book, increasing estate taxes and, perhaps, taxes on inter-vivos transfers and inheritance as well is one of the quickest means of redistributing wealth. Whether it is a fair method is questionable, but it is doubtful, nonetheless, that the government will soon abandon this taxation and policy instrument.

The intergenerational transfer of financial and other resources likely explains many of the patterns I have identified throughout this book. For example, racial differences in wealth ownership may result to a large extent from racial differences in inheritance (Oliver and Shapiro 1995:152–156). White parents are more likely to have accumulated wealth during their lives and are, thus, more able to transfer this wealth to their children. Likewise, there are ethnic differences in wealth ownership and inheritance. There is some evidence that ethnicity or national origin affects both wealth accumulation and inheritance (Clignet 1998). Ethnicity is associated with differences in risk tolerance and preferences for owning certain assets such as businesses versus homes. There are also ethnic differences in inter-vivos transfers and lump-sum inheritance at death. For example, ethnic variations in bequeathing wealth to female children can affect wealth ownership.

Similarly, gender differences in inheritance may also affect wealth accumulation patterns. I have not addressed gender differences in wealth ownership in general because wealth is typically a family-level concept. Trying to disentangle individual ownership of assets and to determine gender differences can become more complicated than the benefits such efforts produce warrant. Inter-vivos transfers and lump-sum inheritance at death generally occur between individuals, and there is evidence that women have long fared worse than men in the United States in the amount they inherit (Gundersen 1998). The effect of gender differences in inheritance likely interacts with family structure, family formation, and marital dissolution in affecting accumulation and distribution processes (Rosenfeld 1998). Unfortunately, however, the majority of writing about inheritance processes is either historical or speculative because so few current, comprehensive data are available to answer questions about who inherits and what it means for inequality. Until such data are available, inheritance will likely remain a black box in most studies of wealth accumulation and distribution.

## Summary and Conclusions

In this chapter, I used the wealth simulation model to explore patterns of wealth mobility and the factors that affect mobility. Because there is so little longitudinal data on wealth mobility, I relied exclusively on simulated estimates to discuss behaviors and processes that are associated with both upward and downward mobility. Ideally, we would have long-term longitudinal data that allows exploration of the life courses that lead to mobility. The Panel Study of Income Dynamics revolutionized the study of income and educational attainment because it allowed researchers to follow the same individuals from adolescence into adulthood and examine their social and economic well-being at different points during their lives. Ideally, a similar data set would document wealth ownership for the same individuals, and preferably families, over time. The PSID did begin to include questions about net worth during the 1980s, but the data are not sufficient to answer questions about long-term mobility.

Short-term mobility data are also available in recent panels of the Surveys of Consumer Finances. Again, these data do allow examination of short-term trends in mobility (see, e.g., Wolff 1998), but questions about escaping poverty and the effects of childhood experience on adult outcomes can only be answered with true longitudinal data. In the absence of such data, I relied on the simulation model to estimate patterns of wealth mobility. The results of short-term mobility estimates from the simulation model proved highly consistent with short-term estimates from survey data (see Table 3–6), and the model estimates are consistent with survey estimates on numerous other aspects of wealth accumulation and distribution (various other tables throughout this volume). While this does not imply that long-term estimates from the model are necessarily historically accurate, it does provide some degree of validation of the simulated estimates.

I presented the results of three separate sets of analyses in this chapter. In the first set, I examined movement into the top 10 percent of the wealth distribution between 1960 and 1995. I found that age, race, education, income, and family structure all affected the odds of becoming rich. The analyses also suggested that net of these other effects, baby boomers were more likely than others to move into the top of the distribution of household wealth. More than any other effect, however, having parents who were upwardly mobile increased the odds of mobility for offspring. Similar patterns were true in the second set of analyses, in which I explored movement out of poverty, that is, out of the bottom quintile of the wealth distribution. I found that nonwhites were much less likely than whites to escape poverty and that education, particularly higher education, was an important means of movement into the middle class. In the third set of analyses, I explored movement into the bottom quintile. The results of these analyses suggested that just as educational attainment may provide a route out of poverty, failing to finish high school dramatically increased the likelihood of movement into poverty. Having children and divorcing also increased the odds of becoming poor.

In the final section of this chapter, I discussed the process of inheritance. Some argue that inheritance is perhaps the single most important deterrent to wealth mobility. Because there is almost no available data on inheritance, I did not produce survey estimates of inheritance processes. For the same reason, I did not model inheritance processes explicitly in the simulation model. Of course, in the simulation model, the process of inheritance is captured by the change coefficients that age people and their wealth holdings. Because the distributional, accumulation, and mobility estimates produced by the model are highly consistent with known survey data, there is reason to believe that the inheritance processes that are included are somewhat accurate. However, in an ideal model, inheritance would be an influence that could be manipulated for experimental purposes. In many ways, the single most important point of this chapter is that while mobility and inheritance are central to understanding wealth ownership and distribution, we do not know enough about either process. Our lack of understanding stems largely from a lack of longitudinal data on the subjects. Simulation modeling can fill some of this gap, but it is not sufficient. Nor will our understanding of wealth inequality be sufficient until we have better data on long-term wealth ownership, mobility, and inheritance.

# CONCLUSIONS AND IMPLICATIONS

Wealth is a sacred trust which its possessor is bound to administer for the good of the community.

(Andrew Carnegie)

If a man is proud of his wealth, he should not be praised until it is known how he employs it.

(Socrates)

I began this volume with a discussion of the importance of wealth as an indicator of social and economic well-being. I observed that while current income can certainly be used to gauge advantage, the ownership of wealth has long separated the truly advantaged from the rest of the population. Social standing, political influence, and, of course, financial security all increase with wealth. Even a relatively small amount of savings can ensure against extreme financial hardship if a family faces the loss of a primary income earner, a major medical expense, or another relatively extreme financial crisis. Yet there is evidence that most families have very little savings. Indeed, empirical evidence from wealth surveys that resumed in the early 1980s, after many years in which they were not conducted, began to provide evidence that inequality of wealth ownership is much more extreme than income inequality. Despite this evidence, social scientists have focused almost exclusively on income in studies of social and economic inequality and related studies of lifetime patterns of mobility. While there is definitely a direct relationship between income and wealth, there is substantial variation in the two measures that suggests that part of the story of well-being is missing in studies that deal with income alone. Research that has been conducted on wealth ownership and inequality in the distribution of wealth has appeared in disparate places and has been almost exclusively descriptive, making it difficult to draw conclusions about the relationship between family-level wealth accumulation processes and aggregate patterns of wealth distribution.

My aim in this study was to synthesize data and theory from various sources to produce a longitudinal picture of household wealth distribution and accumulation processes between 1962 and 1995. Part of the reason that research on wealth ownership has been relatively limited is that data have been scarce. The Federal Reserve Board conducted a fairly comprehensive survey of wealth ownership in 1962. There were several surveys that addressed wealth ownership in the late 1960s and 1970s, but these were relatively weak both in their methodology and their coverage of wealth ownership. It was not until 1983 that the Federal Reserve Board resumed the Survey of Consumer Finances and again began to provide insight into patterns of wealth ownership. Using that survey, researchers have also isolated and examined some of the aggregate and family-level processes that create wealth distribution. In this study, I drew on these surveys to explore patterns of wealth ownership and distribution and to attempt to understand what has caused these patterns. I also drew on data from estate taxes and from the flow of funds. Estate taxes are the taxes filed by the wealthy at the time of death that provide one of the only true glimpses available of the portfolios of these families, and the flow of funds is the government's yearly estimate of total outstanding assets and debts owned by households (and others).

In addition to survey data, I drew extensively on estimates of wealth ownership from a microsimulation model. I used this model for three reasons. First, understanding wealth accumulation and distribution processes requires longitudinal data, but nearly all existing survey data are cross-sectional. The Surveys of Consumer Finances are cross sections, with the exceptions of the 1983–1986 and 1983–1989 panels. The panels are useful for estimating short-term changes in wealth ownership and short-term mobility patterns. However, to truly understand wealth ownership over time, longitudinal data that follow the same individuals and families over many years is necessary. Questions about lifetime patterns of mobility, for example, are central for both basic research and policy studies. Yet it is virtually impossible to study wealth mobility using existing survey data. The Panel Study of Income Dynamics (PSID), a truly longitudinal household survey, began to include wealth questions in the 1980s, but the coverage of this survey is not yet comprehensive enough to study long-term trends.

The simulation model synthesizes survey data, estate tax data, flow of funds estimates, and data from numerous other sources to produce PSID-like estimates of wealth ownership. Second, it is difficult to simultaneously explore patterns of wealth accumulation and distribution using traditional data sources such as survey data. In contrast, the simulation model allows me to tie together accumulation and distribution patterns because it replicates an entire system of behaviors and processes while survey data and other traditional data sources tend to isolate behaviors and patterns, obscuring the larger picture. The third reason that I drew on the simulation model is that it allowed me to experiment with hypothetical historical changes and other changes in behaviors and processes to explore their impact on wealth accumulation and distribution.

## Patterns of Wealth Distribution

In Part II of this book, I explored patterns of wealth distribution. I began by examining overall patterns of wealth distribution between 1962 and 1995, with more emphasis on more recent years. I used both survey data and the simulation model to produce the estimates and demonstrated a high degree of consistency between the two sources. The similarity was not entirely surprising as I aligned the simulation model to the survey data. However, it was important to validate the similarity of the estimates where comparable survey data were available before using the model to produce estimates for processes for which survey data did not exist. The findings suggested that between 1962 and 1995 there was extreme inequality in household wealth ownership in the United States and that inequality increased over that period. Gini coefficients for wealth ownership, an indicator of the degree of inequality ranging from 0 to 1, with 1 being complete inequality, ranged from 0.80 to 0.94. I drew on the simulation model to estimate patterns of wealth mobility over two decades, estimates that are not possible with traditional data sources. The results suggested that there was considerable persistence in household percentile position in the wealth distribution particularly between 1975 and 1995.

I also used the simulation model to explore the effects of a hypothetical increase in historical patterns of middle-class stock ownership and found considerable improvements in wealth distribution. The experiment did not increase middle-class wealth, but rather changed the way middle-class families invested the savings they had. The resulting decrease in inequality suggested that family-level portfolio behavior, particularly willingness to assume risk, affects who owns how much wealth. Evidence regarding the effectiveness of government efforts to encourage middle-class saving in riskier, less-traditional financial instruments such as Individual Retirement Accounts has been inconclusive. However, it may be that not enough time has elapsed to see real increases in saving or changes in the distribution of wealth. The results of the stock experiment suggest that perhaps over a longer time frame, when investments have a chance to grow and to entice even more investors, plans that encourage middle-class stock investing would increase saving and improve the distribution of wealth. Of course, this is only speculative, and longitudinal data on household saving and investment behavior is needed to explain the relationship among such incentive programs, household saving behavior, and the distribution of wealth.

Of course, in order for any real changes in the distribution of wealth to be realized, there must be changes in the upper segments of the distribution. That is, patterns of ownership among those who own the vast majority of all outstanding wealth must change. For this reason, I explored the wealth accumulation patterns of the very richest families in more detail and found that not only did the top 1 percent of wealth owners own vast amounts of wealth during the 1960s and 1990s, but their wealth holdings generally expanded during that time. I found that the rich kept relatively large portions of their savings in high-risk assets such as stocks and bonds. The estimates also indicated that the rich tended to be middle-aged, highly educated, and white. Perhaps the most dramatic finding was that there were virtually no nonwhite families among the top wealth holders.

To explore the effects of racial differences in wealth accumulation on wealth distribution and other outcomes, I used the simulation model to run an experiment that removed the direct effects of race on wealth accumulation. The experiment demonstrated that when these direct racial differences in asset ownership were removed starting in the early 1960s, wealth inequality declined considerably by the mid-1990s. Even with this change, however, top wealth holders were still predominantly white in the 1990s. The persistence of inequality reflected the other behaviors and processes that interact with wealth ownership and that differ by race. Educational attainment, for example, affects wealth ownership patterns, and there are marked racial differences in education. Similarly, fertility, marriage, divorce, life expectancy, and other behaviors and processes all affect wealth accumulation and all differ by race. The simulation results seemed to underscore the need for widespread changes in social inequality in order to change some of the basic patterns of wealth inequality that have been persistent for decades.

I also explored patterns of wealth ownership among the nonwealthy, those in the middle and lower portions of the distribution. Survey and simulation estimates both indicated that these families owned very few assets in the years between 1962 and 1995, particularly relative to top wealth holders. Because my primary goal in the early stages of this book was to describe patterns of wealth ownership, I again focused on the portfolio behavior of these families and explored the fact that their tendency to buy certain assets and debts affected wealth distribution among all families. The survey estimates suggested an association between being middle class or poor and owning fewer high-risk assets. Rather than owning stocks and bonds like wealthy families, if the middle class and poor owned anything, they owned the primary residence and other low-risk assets such as cash accounts. Likewise, the survey estimates suggested higher propensities among the middle class and poor to hold debts. The wealthy did have debt, but their debt was a much lower proportion of net worth than that of the middle and lower classes. Another pattern that began to emerge in my explorations of the wealth ownership of the middle class and poor was the positive relationship between family composition and wealth ownership. Having children reduced wealth ownership nearly unilaterally, and because the middle class and poor tend to have more children than the wealthy, they bore the brunt of the negative effects of family structure more heavily than the rich did.

What is difficult to determine from existing data, even the simulation model, is whether owning low-risk assets leads families to become or remain middle class or whether middle-class families have lower tolerances for risk. Similarly, it is difficult to determine the direction of causation between debt ownership or family composition and wealth. It is possible, however, to explore the implications of these associations for overall wealth distribution using the simulation model. In Chapter 5, I used two experiments to examine the distributional impacts of debt holding and family composition of the middle class and poor. The results of the first experiment indicated that decreasing the debt burden of middle-class and poor families would redistribute wealth away from the rich toward the poor. The implication of these findings is that middle-class and poor families need to be able to raise children *and* save money if inequalities in the distribution of wealth are to be alleviated.

In Chapter 6, I used a somewhat unique method to describe patterns in the distribution of wealth across generations. Researchers have long been interested in intergenerational differences in well-being and have developed methods of using cross-sectional data to examine these differences. A considerable amount of research has developed that focuses on baby boomers and their parents. Much of this research is rooted in questions about whether the Social Security system and related government programs will be able to sustain the shock of the baby boomers' retirement. Basic research also questions whether the baby boomers might be one of the first generations to do worse than their parents. Arguments about cohort crowding and resultant increases in competition for educational and career opportunities, combined with changing demographic patterns such as delays in childbearing, have spawned arguments that this generation may face difficulty financing retirement. Using the simulation model, I projected the wealth ownership of baby boomers into the future to explore their well-being at retirement. I also used the model to compare wealth ownership and mobility patterns of those born during the baby boom with the wealth ownership and mobility patterns of those who were their *actual*, same-sex parents (in the model) at a comparable age (i.e., I compared the wealth of baby boomers at age 30 with the group of people who were their actual, same-sex parents at age 30).

I found that baby boomers will generally do better than their actual parents at retirement age, but consistent with Manchester's report for the Congressional Budget Office, the gains made by baby boomers were not uniform (Manchester 1993). That is, my findings suggested that older baby boomers and those who graduated from college and attained even higher levels of education would do particularly well. By contrast, married couples with only one earner, single women, and nonhomeowners would be at a disadvantage. The results suggested that baby boomers have had, and will continue to have, considerably more wealth than their parents did at all stages of the life cycle. The analyses revealed strong and consistent patterns of continual increases in net worth over the life cycle and provided no support for the life-cycle hypothesis of postretirement dissaving. Similarly, the results suggested that patterns of upward wealth mobility are more pronounced among baby boomers. Again, these patterns were widespread in the baby boom generation, but education, marriage, and investing in high-risk assets were among the things that made upward mobility even more likely for baby boomers. The consistent policy message of these analyses was that there is little reason to be particularly concerned about baby boomers, that is, beyond general concerns about wealth inequality.

## *Aggregate Influences, Family Process, and Wealth*

In Part III, I examined the aggregate-level and microlevel factors that lead to the patterns of wealth distribution that I explored in the first part. I also examined patterns of wealth mobility, drawing almost exclusively on the simulation model. I explored the impact of economic and social trends on wealth inequality, with an emphasis on demographic trends and trends in financial and real estate markets. The findings suggested that cohort size decreased inequality, contrary to some research on the subject. I drew on Easterlin's work (see, e.g., Easterlin 1987 or Easterlin, Schaeffer, and Macunovich 1993) and argued that competition for educational resources and difficult labor market conditions can affect changes in behavior and norms about work, marriage, and childbearing. I simulated a decrease in historical rates of female labor force participation for baby boomers that provided support for these arguments.

Another simulation experiment, this one examining the distributional impact of the 1995 stock market boom, pointed to the importance of market trends in determining the distribution of wealth. The rich benefited most from the boom, of course, because they owned the most stock. Changes in middle-class patterns of stock ownership that began during the 1980s and continued into the 1990s likely mediated the distributional impact of that stock boom. That is, because middle-class families began to buy more stock during the 1980s and 1990s, many of them also benefited during the boom years in the mid 1990s. Had middle-class stock ownership not increased prior to the boom, the effect of the boom on inequality would likely have been greater. Because many middle-class families own their own homes, real estate market trends appear to have less of an impact on wealth distribution than stock market trends.

I then focused on the effects of age, race, family structure, income, education, and other individual and family processes on wealth accumulation, life-cycle patterns of wealth mobility, and the aggregate-level distribution of wealth among all families. The survey and simulated estimates that I found provided support for the life-cycle hypothesis of saving, although there was less evidence of a dramatic decline in wealth after retirement than the life-cycle hypothesis would predict. In my analyses of the effects of individual and family behaviors on wealth accumulation, I discussed the results of an experiment that increased the educational attainment of non-whites. The results suggested that returns to education for nonwhites were considerable. Indeed, it did not take long for the change to increase the median wealth held by nonwhites nearly 20 percent above historical levels. I found similarly dramatic effects of family structure on wealth ownership and mobility. Marriage increased wealth ownership; divorce and children generally decreased it. The effects of marriage and divorce declined over the 30 years in the study, but they continued to be central explanatory variables.

Perhaps more than any other chapter, my examination of wealth mobility in Chapter 9 highlighted the need for improved data on wealth ownership. Some of the answers to the most fundamental questions about wealth accumulation and distribution lie in life-cycle patterns of wealth mobility. Yet answers to these questions continue to elude researchers because longitudinal data on wealth ownership are simply not available. The estimates I included in this book, both survey and simulation, are likely highly accurate for any given year, particularly the years in which surveys were conducted. There are still questions about whether the surveys contain enough high-wealth families to accurately estimate the tail of the wealth distribution, but the inclusion of high-income samples, combined with Federal Reserve Board sample weights, provide a fair amount of assurance that the estimates are, indeed, representative of the population. However, because there is so little data on changes in wealth ownership, my estimates of change processes are more tentative. Validating them against the survey data that do exist suggests that the estimates are highly accurate, but without longitudinal survey data to provide more comprehensive evidence of patterns of change these must be regarded as estimates. And so I end this book in the hope that I will someday be able to write a companion on wealth mobility that can draw on both simulation and survey estimates to provide a more comprehensive picture of the way wealth ownership changes over the life course and the processes that enhance or impede mobility.

While it was tempting to run the model with all of the experimental conditions included, in an effort to create a sort of utopian society, I resisted the temptation. Such an experiment would not only be unrealistic but would also introduce so much room for error in the estimates as to be wholly uninterpretable. In other words, while it is likely that the results of such a combined experiment would produce relatively low levels of inequality, the results would be unbelievable both practically and from a modeling perspective. The experimental results that I did present aimed to isolate and explore the effects of particular processes; combining all of the experiments would detract from the purity, perhaps the most important advantage, of the experiments.

## *Research and Policy Issues*

At the start of this book, I mentioned an important caveat. I cautioned against interpreting the simulated results that I discussed in the book as fact, because they are, indeed, just estimates. When I issued this warning, I also said that I hoped that the estimates I presented in the book, both those from survey data and those derived from the simulation model, might raise questions for researchers interested in both basic research and policy issues. One very basic question that remains is what will happen to wealth inequality in the future? The evidence I presented was consistent with other research that indicates wealth inequality is quite extreme. The most recent trends that I discussed suggested, however, that inequality had improved slightly in the mid 1990s. The 1998 Survey of Consumer Finances will indicate whether this is a trend or merely an anomaly in an otherwise consistently worsening social problem. The new SCF data will not, however, be able to provide more insight into trends in mobility. As I have argued throughout this volume, longitudinal data on wealth own-ership is needed to answer such questions. Future data from the Panel Study of Income Dynamics may fill this gap, but even then the processes underlying patterns of mobility may not be evident without complemen-tary in-depth investigation into the lives of both those who are upwardly mobile and those who are downwardly mobile.

Similarly, the experiments I presented examining the persistence of racial differences in wealth ownership highlighted an extreme difference in the well-being of whites and nonwhites. Oliver and Shapiro's (1995) more detailed investigation into the nature of black-white differences in wealth ownership highlighted the same dramatic disparities, albeit for a shorter period of time. What is not obvious is the reason that these dif-ferences persist. My experiment that simulated removing racial differences in wealth accumulation patterns indicated that while portfolio behavior differences between whites and nonwhites were an important factor leading to racial differences in wealth ownership and resultant wealth inequality, not all of the difference was explained by portfolio behavior alone. Demographic differences, differences in education, income differences, and fertility patterns are all likely involved as well. What exactly is the nature of these differences? And, more importantly, which of the behaviors and processes should be changed to produce more racial equality of wealth ownership? Finally, I dealt here with differences in wealth ownership between whites and nonwhites because the representation of minorities in the Surveys of Consumer Finances was rather weak. Oliver and Shapiro focused on differences in wealth ownership between whites and blacks. How Hispanics, Asians, and other racial minorities accumulate wealth is certainly an important part of the process of wealth accumulation and one that deserves further attention. Because Asians appear to accumulate wealth more quickly than blacks, understanding the differences in wealth ownership and accumulation patterns between blacks and Asians, for example, might point to some of the policy interventions that would affect changes in black wealth accumulation processes.

Another policy tool deserving further investigation is the estate tax. My simulation experiment suggested that of all the interventions I examined, raising estate tax rates was the single most effective means of redistributing wealth. This is not entirely surprising, as estate taxes and inheritance taxes are the only means by which we currently take wealth away from the wealthy and use it for other purposes. Using either of these taxes more vigorously, or instituting a wealth tax of the sort proposed by Wolff (1995b), would likely be an effective way to reduce wealth inequality. As I mentioned in Chapter 9, however, we are unsure as a nation how we feel about intergenerational transfers of wealth. On one hand, we like the notion of equality of opportunity. We like to think that we give every person an equal opportunity to do well in life. If we truly believed this, we would completely redistribute wealth at death by disallowing bequests to future generations. On the other hand, we support the notion that each person should have the right to dispose of his or her property as he or she sees fit. Deciding that the government would take and redistribute one's wealth at death is simply inconsistent with this notion. The bottom line, then, is that we need to decide how much inequality we are willing to tolerate, determine the level of estate or wealth tax that is consistent with that idea, and implement that tax. At the same time, we should address issues of inequality in educational attainment and income in order to create a more level starting ground at whatever levels of inequality we decide to tolerate.

Wealth inequality is still an unresolved issue in America. Levels of wealth inequality are so extreme that most people hardly register any wealth at all, yet wealth is one of the central indicators of financial well-being and security. Wealth inequality was not always as extreme as it was in the early 1990s; indeed, it got considerably worse during the 1980s and 1990s than it had been in the preceding decades. The most recent Federal Reserve Board survey available as I write this book suggested, however, that there might have been some improvement in wealth inequality in the middle of the 1980s. Even if this improvement is genuine, and even if it lasts, inequality in the ownership of wealth is still much more extreme than inequality in income. In other words, it is going to take much more than minor improvements to make wealth inequality less of a problem.

To address this fundamental social problem, we must first acknowledge that it exists. There is so little written on wealth that even many social scientists are unaware of the extreme nature of inequality in its ownership. Once we acknowledge that this is indeed a problem, we need to decide what we want to do about it. Are we going to continue to let vast fortunes transfer from one generation to the next perpetuating the problem? Are we going to use estate taxes, wealth taxes, capital gains taxes, and other policy instruments to lessen the problem? If so, we need to decide how much redistribution is desirable and act on this decision. Finally, we need to create the structural supports that will allow us to further level the playing field. We need to improve access to and attainment of education. Racial inequalities in high school graduation rates no doubt contribute to racial differences in wealth ownership, differences that will persist even if active measures are taken to redistribute wealth. We need to protect the elderly from paying more than their share in taxes. Finally, we need to level income inequalities that also lead to the persistence of wealth inequalities. The collective payoff of increased equality will certainly be worth the effort.

# APPENDIX: RESEARCH DESIGN AND MEASUREMENT ISSUES

## Wealth Definitions

Researchers disagree about the appropriate definition of wealth (see, e.g., Levy and Michel 1991:41 42; Wolff 1987a, 1993, 1994). Some suggest that consumer durables such as automobiles and household appliances should not be considered wealth because they are not fungible (i.e., easily turned into cash) and because their resale value understates their value to the owner (Wolff 1993:37). Similarly, Wolff (1993:37) suggested that retirement assets such as social security assets should not be considered wealth because they are not marketable. Empirical evidence also suggests that including pensions as wealth significantly alters the distribution of wealth among families (McDermed, Clark, and Allen 1989). In my simulated estimates, I included the value of vehicles that are one of the only assets many families own and for which market values are readily available, but I excluded other consumer durables. I also included the value of IRA and Keogh accounts (both of which are fungible) but excluded other pension assets and social security. I included these wealth types in order to be consistent with other published estimates of wealth ownership and distribution.

## Validation of Survey and Simulated Estimates

Throughout this volume, particularly in the early chapters, I included both survey estimates and simulated estimates at least partially in order to validate the simulated estimates. In Tables A–1, A–2, and A–3, I present additional comparisons on my survey estimates and simulation results with actual survey estimates published elsewhere. Consistent with the results presented elsewhere in this book, the results in Tables A–1

Table A-1. *Household Net Worth and Financial Wealth, 1983–1995: Comparison with Wolff (1998)*

| | 1983 | | | 1989 | | | 1992 | | | 1995 | | |
|---|---|---|---|---|---|---|---|---|---|---|---|---|
| | *Survey – Wolff* | *Survey – Chapter 3* | *Simulated* | *Survey – Wolff* | *Survey – Chapter 3* | *Simulated* | *Survey – Wolff* | *Survey – Chapter 3* | *Simulated* | *Survey – Wolff* | *Survey – Chapter 3* | *Simulated* |
| *Net worth* | | | | | | | | | | | | |
| Mean | 170,544 | 170,550 | 173,200 | 195,382 | 195,382 | 195,379 | 189,947 | 189,948 | 190,700 | 175,486 | 175,485 | 176,385 |
| Median | 43,800 | 43,801 | 48,700 | 46,884 | 46,881 | 47,181 | 39,997 | 39,995 | 40,721 | 39,150 | 39,146 | 41,000 |
| Percent with zero or negative | 15.5 | 16 | 17 | 17.9 | 18 | 19 | 18.0 | 18 | 19 | 18.5 | 19 | 19 |
| *Financial wealth* | | | | | | | | | | | | |
| Mean | 123,761 | 123,762 | 124,501 | 145,840 | 145,839 | 146,750 | 144,805 | 144,804 | 146,175 | 134,650 | 134,650 | 135,050 |
| Median | 9,459 | 9,459 | 9,580 | 11,164 | 11,166 | 11,212 | 9,367 | 9,366 | 9,418 | 8,537 | 8,537 | 8,613 |
| Percent with zero or negative | 25.7 | 26 | 27 | 26.8 | 27 | 27 | 28.2 | 28 | 29 | 28.7 | 29 | 29 |

*Note:* Survey estimates labeled "Wolff" are Wolff's (1998:135) estimates from the Surveys of Consumer Finances. Wolff reported these estimates in his Table 1 in 1995 dollars. I have converted them to 1990 dollars (using a standard CPI-U) for comparison. Survey estimates labeled "Chapter 3" are replicated from Table 3–1 in the current volume. These are the author's calculations from the Surveys of Consumer Finances. Simulated results are also replicated from Table 3–1 for comparison. All values are adjusted to 1990 dollars, based on a standard CPI-U.

Table A–2. *Distribution of Net Worth, 1983–1995:*
*Comparison with Wolff (1998)*

| | Share Owned by Top 1% | | |
| --- | --- | --- | --- |
| | Survey – Wolff | Survey – Chapter 3 | Simulated |
| 1983 | 33.8 | 33.8 | 34.8 |
| 1989 | 37.4 | 37.4 | 38.5 |
| 1992 | 37.2 | 37.2 | 39.1 |
| 1995 | 38.5 | 38.5 | 39.1 |

*Note:* Cells indicate the percentage of net worth held by households in the top 1 percent of the household wealth distribution.
Survey estimates labeled "Wolff" are Wolff's (1998:136) estimates
from the Surveys of Consumer Finances, Table 2. Survey estimates
labeled "Chapter 3" are replicated from Table 3–2 in the current
volume. These are the author's calculations from the Surveys of
Consumer Finances. Simulated results are also replicated from
Table 3–2 for comparison. All values are adjusted to 1990 dollars,
based on a standard CPI-U.

through A–3 demonstrate a high degree of consistency across all three
sources. Table A–1 includes estimates of the mean and median net worth
and financial wealth for all households in 1983, 1989, 1992, and 1995.
All survey estimates are from the Surveys of Consumer Finances, and all
simulated results are from the simulation model. My survey estimates and
the simulated estimates are both replicated here from Table 3–1 for comparison. Wolff's estimates are from his 1998 paper appearing in the *Journal
of Economic Perspectives*. I used a standard CPI-U to convert Wolff's estimates to 1990 dollars so that they are comparable to my own estimates.
The table also includes estimates of the percentage of families in the survey
or model for that year that had zero or negative net worth. I included more
significant digits in Wolff's estimates of the percentage of families with
zero or negative net worth in this table because this is how Wolff presented the numbers in his table. There are few differences in the estimates

Table A–3. *Median Ratio of Net Worth to Income, Comparison with Congressional Budget Office (1993)*

|  | 1962 | | 1989 | |
|---|---|---|---|---|
|  | *Survey –*<br>*CBO* | *Survey –*<br>*Chapter 6* | *Survey –*<br>*CBO* | *Survey –*<br>*Chapter 6* |
| *Household head age 25–34* | | | | |
| All households | 0.25 | 0.24 | 0.42 | 0.42 |
| Top income quintile | 0.63 | 0.62 | 1.07 | 1.07 |
| Fourth income quintile | 0.57 | 0.58 | 0.43 | 0.44 |
| Third income quintile | 0.32 | 0.32 | 0.45 | 0.45 |
| Second income quintile | 0.14 | 0.14 | 0.21 | 0.23 |
| Bottom income quintile | 0.02 | 0.02 | 0.02 | 0.02 |
| *Household head age 35–44* | | | | |
| All households | 1.19 | 1.20 | 1.23 | 1.23 |
| Top income quintile | 1.61 | 1.61 | 2.08 | 2.09 |
| Fourth income quintile | 1.64 | 1.64 | 1.32 | 1.32 |
| Third income quintile | 1.19 | 1.19 | 1.73 | 1.73 |
| Second income quintile | 0.72 | 0.73 | 0.84 | 0.85 |
| Bottom income quintile | 0.17 | 0.16 | 0.17 | 0.17 |

*Note*: Survey estimates labeled "CBO" are estimates from Manchester's (1993) report for the Congressional Budget Office, estimated from the 1962 Survey of the Financial Characteristics of Consumers and the 1989 Survey of Consumer Finances. Manchester reported these estimates in her Table 3, p. 13. Survey estimates labeled "Chapter 6" are replicated from Table 6–1 in the current volume. These are the author's calculations from the same survey data.

across the various sources. The simulated estimates are consistent with other published estimates as well. These comparisons are simply a sample of what I might have presented.

Table A–2 includes estimates of the percentage of wealth owned by families in the top 1 percent of the wealth distribution. Again, the table compares estimates from Wolff (1998) with my survey estimates and the simulated estimates. The cells in the table are the percentage of total net worth owned by those in the top 1 percent. I include these estimates to demonstrate that (1) my survey estimates are consistent with others' estimates from survey data, and (2) the simulation model produces distributional estimates that are largely consistent with survey estimates. I included only the top 1 percent of wealth holders in the table because including other segments of the distribution did not add new information. The estimates in Table A–2 demonstrate that my survey estimates are identical to Wolff's. This was true for other segments of the distribution as well. The simulated estimates suggest that the top wealth-holding families actually owned more wealth in the years included in the table. This higher estimate most likely reflects the alignment of the simulation model with estate tax data. Because estate tax data more accurately reflect the true wealth holdings of the rich, and because the rich are likely underrepresented in survey data even in the SCF's high-income sample, including estate tax data in the estimate naturally increases the level of inequality. I discussed estate tax data and their role in the simulation model in more detail in Chapter 2. Barry Johnson and his coauthors offer even greater detail on the comparability of estate tax estimates and survey estimates of wealth ownership (Johnson 1994a, 1994b; Johnson and Eller 1998; Johnson and Woodburn 1994).

The estimates I present in this volume are consistent with published estimates other than Wolff's, and they are also largely consistent across variables. Table A–3 compares my survey estimates of the median ratio of net worth to income with estimates published by the Congressional Budget Office (Manchester 1993). Both my estimates and Manchester's estimates for 1962 are from the Survey of the Financial Characteristics of Consumers. For 1989, both sets of estimates are from the Survey of Consumer Finances. As in the previous two tables, our estimates are nearly identical. Any differences are minor and largely due to rounding differences and slight differences in calculating variable definitions and statistics. My survey estimates are comparable to the estimates I included in Table 6–1. Because Table 6–1 did not include simulated estimates, I do not include them here. Estimates of the ratio of net worth to income from the simulation model for these two years, however, are comparable to the estimates included in the table.

### Simulation Issues

### Stochastic Equations for Initial Values

At each stage in the operation of the simulation model, I used stochastic equations to produce expected values for wealth ownership (yes/no), wealth value (monetary amount), and other aspects of wealth accumulation. The first part of this section describes the equations, estimated on the 1962 Survey of the Financial Characteristics of Consumers (SFCC), used in assigning wealth values to the model's initial sample from the 1960 census. I used these equations to impute ownership and value for each of the assets and debts assigned to the starting sample in the simulation model. The assets included: primary residence, other real estate, business assets, vehicles, stocks and bonds, certificates of deposit, whole life insurance, and other financial assets. The liabilities included: mortgages on the primary residence, other mortgages, and all other debts. There were two dependent variables for each asset and each debt. The first was a dichotomous variable indicating whether the family owned the asset or debt, and the second was a continuous variable for owners indicating the total current value (in current, logged dollars) of the family's holdings. Using a Heckman correction for sample selection bias (Greene 1993) did not significantly alter the estimates. The independent variables included: race (nonwhite = 1), education dummies (did not attend high school, completed some high school, completed high school, completed some college, completed college or more), total household earnings, age (and age squared) for household head, number of children under age 18 still living at home, and marital status. I used logistic regression to estimate the coefficients for the ownership equations and generalized least squares to produce the value estimates. I do not include the coefficient estimates here to conserve space.

## Stochastic Update Equations

Once initial wealth values were assigned to each family for each asset and debt, the values had to be "aged" or "updated." In this step, the ownership (yes/no) and value of each asset and each debt was aged three years for each family. I used additional stochastic equations to accomplish this (the equations are "micro" because they are estimated on family-level data, and they are "dynamic" because they are estimated on panel data and include a lagged term). The equations indicate how the probability of ownership and the value of the family's holdings should increase or decrease over a three-year period as a function of demographic characteristics of the family. To estimate these equations, I used the 1983–1986 Panel of the Survey of Consumer Finances. Using the 1983–1989 panel did not change the coefficient estimates or the resulting simulation results appreciably. I opted to rely primarily on the 1983–1986 estimates in order to have the model update more often.

The model can update wealth every six years using the 1983–1989 SCF panel instead; when this panel is used to age wealth, distributional outcomes do not vary considerably from outcomes obtained when the 1983–1986 panel is used. There were again two dependent variables for each asset and each debt in the model (same categories listed above and in Chapter 2). To produce the coefficient estimates, I used logistic regression to estimate coefficients for ownership and generalized least squares regression to estimate value coefficients. The independent variables included a lagged ownership (did the family own the asset/debt in the period three years prior?) or lagged value (what was the value of the family's holdings of this asset/debt in the period three years prior?), the race of household head (nonwhite = 1), education dummies for the educational attainment of the household head (did not attend high school, completed some high school, completed high school, completed some college, completed college or more), average total household earnings over the three years included in the panel, the age (and age squared) of household head, the number of children under age 18 still living at home, marital status, interactions between education and prior ownership, and interactions between earnings and prior ownership.

The first set of equations was used to assign initial wealth values in 1962. In 1965, the microdynamic ownership equations were used to predict the probability of ownership for each asset and debt for each family, that is, to "age" their wealth. To determine ownership, a random number was drawn from a probability distribution. If the family's calculated probability was greater than the random probability, the family was assigned a value of unity for ownership. Otherwise the family was assigned a value of zero for ownership. Next, the value equation was used to predict a value for all families who were determined to own stock in 1965. This was repeated for all families who were determined to own each asset and debt.

## Alignment with Historical Data

Once aged wealth values were assigned to each family for each asset and debt, the estimates were reestimated and constrained by known values from additional data sources. In this step, I separated families into top wealth holders and non–top wealth holders and constrained the estimates of these families separately. I used regression equations estimated on group-level (rather than at the "micro" or family level) to estimate a proportion of families owning a particular asset/debt and the total value of the holdings of the asset or debt for that group. I then reestimated the module's wealth estimates for each family so that the total for the demographic group of which that family was a part was constrained by the value produced by the group-level regression equation. The basic procedure for reestimating the aged values of wealth ownership and value separately for top wealth holders starts with detailed cross tabulations from the Department of the Treasury's estate tax data. I used cross tabulations of the data because more detailed data were not available. Including more information about the estate tax filers would have allowed me to identify the individuals whose records were included. I estimated stochastic equations on this data, and I used the equations to produce a predicted value for each of 80 demographic groups.

The cross tabs:

a.) are for 1962, 1969, 1972, 1976, 1983, 1986, 1989, and 1992
b.) cross eight asset categories and one debt category (stocks, bonds, cash, life insurance, annuities, real estate, business assets, other financial assets, and debts) against 80 demographic groups, defined by gender (male/female), marital status (single, married, widowed, divorced), and eight age groups (under 40, 40–49, 50–59, 60–69, 70–74, 75–79, 80–84, 85 and older)
c.) contain the proportion of each group that owned each asset and each debt and the total value of each asset and debt owned by that group.

Because wealth is a family-level variable, I aligned wealth ownership of families not of individuals. However, the unit of analysis for estate tax data is the individual. I treated single, widowed, and divorced individuals as separate families. For married couples who die and file estate taxes, however, I needed to estimate the wealth of their family based on the individual's estate. I assumed that the deceased individual owned half of the family's wealth. That is, I doubled the reported wealth to get the family's total wealth. This method of aligning based on individual-level data also prevents another problem. In the simulation model, siblings and other family members who continue to live together into adulthood are considered separate households. By many other accounts, such as the census, these individuals would be considered a single household if they were to continue to live together, so the model tends to have relatively more single-person households. If we were to align these as households, single-person households in the model would have a disproportionate amount of wealth. By aligning against what is essentially person-level data, we prevent this problem from arising. I estimated separate equations for: unmarried males, unmarried females, and married couples because different processes underlie the accumulation of wealth by these groups.

The basic procedure for reestimating the aged values of wealth ownership and value separately for non–top wealth holders starts with detailed cross tabulations from the Surveys of Consumer Finances. I used cross tabulations of the data to get at group means and then used regression to capture patterns underlying the cross tabs. The cross tabs:

a.) are for 1962, 1970, 1983, 1986, 1989, and 1992
b.) are produced for non–top wealth holders only (we eliminate all families who had a net worth in the given year that would have been greater than the estate tax filing requirement)
c.) cross 10 asset categories and one debt category (stocks, bonds, checking and savings accounts, certificates of deposit, IRAs, other financial assets, the primary residence, other real estate, business assets, vehicles, mortgages, and total debts) against 40 demographic groups – defined by gender (male/female), marital status (single, married, widowed, divorced), and five age groups (under 40, 40–49, 50–59, 60–69, 70 and older)
d.) contain the proportion of each group that owned each asset and each debt and the total value of each asset and debt owned by that group.

The predicted values from the equations used to smooth the estate tax and SCF data were then used to produce predicted ownership and value estimates (for 1962, 1965, 1968, 1971, 1974, 1977, 1980, 1983, 1986, 1989, 1992, 1995, and any future years) for 150 demographic groups. The 150 demographic groups include:

a.) 80 groups of top wealth holders defined by gender, marital status (married, single, widowed, divorced), and age (under 40, 40–49, 50–54, 55–59, 60–64, 65–69, 70–74, 75–79, 80–84, 85 and older) b.) 70 groups of non–top wealth holders defined by gender, marital status (married, single, widowed, divorced), and age (under 40, 40–49, 50–59, 60–69, 70 and older).

In each year, after the microdynamic equations were used to update all families' wealth ownership (yes/no) and value, in all 14 wealth categories, the families were separated into one of the 150 demographic groups. The proportion of families in the first demographic group owning the first asset was determined from the model, and this number was compared to the alignment number. If the model number was different from the alignment number, the model number was increased or decreased to equal the alignment number. This procedure was repeated for ownership and value, for each of the 14 assets and debts and for each of the 150 demographic groups. The equations described include hundreds of coefficients. In order to conserve space, I do not reproduce the coefficients here.

### The Use of the Mortality Multiplier

The first step in the alignment procedure described above was determining the proportion of the population that should be considered top wealth holders in each year (where top wealth holder is defined as those who would have had to file an estate tax in that year had they died). Table 2–1 lists the net worth cutoff (in current and constant dollars) for filing an estate tax with the Internal Revenue Service at death. The remainder of this appendix describes the process by which I calculated the proportion of the population to be aligned as wealthy.

I used estate tax data from the Department of the Treasury to determine the proportion of the population that should be aligned as top wealth holders in any given year. In calculating this proportion, certain challenges arose. In particular, the "slice" of the population that is wealthy varies over time because the cut-off for filing an estate tax has changed over time, and because our definition of *wealthy* is those who would have filed an estate tax had they died in that year. In addition, the proportion of the population who are top wealth holders varies by demographic group. For example, a higher proportion of widowed females age 75 and older than single females under 40 would be top wealth holders because the older group includes many women who are "rich widows" and because the younger women have not had time to accumulate significant assets.

Moreover, the most accurate available data on top wealth holders comes from estate tax records filed with the Department of the Treasury; these data are the likely source of information on the proportion of families that are rich. However, this data contains information on a sample of individuals who are rich and have died rather than a sample of all the rich. It would be relatively simple to determine the proportion of all families who have died using widely available mortality rates (the number of live people = the number of dead people / the mortality rate). Yet mortality rates vary not only by demographic group (e.g., women live longer than men) but also by the amount of wealth to which an individual has access. As a result, we need to determine the number of living top wealth holders using demographic group- and wealth-specific mortality rates. A further complication with using estate tax data for this purpose is the fact that the data contain information on individuals rather than families, even though wealth is a family-level variable.

Given these complications, I used the method outlined here for determining what proportion of families are top wealth holders.

**For each demographic group, we know:**

$P$ = probability of death$_t$ (where $t$ = 1962–1995)
*Source:* Vital Statistics

$P|r$ = probability of death given that the person is rich (at $t$ = 1985)
$P|p$ = probability of death given that the person is poor (at $t$ = 1985)
*Source:* 1980–1989 NLMS (National Longitudinal Mortality Survey)

# dead rich$_t$
*Source:* Estate Tax Data

$$\left(\frac{P|r}{P}\right)\left(\frac{\#\,\text{total rich}}{\text{total both}}\right) + \left(\frac{P|p}{P}\right)\left(\frac{\#\,\text{total rich}}{\text{total both}}\right) = 1 \text{ at each } t$$

**We want: total rich$_t$, where:**

$$\#\,\text{dead rich}_t \times \frac{1}{(P|r)_t} = \text{total rich}_t$$

or

$$\#\,\text{dead rich}_t \times \left(\frac{\text{total rich}}{\text{dead rich}}\right)_t = \text{total rich}_t$$

**We need:**

$$(P|r)_t \quad \text{which} = \left(\frac{\text{total rich}}{\text{dead rich}}\right)_t$$

**We assume:**

$$\frac{(P|r)_{85}}{P_{85}} = K(\text{constant})$$

**We can compute:**

$$\frac{(P|r)_t}{(P)_t} = K$$

calculating K from our assumption and rearranging to get:

$$K \times P_t = (P|r)_t$$

We then invert $(P|r)_t$ and multiply this times the number of dead rich from the estate tax data to get the TOTAL rich for that year. Since we want living rich only, we must subtract dead rich from total rich.

**For example:** If P|r in 1985 (from NLMS) is 0.5 and P in 1985 (from vital statistics) 0.8, then K = 0.5/0.8 or 0.625. Then, if P in 1965 is 0.8, we multiply 0.8 by K (or 0.625) and get 0.5 (the probability of death given that the person is rich). We then multiply 1/0.5 by the number of dead rich people in 1965 to get the total number of rich people in 1965. Since we only want the living rich, we must subtract the number of dead rich from the number of total rich.

**Problem with assuming that K is constant over time:**
We know that:

$$1. \left(\frac{P|r}{P}\right)(\#\,\text{rich}) + \left(\frac{P|p}{P}\right)(\#\,\text{poor}) = \#\text{total}$$

And we assume that:

$$2. \left(\frac{P|r}{P}\right) = K$$

We could have assumed that

$$3. \left( \frac{\# \text{total rich}}{\text{total poor}} \right) = K$$

which is actually simpler. This second assumption (3) does not utilize our knowledge about the probability of death and, for that reason, may be the worse assumption. However, given the identity expressed in (1), we know that if we assume (2) we cannot assume that $\frac{(P|p)}{P} = K$ because we are fixing every other term in the equation and $\frac{(P|p)}{P}$, therefore, must be allowed to vary. What this means is that we are assuming that the ratio of the death rate of the rich to the death rate of everyone is constant but the death rate of the poor to the death rate of everyone is not constant.

### Alignment with Aggregate Data

The second stage of alignment is alignment of the value of wealth holdings for all families with historical aggregate wealth estimates. The Federal Reserve Board calculates yearly estimates of more than 30 categories of wealth held by American families and publishes this data in the *Balance Sheets for the U.S. Economy*, alternatively known as the flow of funds (Federal Reserve System 1995). These are the same aggregate estimates I used in the book to indicate total outstanding household wealth within various categories. I used this national accounts data to align most assets and debts, including corporate stock holdings, every third year between 1962 and 1995 (Federal Reserve System 1995).

I used eleven assets and liabilities derived from the flow of funds C.9 tables for the household sector, table B.100 (Federal Reserve System, 1995). I included six categories of financial assets, two real assets, and three debts. Flow of funds household sector wealth estimates also include the wealth holdings of nonprofit organizations. In order to remove the wealth of nonprofit organizations, I subtracted one-sixteenth of the value of each asset and liability per the recommendations of flow of funds staff members. Where our category consists of more than one flow of funds category, I summed the FOF estimates for each year. The amount of wealth I attributed to nonprofit organizations and removed from the FOF was consistent with independent estimates of the wealth held by nonprofit organizations. Beginning in 1969, the FOF began to track separately investments in bank personal trusts (line 31). I used the Z.7 tables to estimate the proportion of investments in bank personal trusts that were held in stocks and added this value to our stocks category. Flow of funds household sector wealth estimates also include the wealth holdings of nonprofit organizations. In order to remove the wealth of nonprofits, I subtracted one-sixteenth of the value of each asset and liability per the recommendations of flow of funds staff members.

Where my category consisted of more than one flow of funds category, I summed the FOF estimates for each year. The amount of wealth I attributed to nonprofit organizations and removed from the FOF was consistent with independent estimates of the wealth held by nonprofit organizations. Beginning in 1969, the FOF began to track separately investments in bank personal trusts (line 31). I used the Z.7 tables to estimate the proportion of investments in bank personal trusts that were held in stocks and added this value to our stocks category. I refer to the first financial asset category as stocks and include in this category the flow of funds categories corporate equities (line 28) and mutual fund shares (line 27). My bonds category includes the flow of funds categories U.S. government securities (line 19), tax-exempt securities (line 23), and corporate and foreign bonds (line 24). Checking and savings accounts refers to FOF categories checkable deposits and currency (line 14) and small time and savings deposits (line 15). Certificates of deposit and money market accounts refers to FOF categories large time deposits (line 16) and money market fund shares (line 17). My cash value of life insurance category refers to the FOF category life insurance reserves (line 29).

Our other financial assets category includes FOF categories mortgages owed to the household (line 25) and miscellaneous assets (line 34). The two real assets I consider are the value of the primary residence and business assets. The value of the primary residence includes the FOF categories owner-occupied housing (line 5) and owner-occupied land (line 10). Business assets refers to the FOF category equity in noncorporate business (line 32). The first of the debts is mortgages on the primary residence that refers to the FOF category home mortgages (line 37). The second is mortgages on other real estate that corresponds to the FOF category other mortgages (line 41), and the final category is total other debts that corresponds to the FOF categories installment consumer credit (line 38), other consumer credit (line 39), bank loans (line 42), and other loans (line 43).

# REFERENCES

Alexander, Karl L. 1976. "High School Context and College Selectivity: Institutional Constraints in Educational Stratification." *Social Forces* 56:199–188.

Alexander, Karl L., Martha Cook, and Edward L. McDill. 1978. "Curriculum Tracking and Educational Stratification: Some Further Evidence." *American Sociological Review* 43:47–66.

Alexander, Karl L., and Bruce K. Eckland. 1975. "Contextual Effects in the High School Attainment Process." *American Sociological Review* 40:402–416

Ando, Albert, and Arthur Kennickell. 1985. "How Much (or Little) Life Cycle Is There in Micro Data? Cases of U.S. and Japan." Unpublished manuscript.

Ando, A., and Franco Modigliani. 1963. "The Life-Cycle Hypothesis of Saving: Aggregate Implications and Tests." *American Economic Review* 53:55–84.

Andrews, Emily S., and Deborah Chollet. 1988. "Future Sources of Retirement Income: Whither the Baby Boom." Pp. 71–96 in *Social Security and Private Pensions: Providing for Retirement in the Twenty-First Century*, edited by S. M. Wachter. Lexington: Lexington Books.

Angle, John. 1986. "The Surplus Theory of Social Stratification and the Size Distribution of Personal Wealth." *Social Forces* 65:293–326.

Angle, John. 1993. "Deriving the Size Distribution of Personal Wealth from 'The Rich Get Richer, the Poor Get Poorer.'" *Journal of Mathematical Sociology* 18:27–46.

Antoniewicz, Rochelle. Forthcoming. "A Comparison of the Household Sector from the Flow of Funds Accounts and the Survey of Consumer Finances." *Review of Income and Wealth*.

Attanasio, Orazio P. 1993. *A Cohort Analysis of Saving Behavior by U.S. Households*. Cambridge, MA: National Bureau of Economic Research Working Paper Series.

Avery, Robert B., Gregory E. Elliehausen, Glenn B. Canner, and Thomas A. Gustafson. 1984a. "Survey of Consumer Finances, 1983." *Federal Reserve Bulletin* September:679–692.

# References

Avery, Robert B., Gregory E. Elliehausen, Glenn B. Canner, and Thomas A. Gustafson. 1984b. "Survey of Consumer Finances, 1983: A Second Report." *Federal Reserve Bulletin* December:857–868.

Avery, Robert B., Gregory E. Elliehausen, Glenn B. Canner, and Thomas A. Gustafson. 1986. "Survey of Consumer Finances, 1983." *Federal Reserve Bulletin* March:163–177.

Avery, Robert B., Gregory E. Elliehausen, Glenn B. Canner, Thomas A. Gustafson, and Julie Springert. 1986. "Financial Characteristics of High-Income Families." *Federal Reserve Bulletin* 72:163–177.

Avery, Robert B., Gregory E. Elliehausen, and Arthur B. Kennickell. 1987. "Changes in Consumer Installment Debt: Evidence from the 1983 and 1986 Surveys of Consumer Finances." *Federal Reserve Bulletin* October: 761–778.

Avery, Robert B., Gregory E. Elliehausen, and Arthur B. Kennickell. 1988. "Measuring Wealth with Survey Data: An Evaluation of the 1983 Survey of Consumer Finances." *Review of Income and Wealth* 34:339–369.

Avery, Robert B., and Arthur B. Kennickell. 1988. *The 1986 Survey of Consumer Finances: Technical Manual and Codebook.* Washington, DC: Board of Governors of the Federal Reserve System.

Avery, Robert B., and Arthur B. Kennickell. 1990. "Household Savings in the U.S." Unpublished manuscript.

Baer, William. 1992. *Race and the Shadow Market in Housing.* Los Angeles: University of Southern California Press.

Bajtelsmit, Vickie L., and Jack L. VanDerhei. 1997. "Risk Aversion and Pension Investment Choices." Pp. 45–66 in *Positioning Pensions for the Twenty-First Century*, edited by M. S. Gordon, O. S. Mitchell, and M. M. Twinney. Philadelphia, PA: University of Pennsylvania Press.

Bane, Mary Jo. 1986. "Household Composition and Poverty." Pp. 209–231 in *Fighting Poverty: What Works and What Doesn't*, edited by S. H. Danziger and D. H. Weinberg. Cambridge, MA: Harvard University Press.

Barringer, Felicity. 1992. "Younger Baby Boomers Are Found Less Well Off." P. B26 in *New York Times*.

Barth, James R., Joseph J. Cordes, and Anthony M. J. Yezer. 1980. "Redlining in Housing Markets." *Journal of Social and Political Studies* 5:221–242.

Baydar, Nazli. 1988. "Effects of Parental Separation and Reentry into Union on the Emotional Well-Being of Children." *Journal of Marriage and the Family* 50:967–981.

Behrman, J. R., and P. Taubman. 1990. "The Intergenerational Correlation Between Children's Adult Earnings and Their Parents' Income." *Review of Income and Wealth* 36:115–127.

Berger, Mark C. 1984. "Cohort Size and the Earnings Growth of Young Workers." *Industrial and Labor Relations Review* 37:582–591.

Berger, Mark C. 1985. "The Effect of Cohort Size on Earnings Growth: A Reexamination of the Evidence." *Journal of Political Economy* 93:561–573.

Berger, Mark C. 1989. "Demographic Cycles, Cohort Size, and Earnings." *Demography* 26:311–321.

Bernheim, B. Douglas. 1991. "How Strong Are Bequest Motives? Evidence Based on Estimates of the Demand for Life Insurance and Annuities." *Journal of Political Economy* 99:899–927.

Bernheim, R. 1987. "Dissaving After Retirement." Pp. 237–276 in *Issues in Pension Economics*, edited by Z. Bodie, J. B. Shoven, and D. A. Wise. Chicago: University of Chicago Press.

Bertaut, Carol C. 1998. "Stockholding Behavior of U.S. Households: Evidence from the 1983–1989 Survey of Consumer Finances." *The Review of Economics and Statistics* 80:263–275.

Blake, Judith. 1989. *Family Size and Achievement*. Berkeley, CA: University of California Press.

Blank, Rebecca M. 1993. "Why Were Poverty Rates So High in the 1980s?" Pp. 21–55 in *Poverty and Prosperity in the USA in the Late Twentieth Century*, edited by D. B. Papadimitriou and E. N. Wolff. New York: St. Martin's Press.

Blau, Francine D., and John W. Graham. 1990. "Black-White Differences in Wealth and Asset Composition." *Quarterly Journal of Economics* May:321–339.

Blau, Peter, and Otis D. Duncan. 1967. *The American Occupational Structure*. New York: Wiley.

Bourdieu, Pierre. 1973. "Cultural Reproduction and Social Reproduction." Pp. 71–112 in *Knowledge, Education, and Cultural Change*, edited by R. Brown. London: Collier-McMillan.

Bovenberg, A. Lans, and Owen Evans. 1990. "National and Personal Saving in the United States: Measurement and Analysis of Recent Trends." *International Monetary Fund Staff Papers* 37:636–639.

Bovenberg, Lans A. 1989. "Tax Policy and National Savings in the United States: A Survey." *National Tax Journal* 42:123–138.

Bowles, Samuel, and Herbert Gintis. 1976. *Schooling in Capitalist America*. New York: Basic Books.

Braun, Denny. 1997. *The Rich Get Richer: The Rise in Income Inequality in the United States and the World*. Chicago: Nelson-Hall Publishers.

Brenner, Joel, and Liz Spayd. 1993. "Separate and Unequal: Racial Discrimination in Area Home Lending." *Washington Post* 6–8 June:A1.

Brimmer, Andrew F. 1988. "Income, Wealth, and Investment Behavior in the Black Community." *American Economic Review* 78:151–155.

Browne, Irene. 1997. "Explaining the Black-White Gap in Labor Force Participation Among Women Heading Households." *American Sociological Review* 62:236–252.

Campbell, Richard, and John Henretta. 1980. "Status Claims and Status Attainment: The Determinants of Financial Well-Being." *American Journal of Sociology* 86:618–629.

Campbell, Richard T., and Angela M. O'Rand. 1988. "Settings and Sequences: The Heuristics of Aging Research." Pp. 58–79 in *Emergent Theories of Aging*, edited by J. E. Birren and V. L. Bengston. New York: Springer Publishing Company.

Cancio, A. Silvia, T. David Evans, and David J. Maume Jr. 1996. "Reconsidering the Declining Significance of Race: Racial Differences in Early Career Wages." *American Sociological Review* 61:541–556.

Canner, Glenn B., Arthur B. Kennickell, and Charles A. Luckett. 1995. "Household Sector Borrowing and the Burden of Debt." *Federal Reserve Bulletin* April:323–338.

Caskey, Richard. 1994. *Fringe Banking: Check-Cashing Outlets, Pawnshops, and the Poor*. New York: Russell Sage Foundation.

Cheal, David. 1983. "Intergenerational Family Transfers." *Journal of Marriage and the Family* 45:805–813.

Cherlin, Andrew J. 1981. *Marriage, Divorce, Remarriage*. Cambridge, MA: Harvard University Press.

Chester, Ronald. 1998. "Inheritance in American Legal Thought." Pp. 23–43 in *Inheritance and Wealth in America*, edited by J. Robert, K. Miller, and S. J. McNamee. New York: Plenum Press.

Clausen, John A. 1991. "Adolescent Competence and the Shaping of the Life Course." *American Journal of Sociology* 96:805–842.

Clignet, Remi P. 1998. "Ethnicity and Inheritance." Pp. 119–138 in *Inheritance and Wealth in America*, edited by J. Robert, K. Miller, and S. J. McNamee. New York: Plenum Press.

Coleman, James S. 1990. *Foundations of Social Theory*. Cambridge, MA: Harvard.

Collins, Julie H., and James H. Wykoff. 1988. "Estimates of Tax Deferred Retirement Savings Behavior." *National Tax Journal* 41:562–572.

Collins, Randall. 1979. *The Credential Society*. New York: Academic Press.

Connelly, Rachel. 1986. "A Framework for Analyzing the Impact of Cohort Size on Education and Labor Earnings." *Journal of Human Resources* 21:543–562.

Cooksey, Elizabeth C. 1997. "Consequences of Young Mothers' Marital Histories for Children's Cognitive Development." *Journal of Marriage and the Family* 59:245–261.

Cooksey, Elizabeth C., and Michelle M. Fondell. 1996. "Spending Time with His Kids: Effects of Family Structure on Fathers' and Children's Lives." *Journal of Marriage and the Family* 58:1–15.

Cooksey, Elizabeth C., Elizabeth G. Menaghan, and Susan M. Jekielek. 1996. "Life-Course Effects of Work and Family Circumstances on Children." *Social Forces* 76:637–667.

Corcoran, M. 1995. "Rags to Riches: Poverty and Mobility in the United States." *Annual Review of Sociology* 21:237–267.

Corcoran, M., and L. P. Datcher. 1981. "Intergenerational Status Transmission and the Process of Individual Attainment." Pp. 269–292 in *Five Thousand American Families: Patterns of Economic Progress*, edited by M. S. Hill, D. H. Hill, and J. N. Morgan. Ann Arbor, MI: Survey Research Center.

Curtin, Richard, F. Thomas Juster, and James Morgan. 1989. "Survey Estimates of Wealth: An Assessment of Quality." Pp. 473–551 in *The Measurement of Saving, Investment, and Wealth*, edited by R. Lipsey and H. S. Tice. Chicago: University of Chicago Press.

Danziger, Sheldon, Jacques Van DerGaag, Eugene Smolensky, and M. Taussig. 1982. "The Life-Cycle Hypothesis and the Consumption Behavior of the Elderly." *Journal of Post-Keynesian Economics* 5:208–227.

Danziger, Sheldon H., Robert H. Haveman, and Robert D. Plotnick. 1986. "Antipoverty Policy: Effects on the Poor and Nonpoor." Pp. 50–77 in *Fighting Poverty: What Works and What Doesn't*, edited by S. H. Danziger and D. H. Weinberg. Cambridge, MA: Harvard University Press.

Danziger, Sheldon H., and Daniel H. Weinberger, eds. 1986. *Fighting Poverty: What Works and What Doesn't*. Cambridge, MA: Harvard University Press.

Darby, Michael R. 1979. *The Effects of Social Security on Income and the Capital Stock*. Washington, DC: American Enterprise Institute.

David, Martin, and Paul Menchik. 1988. "Changes in Cohort Wealth over a Generation." *Demography* 25:317–335.

Davies, J. B. 1981. "Uncertain Lifetime, Consumption, and Dissaving in Retirement." *Journal of Political Economy* 89:561–578.

Davies, J. B. 1982. "The Relative Impact of Inheritance and Other Factors on Economic Inequality." *Quarterly Journal of Economics* 97:471–498.

de Tocqueville, Alexis. 1841 [1966]. *Democracy in America (De la démocratie en Amérique)*. Translated by George Lawrence, edited by J. P. Mayer and Max Lerner. New York: Harper and Row.

Demo, David H., and Alan C. Acock. 1988. "The Impact of Divorce on Children." *Journal of Marriage and the Family* 50:619–648.

Department of Commerce, Economics and Statistics Administration, Bureau of Economic Analysis. 1993. *Fixed Reproducible Tangible Wealth in the United States, 1925–1989*. Washington, DC: Department of Commerce.

Domhoff, G. William. 1970. *The Higher Circles*. New York: Random House.

Domhoff, G. William. 1990. *The Power Elite and the State: How Policy Is Made in America*. New York: Aldine de Gruyter.

Downey, Douglas B. 1995. "When Bigger Is Not Better: Family Size, Parental Resources, and Children's Educational Performance." *American Sociological Review* 60:746–761.

Dreier, Peter. 1982. "The Status of Tenants in the United States." *Social Problems* 30:179–198.

Duncan, Greg J., Timothy M. Smeeding, and Willard Rodgers. 1993. "W(h)ither the Middle Class? A Dynamic View." Pp. 240–271 in *Poverty and Prosperity in the USA in the Late Twentieth Century*, edited by D. B. Papadimitriou and E. N. Wolff. New York: St. Martin's Press.

Duncan, Otis Dudley, David L. Featherman, and Beverly Duncan. 1972. *Socioeconomic Background and Achievement*. New York: Seminar.

Dye, Thomas R. 1995. *Who's Running America? The Clinton Years*. Englewood Cliffs, NJ: Prentice-Hall.

Dynan, Karen E. 1993. "The Rate of Time Preference and Shocks to Wealth: Evidence from Panel Data." *Board of Governors of the Federal Reserve System Working Paper Series, Number 134.*

Easterlin, Richard A. 1980. *Birth and Fortune: The Impact of Numbers on Personal Welfare*. New York: Basic Books.

Easterlin, Richard A. 1987. *Birth and Fortune*, second edition. Chicago: University of Chicago Press.

Easterlin, Richard A., Christine MacDonald, and Diane J. Macunovich. 1990a. "How Have American Baby Boomers Fared? Earnings and Economic Well-Being of Young Adults, 1964–1987." *Population Economics* 3:277–290.

Easterlin, Richard A., Christine MacDonald, and Diane J. Macunovich. 1990b. "Retirement Prospects of the Baby Boom Generation: A Different Perspective." *Gerontologist* 30:776–783.

Easterlin, Richard A., Christine M. Schaeffer, and Diane J. Macunovich. 1993. "Will the Baby Boomers Be Less Well Off Than Their Parents? Income, Wealth, and Family Circumstances over the Life Cycle in the United States." *Population and Development Review* 19:497–522.

Elder, Glen H. 1974. *Children of the Great Depression: Social Change in Life Experience*. Chicago: University of Chicago Press.

Elder, Glen H. 1985. *Life Course Dynamics: Trajectories and Transitions, 1968–1980*. Ithaca, NY: Cornell University Press.

Elder, Glen H. 1995. "The Life Course Paradigm: Social Change and Individual Development." Pp. 101–140 in *Examining Lives in Context: Perspectives on the Ecology of Human Development*, edited by P. Moen, G. H. Elder, and K. Luscher. Washington, DC: American Psychological Association.

Elder, Glen H., and Jeffrey K. Liker. 1982. "Hard Times in Women's Lives: Historical Influences Across 40 Years." *American Journal of Sociology* 88:241–269.

Elder, Glen H., and Richard C. Rockwell. 1977. "The Life Course and Human Development: An Ecological Perspective." *International Journal of Behavioral Development* 2:1–21.

Ellwood, David T. 1988. *Poor Support: Poverty in the American Family*. New York: Basic Books.

Epstein, William M. 1997. *Welfare in America: How Social Science Fails the Poor*. Madison, WI: University of Wisconsin Press.

Falsey, Barbara, and Barbara Heyns. 1984. "The College Channel: Private and Public Schools Reconsidered." *Sociology of Education* 57:111–122.

Featherman, David L., and Robert M. Hauser. 1978. *Opportunity and Change*. New York: Academic Press.

Federal Reserve System, Board of Governors. 1993. *Guide to the Flow of Funds Accounts*. Washington, DC: Board of Governors of the Federal Reserve System.

Federal Reserve System, Board of Governors. 1995. *Balance Sheets for the U.S. Economy, 1945–1993*. Washington, DC: Federal Reserve Board.

Feenberg, Daniel, and Jonathan Skinner. 1989. "Sources of IRA Savings." Pp. 25–46 in *Tax Policy and the Economy, 1989*, edited by L. H. Summers. Cambridge, MA: MIT.

Fischer, Stanley. 1973. "A Life Cycle Model of Life Insurance Purchases." *International Economic Review* 14:132–152.

Fisher, Janet. 1952. "Income, Spending, and Saving Patterns of Consumer Units in Different Age Groups." *Studies in Income and Wealth* 15:89–122.

Frank, Robert H. 1999. *Luxury Fever: Why Money Fails to Satisfy in an Era of Excess*. New York: The Free Press.

Freeman, Richard. 1979. "The Effect of Demographic Factors on Age-Earnings Profiles." *Journal of Human Resources* 14:289–318.

Frenzen, Jonathan, Paul M. Hirsch, and Philip C. Zerrillo. 1994. "Consumption, Preferences, and Changing Lifestyles." Pp. 403–425 in *The Handbook of Economic Sociology*, edited by N. J. Smelser and R. Swedberg. Princeton, NJ: Princeton University Press/Russell Sage Foundation.

Friedman, Milton. 1957. *A Theory of the Consumption Function*. Princeton, NJ: Princeton University Press.

Galbraith, John Kenneth. 1958. *The Affluent Society*. Boston: Houghton Mifflin Company.

Galbraith, James K. 1998. *Created Unequal: The Crisis in American Pay*. New York: Free Press.

Gale, William G., and John Karl Scholz. 1994. "Intergenerational Transfers and the Accumulation of Wealth." *Journal of Economic Perspectives* 8:145–160.

Galenson, Marjorie. 1972. "Do Blacks Save More?" *American Economic Review* 62:211–216.

Gerson, Kathleen. 1985. *Hard Choices: How Women Decide About Work, Career, and Motherhood*. Berkeley, CA: University of California Press.

Gokhale, Jagadeesh, Laurence J. Kotlikoff, and John Sabelhouse. 1996. "Understanding the Postwar Decline in U.S. Saving: A Cohort Analysis." *Brookings Papers on Economic Activity* 1:315–407.

Goldsmith, Raymond W. 1956. *A Study of Saving in the United States*. Princeton, NJ: Princeton University Press.

Goldsmith, Raymond W. 1962. *The National Wealth of the United States in the Postwar Period*. Princeton, NJ: Princeton University Press.

Gottschalk, Peter, and Sheldon Danziger. 1984. "Macroeconomic Conditions, Income Transfers, and the Trend in Poverty." Pp. 185–215 in *The Social Contract Revisited*, edited by D. L. Bawden. Washington, DC: Urban Institute Press.

Gravelle, Jane G. 1991. "Do Individual Retirement Accounts Increase Savings?" *Journal of Economic Perspectives* 5:133–148.

Greene, William. 1993. *Econometric Analysis*. New York: Macmillan.

Greenwood, Daphne T., and Edward N. Wolff. 1990. "Changes in Age-Wealth Profiles: Savings, Revaluation, and Inheritance." Unpublished manuscript. New York: New York University.

Greenwood, Daphne T., and Edward N. Wolff. 1992. "Changes in Wealth in the United States, 1962–1983: Savings, Capital Gains, Inheritance, and Lifetime Transfers." *Population Economics* 5:261–288.

Gundersen, Joan R. 1998. "Women and Inheritance in America: Virginia and New York as a Case Study, 1700–1860." Pp. 91–118 in *Inheritance and Wealth in America*, edited by Robert K. Miller Jr. and S. J. McNamee. New York: Plenum Press.

Hammack, Floyd M., and Peter W. Cookson Jr. 1980. "Colleges Attended by Graduates of Elite Secondary Schools." *The Educational Forum* 44:483–490.

Hendershott, Patrick, and Joe Peck. 1989. "Aggregate U.S. Private Saving: Conceptual Measure and Empirical Tests." in *Measurement of Saving, Investment, and Wealth*, edited by R. E. Lipsey and H. S. Tice. Chicago: University of Chicago Press.

Henretta, John. 1984. "Parental Status and Child's Homeownership." *American Sociological Review* 49:131–140.

Henretta, John, and Richard Campbell. 1978. "Net Worth as an Aspect of Status." *American Journal of Sociology* 83:1024–1223.

Henretta, John C. 1979. "Race Differences in Middle Class Lifestyle: The Role of Home Ownership." *Social Science Research* 8:63–78.

Hill, M. S., and G. J. Duncan. 1987. "Parental Family Income and the Socioeconomic Attainment of Children." *Social Science Research* 16:39–73.

Holloway, Thomas M. 1991. "The Role of Homeownership and Home Price Appreciation in the Accumulation and Distribution of Household Sector Wealth." *Business Economics* 26:38–44.

Homans, George C. 1974. *Social Behavior: Its Elementary Forms*. New York: Harcourt Brace Jovanovich.

Horton, Haywood Derrick. 1992. "Race and Wealth: A Demographic Analysis of Black Ownership." *Sociological Inquiry* 62:480–489.

Huber, Joan, and William H. Form. 1973. *Income and Ideology*. New York: Free Press.

Huber, Joan, and Glenna Spitze. 1980. "Considering Divorce: An Expansion of Becker's Theory of Marital Instability." *American Journal of Sociology* 86:75–89.

Hurd, Michael D. 1987. "Savings of the Elderly and Desired Bequests." *American Economic Review* 77:298–312.

Hurd, Michael D. 1990. "Research on the Elderly: Economic Status, Retirement, and Consumption and Saving." *Journal of Economic Literature* 28:565–637.

Hurd, Michael D., and Gabriela Mundaca. 1989. "The Importance of Gifts and Inheritance Among the Affluent." Pp. 737–758 in *Measurement of Saving, Investment, and Wealth*, edited by R. E. Lipsey and H. S. Tice. Chicago: University of Chicago Press.

Hurst, Erik, Ming Ching Luoh, and Frank P. Stafford. 1996. "Wealth Dynamics of American Families, 1984–1994." Unpublished manuscript. Ann Arbor, MI: University of Michigan.

Ihlanfeldt, Keith R., and Jorge Marinez-Vazquez. 1986. "Alternative Value Estimates of Owner-Occupied Housing: Evidence on Sample Selection Bias and Systematic Errors." *Journal of Urban Economics* November:356–369.

Inhaber, Herbert, and Sidney Carroll. 1992. *How Rich Is Too Rich? Income and Wealth in America*. New York: Praeger.

Internal Revenue Service, Statistics of Income Division. 1975–1983. *Statistics of Income: Individual Income Tax Returns, Various Years*. Washington, DC: Internal Revenue Service.

Jackman, Mary R., and Robert W. Jackman. 1980. "Racial Inequalities in Home Ownership." *Social Forces* 58:1221–1233.

Japan, Bank of. 1989. "Recent Developments in the U.S. Household Savings Rate and Background." Special paper no. 181:100–191.

Jencks, C., M. Smith, H. Acland, M. J. Bane, D. Cohen, M. J Bane, and D. Cohen. 1972. *Inequality: A Reassessment of the Effect of Family and Schooling in America*. New York: Basic Books.

Johnson, Barry W. 1994a. "Estate Tax Returns, 1986–1988." Pp. 20–58 in *Compendium of Federal Estate Tax and Personal Wealth Studies*, edited by I. R. S. Department of the Treasury. Washington, DC: Internal Revenue Service, Statistics of Income Division.

Johnson, Barry W. 1994b. "Estate Tax Returns, 1989–1991." Pp. 59–86 in *Compendium of Federal Estate Tax and Personal Wealth Studies*, edited by I. R. S. Department of the Treasury. Washington, DC: Internal Revenue Service, Statistics of Income Division.

Johnson, Barry W., and Martha Britton Eller. 1998. "Federal Taxation of Inheritance and Wealth Transfers." Pp. 61–90 in *Inheritance and Wealth in America*, edited by Robert K. Miller Jr. and S. J. McNamee. New York: Plenum Press.

Johnson, Barry W., and Louise Woodburn. 1994. "The Estate Multiplier Technique: Recent Improvements for 1989." Pp. 391–400 in *Compendium of Federal Estate Tax and Personal Wealth Studies*, edited by I. R. S. Department of the Treasury. Washington, DC: Internal Revenue Service, Statistics of Income Division.

Katz, Michael B. 1996. *In the Shadow of the Poorhouse: A Social History of Welfare in America*. New York: Basic Books.

Keister, Lisa A. Forthcoming. "Race and Wealth Ownership: The Impact of Racial Differences in Asset Ownership on the Distribution of Household Wealth." *Social Science Research*.

Kendig, Hal L. 1984. "Housing Tenure and Generational Equity." *Aging and Society* 4:249–272.

Kennickell, Arthur, and Janie Shack-Marquez. 1992. "Changes in Family Finances From 1983 to 1989: Evidence from the Survey of Consumer Finances." *Federal Reserve Bulletin* 78:1–18.

Kennickell, Arthur B. 1994a. "Imputation of the 1989 Survey of Consumer Finances: Stochastic Relaxation and Multiple Imputation." Unpublished Federal Reserve Board manuscript.

Kennickell, Arthur B. 1994b. "Multiple Imputation of the 1983 and 1989 Waves of the SCF." Unpublished Federal Reserve Board manuscript.

Kennickell, Arthur B. 1995. "Saving and Permanent Income: Evidence from the 1992 SCF." Unpublished Federal Reserve Board manuscript.

Kennickell, Arthur B., and Myron L. Kwast. 1997. "Who Uses Electronic Banking? Results From the 1995 Survey of Consumer Finances." Unpublished Federal Reserve Board manuscript.

Kennickell, Arthur B., and Martha Starr-McCluer. 1994. "Changes in Family Finances From 1989 to 1992: Evidence from the Survey of Consumer Finances." *Federal Reserve Bulletin* October:861–882.

Kennickell, Arthur B., and Martha Starr-McCluer. 1997. "Household Saving and Portfolio Change: Evidence from the 1983–89 SCF Panel." *Review of Income and Wealth* December:381–399.

Kennickell, Arthur B., Martha Starr-McCluer, and Annika E. Sunden. 1997. "Family Finances in the United States: Recent Evidence from the Survey of Consumer Finances." *Federal Reserve Bulletin* January:1–24.

Kennickell, Arthur B., and R. Louise Woodburn. 1992. "Estimation of Household Net Worth Using Model-Based and Design-Based Weights: Evidence from the 1989 Survey of Consumer Finances." Unpublished Federal Reserve Board manuscript.

Kerbo, Harold R. 1991. *Social Stratification and Inequality: Class Conflict in Historical and Comparative Perspective*. New York: McGraw Hill.

Kerckhoff, Alan C. 1976. "The Status Attainment Process: Socialization or Allocation?" *Social Forces* 55:368–381.

Keynes, John Maynard. 1936. *The General Theory of Employment, Interest, and Money*. New York: Harcourt Brace.

Kiker, B. F., and C. M. Condon. 1981. "The Influences of Socioeconomic Background on the Earnings of Young Men." *Journal of Human Resources* 16: 94–105.

King, M. A., and L.-D. L. Dicks-Mireaux. 1982. "Asset Holdings and the Life-Cycle." *Economic Journal* 92:247–267.

Kingson, Eric. 1992. *The Diversity of the Baby Boom Generation: Implications for Their Retirement Years*. Washington, DC: American Association of Retired Persons.

Kluegel, J. R., and E. R. Smith. 1986. *Beliefs About Inequality: Americans' Views of What Is and What Ought to Be*. New York: Aldine de Gruyter Press.

Kornstein, D. J. 1984. "Inheritance: A Constitutional Right?" *Rutgers Law Review* 36:741.

Kotlikoff, Laurence J., and Lawrence H. Summers. 1981. "The Role of Intergenerational Transfers in Aggregate Capital Accumulation." *Journal of Political Economy* 89:706–732.

Kurz, Mordecai. 1984. "Capital Accumulation and the Characteristics of Private Intergenerational Transfers." *Economica* 541:1–22.

Kuttner, Robert. 1987. "The Patrimony Society: What Happens When the First Generation of Mass Affluence Passes On?" *The New Republic* May 11:18–21

Lampman, Robert J. 1962. *The Share of Top Wealth-Holders in National Wealth, 1922–56*. Princeton, NJ: Princeton University Press.

Land, Kenneth C., and Stephen T. Russell. 1996. "Wealth Accumulation Across the Adult Life Course: Stability and Change in Sociodemographic Covariate Structures of Net Worth Data in the Survey of Income and Program Participation, 1984–1991." *Social Science Research* 25:423–462.

Lane, Randall, and Stephen S. Johnson. October 16, 1995. "Secrecy Is Success." *Forbes*, vol. 156, no. 9, pp. 46–54.

Lawrence, Emily C. 1991. "Poverty and the Rate of Time Preference: Evidence From Panel Data." *Journal of Political Economy* 99:54–77.

Lawton, M. P. 1980. "Housing the Elderly." *Research on Aging* 2:309–327.

Lenski, Gerhard E. 1966. *Power and Privilege: A Theory of Social Stratification*. New York: McGraw-Hill.

Lerman, Donald L., and James J. Mikesell. 1988. "Rural and Urban Poverty: An Income/Net Worth Approach." *Policy Studies Review* 7:765–781.

Levy, Frank S. 1980. "The Intergenerational Transfer of Poverty: Final Project Report." Washington, DC: Urban Institute.

Levy, Frank S., and Richard C. Michel. 1986. "An Economic Bust for the Baby Boom." *Challenge* 29:33–39.

Levy, Frank S., and Richard C. Michel. 1991. *The Economic Future of American Families: Income and Wealth Trends*. Washington, DC: Urban Institute.

## References

Lewin-VHI, Inc. 1994. *Baby Boomer Pension Benefits: Will They Be Adequate for the Future?* Washington, DC: American Association of Retired Persons.

Lewis, Frank D. 1989. "Dependents and the Demand for Life Insurance." *American Economic Review* 79:452–467.

Lewis, Lionel S., and Richard A. Wanner. 1979. "Private Schooling and the Status Attainment Process." *Sociology of Education* 52:99–112.

Logan, John R., and O. Andrew Collver. 1983. "Residents' Perceptions of Suburban Community Differences." *American Sociological Review* 48:428–433.

Long, James E., and Steven B. Caudill. 1992. "Racial Differences in Homeownership and Housing Wealth, 1970–1986." *Economic Inquiry* 30:83–100.

Maddala, G. S. 1977. *Econometrics.* New York: McGraw-Hill.

Manchester, Joyce M. 1993. *Baby Boomers in Retirement: An Early Perspective.* Washington, DC: Congress of the United States, Congressional Budget Office.

Massey, Douglas S., Gretchen A. Condron, and Nancy A. Denton. 1987. "The Effect of Residential Segregation on Black Social and Economic Well-Being." *Social Forces* 66:29–56.

Mayer, Susan E., and Christopher Jencks. 1989. "Poverty and the Distribution of Material Hardship." *Journal of Human Resources* 24:88–114.

Mayhew, Bruce H., and Paul T. Schollaert. 1980. "The Concentration of Wealth: A Sociological Model." *Sociological Focus* 13:1–35.

McDermed, Ann, Robert Clark, and Steven Allen. 1989. "Pension Wealth, Age-Wealth Profiles, and Distribution of Net Worth." Pp. 435–443 in *The Measurement of Saving, Investment, and Wealth*, edited by R. Lipsey and H. S. Tice. Chicago: University of Chicago Press.

McNamee, Stephen J., and Robert K. Miller Jr. 1998. "Inheritance and Stratification." Pp. 193–213 in *Inheritance and Wealth in America*, edited by Robert K. Miller Jr. and S. J. McNamee. New York: Plenum Press.

Medoff, James, and Andrew Harless. 1996. *The Indebted Society: Anatomy of a Ongoing Disaster.* New York: Little, Brown, and Company.

Menaghan, Elizabeth G. 1991. "Work Experiences and Family Interaction Processes: The Long Reach of the Job?" *Annual Review of Sociology* 17:419–444.

Menaghan, Elizabeth G., and Toby L. Parcel. 1991. "Determining Children's Home Environments: The Impact of Maternal Characteristics and Current Occupational and Family Conditions." *Journal of Marriage and the Family* 53:417–431.

Menchick, Paul, and Martin David. 1983. "Income Distribution, Lifetime Savings, and Bequests." *American Economic Review* 73:672–690.

Menchik, Paul L., and Nancy A. Jiankoplos. 1998. "Economics of Inheritance." Pp. 45–59 in *Inheritance and Wealth in America*, edited by Robert K. Miller Jr. and S. J. McNamee. New York: Plenum Press.

Millar, John. 1806. *The Origin of the Distinction of Ranks*, Fourth edition. Edinburgh: William Blackwood.

Miller, Robert K., Jr., and Stephen J. McNamee. 1998. *Inheritance and Wealth in America*. New York: Plenum Press.

Mirer, Thad W. 1979. "The Wealth-Age Relation Among the Aged." *American Economic Review* 69:435–443.

Mirer, Thad W. 1980. "The Dissaving Behavior of the Retired Aged." *Southern Economic Journal* 46:1197–1205.

Modigliani, Franco. 1986. "Life Cycle, Individual Thrift, and the Wealth of Nations." *American Economic Review* 76:297–313.

Modigliani, Franco. 1988a. "Measuring the Contribution of Intergenerational Transfers to Total Wealth: Conceptual Issues and Empirical Findings." Pp. 21–52 in *Modelling the Accumulation and Distribution of Wealth*, edited by D. Kessler and A. Masson. New York: Oxford.

Modigliani, Franco. 1988b. "The Role of Intergenerational Transfers and Life Cycle Saving in the Accumulation of Wealth." *Journal of Economic Perspectives* 2:15–40.

Modigliani, Franco. 1992. "Life Cycle, Individual Thrift, and the Wealth of Nations." Pp. 150–171 in *Nobel Lectures: Economic Sciences, 1981–1990*, edited by K. G. Maler. New Jersey: World Scientific.

Modigliani, Franco, and A. K. Ando. 1957. "Tests of the Life Cycle Hypothesis of Saving." *Bulletin of the Oxford Institute of Statistics* 19:99–124.

Modigliani, Franco, and Richard Brumberg. 1952. "Utility Analysis and Aggregate Consumption Functions: An Attempt at Integration." Unpublished manuscript.

Modigliani, Franco, and Richard Brumberg. 1954. "Utility Analysis and the Consumption Function: An Interpretation of Cross-Sectional Data." Pp. in *Post-Keynesian Economics*, edited by K. K. Kurihara. New Brunswick, NJ: Rutgers University Press.

Montesquieu, Charles de. 1748. *De l'Espirit de Loix. Tome I*. Geneve: Barrillot et fils.

Norris, Floyd. January 5, 1996. "Flood of Cash to Mutual Funds Helped Fuel '95 Bull Market." P. A1 in *New York Times*.

Oliver, Melvin L., and Thomas M. Shapiro. 1989. "Race and Wealth." *Review of Black Political Economy* 17:5–25.

Oliver, Melvin L., and Thomas M. Shapiro. 1990. "Wealth of a Nation: At Least One-Third of Households Are Asset Poor." *American Journal of Economics and Sociology* 49:129–151.

Oliver, Melvin L., and Thomas M. Shapiro. 1995. *Black Wealth/White Wealth*. New York: Routledge.

O'Neil, Cherie J., and G. Rodney Thompson. 1987. "Participation in Individual Retirement Accounts: An Empirical Investigation." *National Tax Journal* 40:617–624.

Ong, Paul, and Eugene Grigsby III. 1988. "Race and Life Cycle Effects on Home Ownership in Los Angeles, 1970 to 1980." *Urban Affairs Quarterly* 23: 601–615.

Orcutt, Guy. 1957. "A New Type of Socio-Economic System." *Review of Economics and Statistics* 58:773–797.

Orcutt, Guy, Steven B. Caldwell, and Richard Wertheimer. 1976. *Policy Exploration Through Microanalytic Simulation*. Washington, DC: The Urban Institute.

Orcutt, Guy, Martin Greenberger, John Korbel, and Alice M. Rivlin. 1961. *Microanalysis of Socioeconomic Systems: A Simulation Study*. New York: Harper and Row.

Osberg, Lars. 1984. *Economic Inequality in the United States*. New York: M. E. Sharpe.

Parcel, Toby L. 1982. "Wealth Accumulation of Black and White Men: The Case of Housing Equity." *Social Problems* 30:199–211.

Perin, Constance. 1977. *Everything in Its Place: Social Order and Land Use in America*. Princeton, NJ: Princeton University Press.

Persell, Caroline Hodges, and Peter W. Cookson Jr. 1986. "Chartering and Bartering: Elite Education and Social Reproduction." *Social Problems* 33:114–129.

Peters, E. 1992. "Patterns of Intergenerational Mobility in Income and Earnings." *Review of Economics and Statistics* 24:456–466.

Peterson, Richard R. 1996. "A Re-Evaluation of the Economic Consequences of Divorce." *American Sociological Review* 61:528–536.

Petterson, Stephen M. 1997. "Are Young Black Men Really Less Willing to Work?" *American Sociological Review* 62:605–613.

Pissarides, C. A. 1980. "The Wealth-Age Relation with Life Insurance." *Economica* 47:451–457.

Projector, Dorothy S., and Gertrude S. Weiss. 1966. *Survey of the Financial Characteristics of Consumers*. Washington, DC: Federal Reserve Board.

Quinn, Joseph F. 1985. "Retirement Income Rights as a Component of Wealth in the United States." *Review of Income and Wealth* 31:223–236.

Radner, Daniel B. 1989. "Net Worth and Financial Assets of Age Groups in 1984." *Social Security Bulletin* 52:2–15.

Rodgers, J. 1995. "An Empirical Study of Intergenerational Transmission of Poverty in the United States." *Social Science Quarterly* 76:178–194.

Rosenfeld, Jeffrey P. 1998. "Women and Inheritance in America: Virginia and New York as a Case Study, 1700–1860." Pp. 173–192 in *Inheritance and Wealth in America*, edited by Robert K. Miller Jr. and S. J. McNamee. New York: Plenum Press.

Ross, C. M., Sheldon Danziger, and E. Smolensky. 1987. "Interpreting Changes in the Economic Status of the Elderly, 1949–1979." *Contemporary Policy Issues* 5:98–112.

Ruggles, Richard, and Nancy Ruggles. 1982. "Integrated Economic Accounts for the United States, 1947–1980." *Survey of Current Business* 62:1–53.

Russell, Louise B. 1982. *The Baby Boom Generation and the Economy*. Washington, DC: Brookings Institution.

Sabelhaus, John, and Joyce Manchester. 1995. "Baby Boomers and Their Parents: How Does Their Economic Well-Being Compare in Middle Age?" *Journal of Human Resources* 30:791–806.

Schervish, Paul G., Platon E. Coutsoukis, and Ethan Lewis. 1994. *Gospels of Wealth: How the Rich Portray Their Lives*. Westport, CT: Praeger.

Schor, Juliet B. 1991. *The Overworked American: The Unexpected Decline of Leisure*. New York: Basic Books.

Schrag, Peter. 1970. *Out of Place in America*. New York: Random House.

Sewell, William H., and Robert M. Hauser. 1975. *Education, Occupation, and Earnings: Achievement in the Early Career*. New York: Academic Press.

Sheiner, Louise, and David N. Weil. 1992. "The Housing Wealth of the Aged." National Bureau of Economic Research Working Paper Number 4115.

Shorrocks, A. F. 1975. "The Age-Wealth Relationship: A Cross-Section and Cohort Analysis." *Review of Economics and Statistics* 57:158–163.

Sloane, Leonard. December 30, 1995. "Dow Climbs 21.32 Points; Gain for the Year is 33.5%." P. B45 in *New York Times*.

Smith, James D. 1984. "Trends in the Concentration of Wealth in the United States, 1958–1976." *Review of Income and Wealth* December:419–428.

Smith, James D. 1987. "Recent Trends in the Distribution of Wealth in the United States: Data, Research Problems, and Prospects." Pp. 72–90 in *International Comparisons of the Distribution of Household Wealth*, edited by E. N. Wolff. New York. Oxford University Press.

Solon, G. 1992. "Intergenerational Economic Mobility in the United States." *American Economic Review* 82:393–408.

Spencer, Herbert. 1882. *Principles of Sociology*, Volume II, Part V. New York: D. Appleton Press.

Steckel, Richard H., and Jayanthi Krishnan. 1992. "Wealth Mobility in America: A View from the National Longitudinal Survey." National Bureau of Economic Research Working Paper Series, Working Paper Number 4137. Cambridge, MA: National Bureau of Economic Research.

Stinchcombe, Arthur L. 1975. "Merton's Theory of Social Structure." Pp. 11–33 in *Social Structure: Papers in Honor of Robert K. Merton*, edited by L. A. Coser. New York: Harcourt Brace Jovanovich.

Stirling, Kate. 1989. "Women Who Remain Divorced: The Long-Term Economic Consequences." *Social Science Quarterly* 70:549–561.

Straw, K. H. 1956. "Consumer's Net Worth: The 1953 Savings Survey." *Bulletin of the Oxford Institute of Statistics* 18:1–60.

Terrel, Henry S. 1971. "Wealth Accumulation of Black and White Families: The Empirical Evidence." *Journal of Finance* 26:363–377.

Thomas, Rich. 1995. "A Rising Tide Lifts the Yachts." *Newsweek* May 1.

Torrey, Barbara Boyle. 1988. "Assets of the Aged: Clues and Issues." *Population and Development Review* 14:489–497.

Torrey, Barbara Boyle, and C. Taeuber. 1986. "The Importance of Asset Income Among the Elderly." *Review of Income and Wealth* 4:443–449.

Treas, Judith. 1987. "The Effect of Women's Labor Force Participation on the Distribution of Income in the United States." *Annual Review of Sociology* 13:259–288.

Useem, Michael. 1984. *The Inner Circle.* New York: Oxford University Press.

Vanderhart, Peter G. 1993. "A Binomial Probit Analysis of the Home Equity Decisions of Elderly Homeowners." *Research on Aging* 15:299–323.

Venti, Steven F., and David A. Wise. 1993. "The Wealth of Cohorts: Retirement Savings and Changing Assets of Older Americans." National Bureau of Economic Research Working Paper Series, Working Paper no. 4600.

Weicher, John C. 1995. "Changes in the Distribution of Wealth: Increasing Inequality?" *Federal Reserve Bank of St. Louis Review* 77:5–23.

Weicher, John C. 1997. "Wealth and Its Distribution: 1983–1992: Secular Growth, Cyclical Stability." *Federal Reserve Bank of St. Louis Review* 79: 3–23.

Weitzman, Lenore J. 1985. *The Divorce Revolution: The Unexpected Social and Economic Consequences for Women and Children in America.* New York: Free Press.

Welch, Finis. 1979. "Effect of Cohort Size on Earnings: The Baby Boom Babies' Financial Bust." *Journal of Political Economy* 87:S65–97.

White, Betsy Buttrill. 1978. "Empirical Tests of the Life Cycle Hypothesis." *American Economic Review* 68:547–560.

Williams, Robin M. 1975. "Race and Ethnic Relations." *Annual Review of Sociology* 1:125–164.

Willis, Paul E. 1981. *Learning to Labor: How Working Class Kids Get Working Class Jobs.* New York: Columbia University Press.

Wilson, William J. 1987. *The Truly Disadvantaged: The Inner City, the Underclass, and Public Policy.* Chicago: University of Chicago Press.

Winnick, Andrew. 1989. *Toward Two Societies: The Changing Distributions of Income and Wealth in the United States Since 1960.* New York: Praeger.

Wolff, Edward N. 1979. "The Distributional Effects of the 1969–75 Inflation on Holdings of Household Wealth in the United States." *Review of Income and Wealth* 2:195–208.

Wolff, Edward N. 1987a. "The Effects of Pensions and Social Security on the Distribution of Wealth in the United States." Pp. 208–247 in *International Comparisons of the Distribution of Household Wealth*, edited by E. N. Wolff. New York: Oxford University Press.

Wolff, Edward N. 1987b. "Estimates of Household Wealth Inequality in the United States, 1962–1983." *Review of Income and Wealth* 33:231–256.

Wolff, Edward N. 1988. "Life Cycle Savings and the Individual Distribution of Wealth by Class." Pp. 261–280 in *Modelling the Accumulation and Distribution of Wealth*, edited by D. Kessler and A. Masson. New York: Oxford University Press.

Wolff, Edward N. 1990. "Wealth Holdings and Poverty Status in the United States." *Review of Income and Wealth* 36:143–165.

Wolff, Edward N. 1992. "Changing Inequality of Wealth." *American Economic Review* 82:552–558.

Wolff, Edward N. 1993. "Trends in Household Wealth in the United States During the 1980s." Unpublished manuscript. New York: New York University.

Wolff, Edward N. 1994. "Trends in Household Wealth in the United States 1962–1983 and 1983 1994." C. V. Starr Center for Applied Economics, New York University, #94-03.

Wolff, Edward N. 1995a. "The Rich Get Increasingly Richer: Latest Data on Household Wealth During the 1980s." Pp. 33–68 in *Research in Politics and Society*, vol. 5, edited by R. E. Ratcliff, M. L. Oliver, and T. M. Shapiro. Greenwich, CT: JAI Press.

Wolff, Edward N. 1995b. *Top Heavy: A Study of the Increasing Inequality of Wealth in America*. New York: Twentieth Century Fund.

Wolff, Edward N. 1998. "Recent Trends in the Size Distribution of Household Wealth." *Journal of Economic Perspectives* 12:131–150.

Wolff, Edward N., and Maria Marley. 1989. "Long Term Trends in U.S. Wealth Inequality: Methodological Issues and Results." Pp. 765–839 in *The Measurement of Saving, Investment, and Wealth*, edited by R. Lipsey and H. S. Tice. Chicago: University of Chicago Press.

World Bank. 1992. *World Development Report*. Washington, DC: World Bank/Oxford University Press.

Yaari, Menahem E. 1965. "Uncertain Lifetime, Life Insurance, and the Theory of the Consumer." *Review of Economic Studies* 32:137–50.

Zedlewski, S. R., and J. A. Meyer. 1989. "Toward Ending Poverty Among the Elderly and Disabled Through SSI Reform." Washington, DC: Urban Institute.

Zimmerman, D. 1992. "Regression Towards Mediocrity in Economic Stature." *American Economic Review* 82:409–429.

# INDEX